The Baltimore Rowhouse

The Baltimore Rowhouse

MARY ELLEN HAYWARD

AND

CHARLES BELFOURE

Foreword by James Marston Fitch

PRINCETON ARCHITECTURAL PRESS   *New York*

PRINCETON ARCHITECTURAL PRESS
37 East 7th Street
New York, NY 10003

For a free catalog of books published by Princeton Architectural Press,
call toll free 1.800.722.6657 or visit www.papress.com

© 2001 Princeton Architectural Press
First paperback edition
Hardcover edition © 1999 Princeton Architectural Press
All rights reserved
Printed and bound in the United States
04 03 02 01   4 3 2 1
ISBN 1-56898-283-6

This book was made possible by a grant from
The James Marston Fitch Foundation and the Samuel H. Kress Foundation

EDITING: Jan Cigliano

BOOK DESIGN: Sara E. Stemen

PHOTOGRAPH INSERT DESIGN: Karla Roberts

COVER PHOTOGRAPH: 900 block, Fulton Avenue, Baltimore. Alain Jaramillo

FRONTISPIECE:
900 block North Bradford Street, circa 1909; John Dubas Collection, Maryland Historical Society

SPECIAL THANKS:
Eugenia Bell, Jane Garvie, Caroline Green, Clare Jacobson, Mark Lamster,
and Anne Nitschke of Princeton Architectural Press   —Kevin C. Lippert, publisher

**THE LIBRARY OF CONGRESS HAS CATALOGED
THE HARDCOVER EDITION OF THIS BOOK AS:**
Hayward, Mary Ellen, 1947–
The Baltimore rowhouse / Mary Ellen Hayward and
Charles Belfoure ; foreword by James Marston Fitch.
New York : Princeton Architectural Press, 1999.
p. cm.
Includes index.
1. Row houses—Maryland—Baltimore. 2. Architecture, Domestic—Maryland—Baltimore.
I. Belfoure, Charles, 1954– . II. Title. III. Title:
NA7238.B3H38   1999
312.097'526—dc21   99-014573
CIP

Contents

TO MY MOTHER, ELEANOR BERRY HAYWARD

MY DAD, JOHN HAYWARD

AND MY DAUGHTER, MILLY

Mary Ellen Hayward

TO CHRIS, JULIE, GLORIA, AND MY MOM

Charles Belfoure

Acknowledgments

THIS BOOK BEGAN WITH a special collaboration between a historian of architecture and urbanism and an architect interested in renovations and real estate development. Each had been working independently on Baltimore rowhouses for some time, and they finally met in 1995 to write this book together.

Charles Belfoure, an architect who had studied at Columbia University and worked as a preservation architect in Connecticut, returned to his hometown of Baltimore in 1995 with the idea of writing a history of the Baltimore rowhouse. Mary Ellen Hayward's fascination with the Baltimore rowhouse began in 1978 when, with the support of the Maryland Historical Trust and Struever Bros. and Eccles, she completed a survey of structures in Federal Hill, one of Baltimore's oldest communities. During the survey, Michael Isekoff led her through the intricacies of deed research in the Baltimore City Land Records; the Maryland Historical Society, with a complete set of Baltimore City Directories, provided the answers to questions that arose at Land Records: who was buying houses in 1795, 1810, 1860, and 1880? did rowhouse owners build the houses themselves, or did they hire someone? Patterns emerged and the mass of data became history. In 1981 Baltimore's historic Peale Museum, after a major renovation, re-opened with a large permanent exhibition, *Rowhouse—A Baltimore Style of Living*, created by assistant director Barry Dressel, Ms. Hayward, curator Robert Weis, and photographer Jane Webb Smith (whose images appear in the book). Exhibition designers Patricia Chester and David Root produced elevations and isometric drawings of typical rowhouse types, which illustrate the text.

In 1997 the authors were awarded a major grant from the James Marston Fitch Charitable Trust to support final research and publication. The Baltimore Architecture Foundation also provided support and information regarding Baltimore architects. We would like to especially thank James F. Wollon, president of the Historic Architect's Roundtable (a.k.a. Dead Architect's Society); Charles B. Duff, president of the Baltimore Architecture Foundation; and Jillian Storms, past president, who shared information and were very helpful. In addition, we are grateful to the invaluable assistance of Baltimore Heritage, Inc., a private preservation organization, and Baltimore's Commission on Historical and Architectural Preservation (CHAP), particularly director, Kathleen Kotarba, and staff member Eric Holcomb. Thanks also go to Dean Krimmel, a local expert on Baltimore rowhouses; Barry Dressel, Director of the Chrysler Museum; Dr. Jeffrey A. Cohen at Bryn Mawr College and an expert on Philadelphia rowhouses; Bill Pencek, deputy director of the Maryland Historical Trust and president of Baltimore Heritage; and Karen Lewand, director of AIA Baltimore.

For archival information and illustrations, the authors are indebted to the invaluable collections at the Winterthur Museum and Library; the Hagley Museum and Library; the Museum of Early Southern Decorative Arts; the Maryland Room and the periodical department of the Enoch Pratt Free Library—particularly Jeff Corman, Eva Slezak, and John Sondheim; the Maryland Historical Society, notably Barbara Weeks, Ann Verplanck, Rob Schoeberlein, Jennifer Bryan, Mary Markey, and Robert I. Cottom Jr.; the Baltimore Equitable Society, an early city fire insurance company (1794) that retains complete records and old policy books, and its past president Steve Bernhardt; the University of Baltimore Archives, directed by Tom Hollowak; the research and photograph collections of the Baltimore Neighborhood Heritage Project, directed by Dr. Theodore Durr in the late 1970s; and the Goucher College Library, which archives microfilm of the Baltimore *Sun*, 1850 through the present. Dr. Phoebe B. Stanton, retired professor of architectural history at the Johns Hopkins University, shared invaluable research from early-nineteenth-century Baltimore *Sun* editions, and Charles Belfoure's mother, Kris, provided the wonderful service of translating records of the Polish Kosciusko Savings and Loan, which enabled the authors to identify clients and services.

As research proceeded and new topics emerged, we depended on the good offices of several local scholars, including: Dr. Garrett Power, of the University of Maryland Law School at Baltimore, an expert on land tenure, ground rents, and segregation; Philip Merrill provided information on black-operated savings and loans; Linda Shopes, a coauthor of *The Baltimore Book: New Views of Local History* (1991), shared her research on the Polish community in Fells Point and East Baltimore; and the late Martha Vill, a geography professor at the University of Maryland, who was one of the first scholars to investigate local land development processes. We were also fortunate to interview the descendants of leading rowhouse builders: Jim and Norman Gallagher, Jack Coady (the son of Gallagher's attorney), Joseph Keelty, Amy Macht, and Harvey Meyerhoff—as well as those active in the homebuilding business today, including Lee Rosenburg and Jim Joyce of Ryland Homes; Don Taylor and Gloria Mikolajszyk of D. W. Taylor Associates, Inc. Architects; and Cheryl O'Neill of CHK Planners and Architects. We are also indebted to the personal expertise of Robert C. Embry Jr., and Dr. Phoebe Stanton on Baltimore's Renaissance; and Robert L. Eney and Lucretia Fisher, key activists in protesting the planned interstate highway that would have demolished two of Baltimore's oldest neighborhoods in the 1960s; Jeff Tunney, an architectural wood-worker, Catherine Black and James Dilts; Andrew Colletta, a realtor and Baltimore Heritage Board member.

For superb contemporary photographs of rowhouses, we gratefully thank J. Brough Schamp, one of the most important architectural photographers in the area; Steven Allan; and photographer Alain Jaramillo, a long-time friend who jumped in on short notice to produce the striking cover image. Gloria Mikolajczyk, architect, helped translate old blueprints into the clear elevations and floor plans illustrating the different rowhouse types. For excellent maps showing the location of various rowhouse types, as well as the extent of various transportation systems, we are deeply grateful to Steven Allan. Thanks also go to Craig H. Huntley for his expertise in preparing final map art; the Greater Homewood Community Association for their generous in-kind donation of their Geographic Information Systems equipment;

Our text owes much to Catherine E. Hutchins, formerly on the staff of the *Winterthur Portfolio*, who edited various drafts of the manuscript and combined vast quantities of fascinating details we were loathe to give up. Kate was a joy to work with, always in good spirits, and had a never-flagging sense of humor and undaunted work ethic. In like manner, Jan Cigliano, our editor at Princeton Architectural Press, shepherded the manuscript through its final trials and tribulations. Our devoted thanks to her and to our hard-working-and-in-constant-communication fax machines.

Unless authors are independently wealthy, a book needs financial support to get written. In our case, it came from the James Marston Fitch Foundation and the Samuel H. Kress Foundation, which made this book possible. We would especially like to thank Richard Blinder and Eric DeLony, members of the Fitch board of trustees, for their confidence in this book's value, and James Marston Fitch for his gracious foreword.

We also thank our personal friends, who have helped make this book a reality. For Charles, special thanks go to Jim and Norman Gallagher for their foresight in donating the business records and archive of Edward J. Gallagher to the University of Baltimore. Their personal interviews were of great help. Joseph Keelty, son of rowhouse builder James Keelty, was very kind in providing information about his father's Rodger's Forge development. For Mary Ellen, special thanks go to a very old and dear friend, Robert L. Tarring Jr., whose family came to Baltimore from Germany before the Civil War and had been in the hat-making business in Fells Point before subsequent generations became doctors, bankers, and professors. His late mother and aunt had already researched the family and knew the names of the first Singewalds to come to Baltimore—Gottleib and Traugoth. Mary Ellen searched land records to identify the Singewalds' various real estate transactions beginning in 1840; Charles searched immigration records at the Maryland Historical Society and documented various trips the family took back to Germany. Working together Bob Tarring and Mary Ellen reconstructed a fairly complete history of the Singewald family in Baltimore.

Throughout the course of our research, and particularly when we were photographing houses, we met many wonderful people who invited us in, shared what they knew about their houses, and allowed us to photograph them. This is how we met Richard Gibson of Pleasant View Gardens and how we learned about what life in Baltimore's newest rowhouses means to the people who live there. Finally for Mary Ellen, special thanks extend to her dad, John Hayward, who actually understood about ground rents since he grew up in St. Louis County, Missouri (where they have them); daughter Milly Brugger, who has been looking at houses for years; and aunt Helen Berry, who shared information on the family's roots in Baltimore's early nineteenth-century brickmaking industry; and a few very special, supportive friends who always provided shoulders to lean on, patience during periods of intense research and writing hibernation, and, most of all, understanding.

Mary Ellen Hayward
Charles Belfoure
Baltimore, Maryland

Foreword

BEGINNING WITH ITS ADOPTION by Baltimoreans in the eighteenth century, the British rowhouse became the dominant house type of the city. This book demonstrates with admirable clarity the changes and lack of changes that have occurred across two centuries in Baltimore. The rowhouse itself was a practical invention for the preindustrial city and nowhere else in the United States has it been employed with such persistence and tireless ingenuity. In its simplest form, the Baltimore rowhouse remained a two-story, single gable structure built on the typical 18-foot by 21-foot module of the early land developers. The history of this development is told in fascinating detail by the authors, who trace the evolution of this type from its earliest and simplest form to the increasingly elaborate mutations at the end of the nineteenth century.

Despite its size and its age, Baltimore appears to be a very little known city to contemporary Americans. The Baltimore cityscapes that travelers on Amtrak see after leaving the central train station display the typical townhouse in row after row strung across the gently rolling landscape. The amazing ability of this basic houseform to adapt to various conditions of both social class and topographical contour is beautifully dramatized in this book. The authors show us quite convincingly the morphological changes in the basic housetype that has served the city in its growth across two centuries.

The two-story, three-bay house in the beginning was, of course, an English invention and represented an efficient development policy that proved viable over decades of use. At the same time, it is impressive to see the way this houseform has been modified across time to meet the needs of different population groups within the city. The starkly functional façades of the earliest rowhouses gave way in later times to all sorts of ornamental façadism. This took many different forms, but the most spectacular was the device of utilizing entire rows of houses to create monumental streetscapes by manipulation of façades alone.

This book is notable for the convincing way the authors have delineated the Baltimorean use of this form. While the illustrative materials of this study are impressive, it is by no means a picture book. The authors have attempted to delineate the major social and economic forces that resulted in the rowhouse's development. Perhaps the most ironic aspect of the story they tell is that of the demolition of thousands of rowhouses during the mid-twentieth century to make way for high-rise housing projects. The latter proved so disastrously unsuccessful that in the 1990s the city received a $293 million grant to demolish these projects and replace them with rowhouses—contemporary versions of the old standby housetype they slaughtered forty years before.

James Marston Fitch
New York City, New York
December 1998

Introduction

The two story houses that were put up in my boyhood, forty years ago, all had a kind of unity, and many of them were far from unbeautiful. Almost without exception, they were built of red brick, with white trim—the latter either of marble or of painted wood. The builders of the time were not given to useless ornamentation: their houses were plain in design and restful to the eye. A long row of them to be sure, was somewhat monotonous, but it at least escaped being trashy and annoying. Before every row, in those days, ranged a file of shade trees. The green against the red, with flecks of white showing through, was always dignified and sometimes very charming. Many such rows survive, but the trees are gone, and new storefronts, plate glass front doors, concrete steps, and other such horrors have pretty well corrupted their old placid beauty.

H. L. Mencken, *Baltimore Evening Sun*, February 7, 1927

ON A WINTER'S MORNING in 1955, a bulldozer started up and plowed into a group of brick rowhouses at the corner of Lexington and Aisquith Streets. When it was through, every rowhouse in the area bounded by Aisquith, Colvin, Fayette, and Orleans Streets was gone. In its place came a high rise housing project called Lafayette Courts.

Forty years later, on a summer's morning in 1995, an electronic signal ignited 995 pounds of dynamite and the six, eleven-story high-rise towers of Lafayette Courts came crashing down. In its place came 228 rowhouses.

The rowhouse has come full circle. For more than one hundred fifty years it symbolized homeownership and stability for Baltimore's working and middle class. After World War II, the rowhouse was spurned in favor of the single-family suburban home and the apartment. Derided in the 1940s and 1950s as an outmoded housing type, it was not the choice of postwar planners to cure the country's urban housing crisis.

In fact, older rowhouses were seen as the enemy: overcrowded, dilapidated, and neglected by absentee landlords. Even worse, many rowhouses in the inner city had become the homes of the poor, those Baltimoreans

1

who could not escape to the suburbs. Idealistic planners imagined the way to rid the city of these evils was to clear "slums" and build in their place new housing that could provide a better living environment for the poor. Some of it worked—low-rise garden apartments that at least retained the scale of the old rowhouse neighborhoods. But when architects looked to high density solutions like Lafayette Courts, the results were dismal. Lafayette Courts was a total failure as a neighborhood. Modern plumbing and elevators could not replace the sense of community that living in a real neighborhood, at street level, created. Forty years later, the projects themselves were the slums, with high crime rates, active drug trafficking, and long-time residents threatened on all sides. Now the rowhouse has been redeemed as a humanely scaled housing form that can help solve inner city housing problems by creating a strong sense of neighborhood.

From any vista Baltimore overwhelms the viewer with tens of thousands of rowhouses. Seen from a moving automobile they seem to stretch forever, forming endlessly repeated miles of look-alike houses. Yet a walk along the same streets, with an alert eye, reveals that there is more to rowhouses than repetition. Built in Baltimore for two centuries now, the houses have defined the urban environment and changed with it. Most major styles of American residential architecture can be seen reflected in Baltimore's rowhouses, from the Federal and Greek Revival to the Italianate, Queen Anne, and Renaissance Revival, and this century's English cottage style and American neocolonial. The very location of the various styles of rowhouses speaks directly to patterns of city growth, changes in public transportation, improvements in infrastructure, and changing demographics. It's true that other American cities like Boston, Philadelphia, New York, Richmond, and St. Louis have rowhousing, but few other cities' psyche and identity are so closely tied to this architectural form as Baltimore's.

The story of Baltimore's rowhousing is the story of residential development in American cities. American cities look the way they do not as the result of any grand urban planning scheme or architectural philosophy, but because of the decisions made by thousands of anonymous speculative builders, each acting on his own to make a profit. It was up to these builders to fill the city's plat with a building form and a density they knew would sell. Collectively they produced a city of homeowners. Thus cities across America were built.

Considered merely a mundane vernacular building form, America's rowhousing (as well as the men who built the houses) has been ignored by most scholars. The process of acquiring land, arranging financing, and constructing and selling houses is absent from most urban histories. But to understand the growth of American cities, one must understand this residential development process. Along with analyzing the critical roles of infrastructure, technology, social, and economic growth, this book will examine builders' records and land records transactions to explain how this real estate development process evolved from small-scale builders, building a few houses at a time in the early nineteenth century, to large-scale building developers, with access to large amounts of capital and land, filling whole tracts in the twentieth century.

In his seminal work *Streetcar Suburbs* (1962) Sam Bass Warner was one of the first American scholars actually to investigate an aspect of the urban development process (in his case, the growth of the first suburbs that ringed the city of Boston). Walter Muir Whitehill's even earlier *Boston, A Topographical History* (1959) provided a fascinating analysis of the forces and people behind the three-hundred-year growth of one of America's oldest cities. Both shed light on the fact that the building of the Boston metropolis was the product of hundreds of thousands of separate decisions. The same can be said of Baltimore, as well as other American cities. The goal of builders to make a profit, the desire of most residents to own a home, investors looking for a return on their money, transit companies seeking to expand, and the government's growing sense of responsibility for public health all came together to create a city. In Baltimore, a special glue held it all together, the ground rent, which made homeownership possible for a much larger cross-section of people.

During the nineteenth century, rowhouses sheltered almost all Baltimoreans from the very rich to the very poor. Those for the wealthy were architect-designed; those for everyone else were built on speculation and, for the most part, designed by the builders themselves. To attract customers and to make their product stand out among the thousands of rowhouses available to purchase, builders kept up with the latest styles, making modifications to cornice designs, window treatments, and the brick façade itself, adding bay windows, peaked roofs, stick-style porches, and carved or molded embellishments when changing fashions dictated. When first the wealthy and then many members of the upper-middle class moved to detached housing in the suburbs in the early twentieth century, builders responded by making rowhouses that had amenities such as front porches and small lawns, building such houses successfully into the mid-1950s.

By this time, however, governmental policies such as zoning and FHA financing discriminated against the city's older housing stock and it began to deteriorate. Planning officials felt the rowhouse had outlived its usefulness as an urban housing form and oversaw the demolition of dozens of inner-city rowhouse blocks. By the late 1960s, however, preservationists had discovered the charm of old rowhouse neighborhoods and throughout the 1970s and early 1980s whole sections of the city were reclaimed and "gentrified."

The rowhouse has always been important to Baltimore's urban health. In the late nineteenth century, city officials understood that Baltimore's high rate of homeownership (about 70 percent) meant economic stability. In the 1990s, after a hiatus of some forty years, the officials once again understand the importance of the rowhouse as the basic building block of city neighborhoods. Contemporary rowhouses, designed with traditional treatments, are replacing public housing towers like Lafayette Courts, while historic rowhouse neighborhoods with renovated houses still attract buyers. Together they are playing an important role in remaking the city. To residents of the nineteenth-century city, the rowhouse offered the dream of homeownership. To those of the 1990s it means exactly the same.

One of the more remarkable qualities about Baltimore is that its growth as a city began very late in the eighteenth century and continued steadily throughout the nineteenth and twentieth centuries. Because development spread outward from the harbor basin, the layers of the city's growth can be read like a series of concentric rings around this central core. Until the 1920s builders offered different housing choices for people of different means as they developed sections of the city. The grandest houses were located on the main streets, often facing parks or squares, lesser houses on the side streets, on down to the smallest of houses located on the narrow "alley" streets that bisected every block. By the 1920s the very wealthy no longer lived in the city. New two-story rowhouse developments were skewed to either middle-class or working-class occupants, depending on the location selected by the builder.

Land records across time allow us to reconstruct the development process and hone in on the activities of individual builders throughout these two centuries. Building was an arduous and risky task and very few men built more than one hundred houses in their lifetime. In the late nineteenth century a few "building developers" emerged, men who built hundreds, or even over a thousand, houses in their careers. But it was not until the early twentieth century that a handful of builders rose to the upper ranks of the trade, building thousands of houses over long careers and establishing companies that continued on after the principal's retirement and death.

Research into land records also enables us to focus on the buyers of rowhouses—who they were, where they came from, what they did for a living, and what they paid for their house. One particular group of row-house buyers, Traugoth Singewald and his descendants, are traced in these pages through seven generations of life in Baltimore rowhouses, from their arrival from Germany in 1840 down to the present day. They started in Baltimore as modest shopkeepers and fulfilled the American dream of rising to the professional classes in three generations. But still they lived in row-houses. We can also trace other inhabitants, most of whom improved their condition in life, moving to new and more stylish rowhouses when they did so. Their housing choice always reflected their understanding of their status in life.

Because this book traces the appearance and development of each rowhouse style through the various classes of society, readers will find that the dates on the chapters overlap. For instance, builders were still constructing houses with Federal-style elements for the working classes and Greek Revival touches for the middle class at the same time they were beginning to erect newly fashionable houses for the very wealthy. This overlap allows us to trace the evolution of specific styles and to clarify how they waxed and waned across the city. It also allows us to discover how builders sought to compete with one another for the middle- and working-class market by adding embellishments designed to suggest that their houses were the most up-do-date and fashionable versions in that particular price range.

As a writer in *American Architect and Buildings News* observed in 1888, dwelling house architecture is really "the architectural type that tells the story of a people more accurately than any other, being the clearer exponent of their habits and taste, in that it is more intimately associated with their lives than any public building, secular or otherwise." Any city's residential architecture deserves study and can tell volumes about almost any aspect of a city's history. It is the one material culture object that directly illuminates inquiries on patterns of city growth, patterns of economic development, demographics, transportation history, business and financial history, evolving technological developments, changing aesthetic tastes and their meaning to the society that embraced them. Most importantly of all it can tell us how people actually *lived* in any given time.

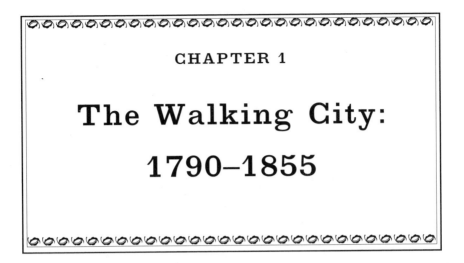

CHAPTER 1

The Walking City:
1790–1855

...even the private dwellings have a look of magnificence, from the abundance of white marble with which many of them are adorned. The ample flights of steps and the lofty door frames are in most of the best houses formed of this beautiful material.

Frances Trollope, *Domestic Manners of the Americans*, 1830

Baltimore from Federal Hill, *painted and engraved by W. J. Bennett, New York, 1831,*
shows the bustling port with its long rows of warehouses extending into the harbor. (Maryland
Historical Society)

IN MAY 1846 Traugoth Singewald, a twenty-year-old who had arrived in
Baltimore from Germany only the year before, bought the first of many
rowhouses in which generations of his family would live and work. It was a
two-and-a-half-story Federal-style house on Liberty Alley, a block east of
the Jones Falls in Old Town, and it cost him $420. Built in 1817, 10
Liberty Alley had already been home to carpenters, a bricklayer, a black-
smith, and a tailor—common occupations for the residents of Old Town,
which had got its start as a center for flour milling. Nearby lived Gottlieb
Singewald, Traugoth's older brother who had arrived in Baltimore in 1840
and operated a hat-making business out of his small home.

The Singewald brothers were part of an enormous wave of German
immigrants who came to Baltimore between 1820 and 1848, largely for
economic reasons. Most were merchants, tradesmen, and professionals,
and many arrived with sufficient capital to set up their businesses quickly.
Baltimore proved to be an ideal location for them. The city had a population of more than 100,000 and by mid-century one in four residents was of
German extraction. Each of the city's original settlements—Baltimore
Town, Old Town, and Fells Point—still had its own commercial streets and
mix of craftsmen and tradesmen to service the immediate community.

Just a few years after his arrival in Old Town Traugoth Singewald
decided to expand the family business by opening a second shop in Fells
Point. He chose a location a few blocks north of the waterfront on South

Broadway, the bustling commercial center of the district. This two-and-a-half-story house was even older, built about 1798, but it was larger and much more finely finished than his house on Liberty Alley, and faced a main commercial street. In 1852 Singewald paid $1,800 for the building, one of a pair of Federal-style houses with a Flemish bond brick façade, stone keystones decorating the window lintels, and an elegant trimmed dormer. When new, the house had been home to a sea captain, one of many who lived in Fells Point and who, with shipbuilders, formed the wealthiest segment of the community. The hat business prospered, Singewald married, and in 1858 he invested $4,500 in a much larger, three-and-a-half-story Federal-style house one block to the south. In this building he consolidated his store, a small manufactory, and, on the upper floors, his residence.[1] This time he owned both the building and the land it stood on (FIGURE 1).

Similar to Philadelphia in these years, Baltimore property transactions operated on a ground rent system. Most homebuyers paid for their house but only rented the land beneath it for a small annual fee, called a ground rent. For houses built in the eighteenth or very early nineteenth centuries, this fee was low—a shilling, a penny, a few dollars (Singewald paid only $3 twice a year for his first house on Broadway). But affluent citizens who could afford to own their land, bought properties in fee or bought the land under their house later in a separate transaction. This is what Singewald did when he purchased the large building that served as his shop and residence. He lived in an active location. The Fells Point Market, which sold fresh seafood, meat, and produce, stood across the street. Every few blocks there was a coal yard where he or one of his employees could fill the scuttle with coal to keep the house, factory, and store warm for several days. At the nearby wharves he could take delivery on the hat fabrics and beaver, muskrat and rabbit pelts purchased through a wholesaler, or he could pay a few pennies and hire a drayman to deliver them to the shop (FIGURE 2).

Fells Point was full of day laborers—from sailors between voyages to recently arrived immigrants—looking for jobs; Singewald had little trouble finding help to set up his machinery, clean his shop, or cook his meals. To promote the relocated business, he paid extra to have the shop listed in capital letters in the city directory and hoped to attract a much broader trade than he had formerly. His immediate neighbors also ran shops on the ground floor of their houses. All were German-born. His neighbor to the north was a clothier; his neighbors to the south were a tailor and another hatter.

Because walking remained the major mode of city travel for all but the wealthiest citizens, the average Baltimorean's whole world existed within walking distance. The limits of the city's development were set by the distance most people were willing to walk—to work, to transact business, shop, or to pay social calls. At mid-century people of all classes still lived close to one another: well-to-do merchants, professional men, and shopkeepers on the main streets; craftsmen and skilled laborers on the side streets; and a mix of skilled and unskilled laborers on the narrow "alley" streets that ran down the center of each block. Baltimore had the nation's largest population of free blacks, and many African-Americans were counted among the city's skilled and unskilled laborers. In the Fells Point section they lived on main, side, and alley streets, providing a vibrant racial mix that added to the cultural life of the "Point." Directly behind Singewald's property, on Bethel Street (formerly called Apple Alley), he could find a German-born shoemaker and a street paver, as well as two African-American seamen, and a drayman. He could walk two blocks up Broadway to attend the German Methodist Episcopal Church; his free black neighbors had about the same trip—the African-American Methodist Episcopal Church stood one block west and two blocks north.[2]

All of these people, wealthy or poor, of English descent, or German, Irish, or African-American origin, lived in rowhouses. Singewald's was the largest type of rowhouse built in the Federal period—a full three-and-a-half-stories tall and three bays wide. On Bethel Street, the rowhouses were two-and-a-half-stories high, only two bays wide, and some were only one room deep. Baltimore's growth as a city of rowhouses is a tale that begins two centuries before this. It was shaped by events in London and other major cities such as Bath in England and Boston and Philadelphia in the American colonies.

The English Background

American rowhouse building derives from English precedent. In mid-eighteenth-century London, imposing, architect-design rows—or "terraces" as they were called in England—arose in affluent areas of the city. Modeled after earlier seventeenth-century Palladian grand *palazzo* façades, such as the continuous block-face around Covent Garden Piazza (begun 1630) by Inigo Jones, new rows of multiple houses emphasized unity and monumentality in design. To create the appearance of a grand town palace, façades within the row were articulated with central and end pavilions marked by giant classical orders; a deep cornice unified the composition, often masking a gable roof with a high balustrade. Eminent designers

Robert and James Adam first used the term *terrace* to describe their design of Adelphi Terrace (1769) (FIGURE 3). The four-story Adelphi was one of the first block-long rows to go up in London; the Adam brothers designed the joined units to suggest the block-long façade of a grand town palace articulated with pedimented and projecting end pavilions and a central projecting unit. Another row is Bedford Square (1775–80), which remains the most complete and best preserved of London's Georgian squares. Each unit is three bays wide, three-and-a-half stories tall, with a basement below.

While only the grandest of terraces were clad with such decorative elements as full-height columns and pilasters or central pavilions, even simplified and lower-cost rows maintained the proportions of the elegant Palladian façades: high, clearly articulated basements, tall first stories, and reduced second (and sometimes third) stories; the whole capped by a significant cornice and a low-pitched gable roof, often with dormer windows to light the garret space. In these buildings the standard floor plan consisted of a two-room-deep main block with entryway and stairhall at one side, and a narrow rear extension housing the kitchen (if it was not in the basement of the main block), a wash house, and extra bedrooms. Soon such dwellings were being built to house all levels of British society. Those for working people were modest, narrow two-story units built along the lesser streets, courts, mews, and alleys, as well as in the newly industrializing areas of the city. Those for the middle-class were fairly regularized two- and three-story rows often laid out around planted and gated squares, though somewhat removed from the most fashionable areas. And those for the affluent were the luxurious large-scale terrace houses sited in planned developments encircling wider expanses of green space, such as Bloomsbury Square, Bedford Square, and Regents Park.[3]

London's Building Act of 1774 consolidated the many code reforms that had been enacted in the century since the Great Fire of 1666, and established four "rates" of houses, of different sizes, cost, and structural requirements. The finest and highest rated was a house valued at more than £850 and having more than 900 square feet. The lowest was one valued at less than £150 and having only 350 square feet. Building laws mandated specific requirements for foundations and party walls for each class of house and outlawed any projecting exterior woodwork. The code was also intended to regulate the homebuilding market, according to architectural historian John Summerson:

> the real importance of this system was not so much that it facilitated
> the enforcement of a structural code but that it confirmed a degree of

standardization in speculative building. This was inevitable; for the limitation of size and value set out in the rating tended to create optimum types from which there was no escape and within which very little variation was possible. Especially did the second, third, and fourth rates of houses tend to become stereotyped. This was, in many ways, an excellent thing: it gave some degree of order and dignity to the later suburbs and incidentally laid down minimum standards for working- class urban housing.... [4]

Virtually all the post-Great Fire rowhousing in London was speculatively built by men investing their own capital, hoping that the houses would sell and earn a profit. These men shaped the look of the city. Their development process followed a consistent pattern decade after decade. Most of the land was owned by a handful of very wealthy individuals, who in order to derive an income from it, leased plots to builders for a low initial rent—called a peppercorn rent. During the first year, the builder would erect the houses as quickly as possible, then sell them to a buyer who would also assume the land (or ground) rent, which ran for a period of ninety-nine years. The builder's rent for the land was practically nothing, so long as he found a buyer for the houses before the peppercorn period ended. The money from the sale of each house enabled the builder to pay off mortgage loans, make a profit on the sale of the house, and start another deal. Generally the men who leased land and built for the speculative market were carpenters, masons, joiners and others in the building trades. As they usually lacked the investment capital and labor supply to erect large numbers of contiguous houses, most built pairs of houses on scattered sites throughout the city. They acted as their own designer, using pattern books compiled especially for builders, such as Batty Langley's *The Builder's Compleat Assistant*, William Halfpenny's *Practical Architect*, and even Isaac Ware's edition of Palladio. To underwrite construction costs they turned to private individuals such as businessmen, shopkeepers, or widows looking for a five percent return on their money. [5]

Ground Rents in England and America

Ground rent, or the system of renting the land on which the houses were built, proved crucial to London's rowhouse development. A ground rent is the amount of money an individual must pay annually for the privilege of using a piece of land. In England the custom was well established within the legal system, having been derived from the feudal practice of exacting a tithe or share of the crop from each yeoman farmer who lived on a nobleman's domain. It was encouraged by two other customary practices: primogeniture, which required that an estate pass from the eldest son of one generation to the eldest son in the next; and entail, which prevented any one of the owners from selling the land outright. The effect of these was to make the income of many of the members of the nobility dependent upon tenant farmers. As English cities started to expand, some nobles realized that their land was worth much more for building than for farming. They also discovered that although they could not sell their land, they could lease it for ninety-nine years. (Ninety-nine years was considered the adult life span of three men: father, son, and grandson; it was also presumed to be the useful life of an eighteenth century house.) The builder himself could retain the lease or he could rent the house and land to tenants. In ninety-nine years the land and the house automatically reverted to the families of the estates, and they could then rehabilitate the property, tear it down and build anew, or rent out the property at a sizable rent increase called a rack rent.

The ground rent became a method of land tenure in British-American colonies such as Maryland and Pennsylvania, particularly in the cities of Baltimore and Philadelphia. In both, the lord proprietors drew upon their personal experience as landowners and encouraged the perpetuation of the traditional English form of development: lease the land to builders (and by extension the house buyers) and annually collect a rent for the use of that land. Under the Maryland Charter, the Lords Baltimore exercised their proprietary land rights to traditional feudal "quit rents." This practice was abolished with the new state constitution of 1782, but the practice of creating leaseholds for 99-year terms, renewal forever, continued. Baltimore, laid out in 1729, grew more slowly than Philadelphia, platted in 1682, and thus while Annapolis, Philadelphia, and Boston in 1750 gloried in Georgian architectural splendor, the tiny hamlet of Baltimore on the Patapsco River numbered houses only in the hundreds (FIGURE 4). Initially established as a local tobacco shipping point, Baltimore's fortunes changed dramatically in the 1760s when an enterprising group of immigrant Scots-Irish merchants began shipping wheat and flour to Great Britain and later the West Indies. These same merchants reaped substantial profits during the American Revolution and the Napoleonic Wars and by 1800 Baltimore had become the third largest city in the nation. The swelling population necessitated immense building activity and employed aspiring builders drawn from the ranks of carpenters and masons. Buyers and builders alike embraced the concept of renting the land on which to build houses, instead of purchasing it.

Thomas Harrison introduced ground rents to Baltimore. A shipping merchant, Harrison had arrived from England in 1742 and established his business at the end of South Street on the waterfront. Five years later he bought the twenty-eight-acre marsh that separated the two parts of the newly incorporated Baltimore Town: Baltimore and Jones Town (later called Old Town). In 1750 he began putting lots on the market, selling some outright but also offering to make the lots (most of which needed reclamation) more affordable by leasing them for an annual sum, "for and during the full term of ninety-nine years," with perpetual renewals and no down payment. Among the lessees were the Town Commissioners, who in 1763 obtained the site for the city's first market house, called "Marsh Market."[6]

In 1761 another major figure emerged in local land development. Edward Fell the younger consolidated the Fell family's several holdings on the Point. Two years later he laid out streets, using a grid system. After his death in 1766, his widow Ann successfully marketed the family land holdings, relying on the allure of the ground rent system to keep initial costs low. To ensure that her property would increase in value, Fell attached covenants requiring that a substantial dwelling or commercial structure be erected on each lot within two years, or the property would revert to her for re-leasing.

John Eager Howard, a hero in the Revolutionary War, also became a leading supplier of land for Baltimore's development using the ground rent system. Perhaps in response to new legislation after the war abolishing entailments in Maryland, he carved up Lunn's Lott, a vast acreage to the west and south of the harbor, which he had inherited from his father, Cornelius Howard, who had acquired the land in 1763 when he married Ruth Eager, daughter of the original patentee. On it John laid out "Howard's Addition" with some 350 sixty-foot building lots punctuated by a new north-south axis named Howard Street and also offered to sell outright some larger tracts, such as the section extending south of the basin into Federal Hill. At about the same time the Moale family, owners of the 257-acre David's Fancy, which encompassed the whole southern end of the peninsula just south of Howard's land, began offering portions of the property for lease or sale to individual farmers or investors.

These landowners sometimes offered builders another incentive: an advance mortgage. Simply put, this was a loan to cover construction costs, which thereby provided landowners with another source of investment income. They executed the advance mortgage at the same time they leased the unimproved lot to the builder. The builder was lent fifty percent of the value of the finished house, payable on an incremental schedule based on staged completion of the dwelling: one-fourth when the second floor joists had been laid; one-fourth when roofed in; one-fourth when the floors were laid; and the last payment when the house was finished and ready for occupancy. Most advance mortgages also specified the type and size of house that would be financeable on the lot: whether two or three stories, the building's depth (front footage being fixed by the lot size), ceiling heights, the materials to be used, and the timetable for construction. Such specifications protected the landowner's investment in the land (and his ground rent) by ensuring that a house commensurate to the ground rent being charged would be built. The practice also gave landowners the power to set the quality standards for the neighborhoods they were developing. Thus, by specifying and financing the cost of a three-story house of certain proportions and level of finish raised on the lots they owned, they were assured a certain economic and social level of purchaser and, they hoped, a fashionable neighborhood.

Unlike in England, where entailments kept the ground rent within the landowner's family, in Baltimore ground rents quickly became highly negotiable investment vehicles. In a time when savings accounts paid 2 percent to 3 percent, and bonds 4 percent to 5 percent, ground rents were considered dependable 6-percent investments, secured by the land and a first lien. If a householder defaulted on the ground rent, the landlord had the right to take both the land and the house. This did not happen often, an individual who paid $500 for his house would not risk losing it because of a $38 annual payment. The attractiveness of ground rents as investment vehicles soon made them important to future rowhouse development in Baltimore.

America's First Rows

The rowhouse form appeared in the British-American colonies early on: archaeological evidence suggests some were built in colonial Virginia at Jamestown and pictorial evidence suggests they existed in early-to-mid-eighteenth-century Boston and Philadelphia.[7] But the rowhouse as an expensive, fashionable dwelling—emulating the grand terraced houses of London—did not make an appearance in the United States until the 1790s. One of the first architects to design such a project in America was young Charles Bulfinch who in 1793, shortly after returning to Boston from a Grand Tour of Europe, proposed to build a radically new form of housing—a crescent of sixteen three-story, three-bay-wide houses, much resembling those in London designed by Scottish-born architects Robert and James Adam and those in Bath, England. Across from this elliptical-shaped row, Bulfinch set eight houses in a straight row. Between the two structures, he sited a semi-oval park. To obtain financing he adopted an English scheme, called a "tontine," whereby the capital raised for construction was secured by stock that would eventually be divided among surviving subscribers. The project thus was given the name "Tontine Crescent." Bulfinch's design for the façade echoed that on the Palladian-inspired examples he had recently seen in London: he marked the central portion of the row with giant pilasters set over the central arched opening that led to the rear of the block. Some years later, in 1805, Bulfinch began another fashionable row, this one comprised of four houses, four-and-a-half-stories, on Park Street near the new State House. For these he used wide, recessed arches to mark ground-floor openings, similar to those he designed in the earlier Harrison Gray Otis houses, which had drawn on the work of classicist Sir John Soane in London. Otherwise, the houses are quite restrained. Five years later Bulfinch introduced something new again—for Colonnade Row on Tremont Street he unified the long façade made up of nineteen four-story houses by extending a two-storied portico along the entire façade.[8]

In Philadelphia, elegant rowhouses for affluent owners also made their first appearance in the 1790s. An unknown builder introduced the form early in the decade with Norris Row on Chestnut Street. Thomas Carstairs built along Sansom and Walnut Streets for William Sansom around 1799–1803; these three-and-a-half-story houses measured twenty feet by forty feet and had such old-fashioned Georgian decorative elements as white belt courses, high basements, and modillion cornices. The three-and-a-half-story, three-bay houses in York Row, 1807–08, combined the older Georgian taste of splayed lintels and slightly projecting keystones with contemporary Adamesque elements, such as doorways with arched fanlights and delicate sidelights. A year or so later, Robert Mills, the first professionally trained American-born architect, designed fashionable rowhouses in an entirely different style; these reflected the spare classicism of Sir John Soane, as seen in his 1798 *Sketches in Architecture*, with signature tripartite windows, recessed arches, and a planar façade. As a part of this development scheme Mills also prepared a plan for an entire square, solidly in the current London tradition. Only ten of the forty-two houses were ever built, and the group was named Franklin Row, after Benjamin Franklin, just as Bulfinch's row opposite Tontine Crescent in Boston had been named.[9] In Washington, D.C., Wheat Row, a block-long row with Palladian-style central and end pavilions, went up on Fourth Street, SW, near the waterfront, followed in subsequent decades by several long rows on Capitol Hill and Georgetown.

The Fashionable Row in Baltimore

The earliest grand rows to appear in Baltimore date from the mid-1790s, about the same time Bulfinch was building Tontine Crescent in Boston. The initiative came not from an architect but from the landowner specula-tors who developed their properties.[10] In 1796 flour merchants Thomas McElderry and Cumberland Dugan built matching 1,600-foot-long wharves extending south from Market Place (the site of Centre Market and the commercial hub of the town). On the wharves, they built long rows of grand houses on either side, following the model established by the Adam brothers at London's Adelphi Terrace (FIGURE 5). Three-and-a-half stories high, with hipped roofs and dormer windows, high English basements defined by a prominent belt course, and stone window lintels with project-ing keystones, the rows made a monumental design statement. As at Adelphi Terrace, the high basement provided commercial space for mer-chants, grocers, and storekeepers at wharf level, while the upper floors served as residences. (Further down each wharf less elaborate buildings served strictly as warehouses, mainly for the flour trade.) McElderry insured the rowhouses on his wharf in 1800 and 1802, each house valued at $3,200; his renters included a group of commission merchants, flour mer-chants, lumber merchants, and grocers.[11]

Dugan and McElderry also built facing mixed-use rows just north of the wharves, on either side of Market Place. St. Patrick's Row, McElderry's pro-ject, was occupied initially by a ship chandler, merchants, a cabinetmaker, and a gentlewoman. Cumberland Row, Dugan's project, was home to two commission merchants, a grocery merchant, a composition manufacturer, a shoemaker and tailor sharing one unit, and an innkeeper who lived in one unit and operated his beefsteak and oyster house in another.[12] The impor-tance of Dugan's and McElderry's rows became clear when they were used as one of two illustrations of important public buildings (the other was the Assembly Rooms) on a major map of the city published in 1801 (FIGURE 6). Their status also appealed to other landowners, such as Daniel Bowly, who advertised the same year the auction sale of his "very valuable city lots," one group of which was located "on St. Patrick-street, at the back of and parallel to that elegant range of buildings on McElderry's wharf."[13]

Other wealthy Baltimoreans also initiated grand rowhouse projects. In 1795 John O'Donnell, the merchant who opened Baltimore's trade with China in 1787, erected two rows of six houses each on opposite sides of Commerce Street, three-and-a-half stories and three bays wide, just north of Pratt Street and the waterfront. The spacious houses had 23-1/2-foot fronts, a depth of 36 feet, and a 12-by-21-foot, two-story back building that housed the kitchen. Like Dugan and McElderry, O'Donnell built the rowhouses to produce rental income, and when he took out his insurance policy the first two houses, 6 and 8 Commerce, were already occupied. Soon he added a merchant and a broker as first-floor tenants and a painter and a baker as renters upstairs. On other occasions the merchant-tenant used the ground floor for his office and lived on the upper floors.[14]

In 1796 Richard Caton, son-in-law of Charles Carroll of Carrollton, Maryland's wealthiest citizen and a signer of the Declaration of Independence, built four three-and-a-half-story, three-bay-wide rowhouses on the north side of King George Street near Still House Street (present-day Lombard and Front Streets), bordering the east side of Jones Falls in Old Town. The fashionable façades had tall windows marked by stone lintels with projecting keystones, and twelve-over-twelve sash, and, as was common at the time (and for most of the nineteenth century) porches called "Balconys" extending along the first and second floors of the back building (FIGURE 7). Presenting a similar appearance were merchant John Carrere's four three-and-a-half-story rowhouses (built by 1798) on Harrison Street, northeast of Market Place on land that had once been the site of Harrison's Marsh. Further from the center of town, Carrere's houses were slightly smaller than those of O'Donnell or Caton. But like his counterparts, Carrere had invested in these buildings for their rental income, and he advertised two of them in the *Baltimore American* on March 24, 1801:

To Let,

A CONVENIENT three story brick House, in Harrison-street, near the centre market, having a convenient two story brick kitchen, large yard and a commodious brick Warehouse on the lot, and near the Falls, convenient for water carriage. This house and back buildings are suitable for a merchant in extensive business. Possession may be had the first of April next.

Also,

A convenient three story brick HOUSE, with convenient back buildings, and the lot extending to the water, near the above mentioned house, in Harrison-street, now in the tenure of Mr. Andrew Parks. Possession may be had the first of May next. Enquire in East-street, of

JOHN CARRERE

By 1804 the residents in the area included a variety of craftsmen—a silversmith, umbrella maker, shoemaker, chairmaker, clock and watch-maker, and a saddle and harnessmaker. [15]

Perhaps the last fashionable row designed in the early Federal style was built some blocks north of the waterfront in a stylish residential area emerging on the square facing the court house. There Revolutionary War hero Dr. James McHenry, for whom Fort McHenry is named, built a row of five elegant three-and-a-half-story houses in 1802, 25 feet wide by 40 feet deep, with high basements housing the kitchen and dining room, and tall front steps with iron railings that gave the row a distinguished appearance (FIGURE 8). By 1804 the five houses were occupied by McHenry, two attorneys, a merchant, a Mrs. Goodwin, who ran a boarding house, and a Mrs. Groombridge, who operated a ladies' boarding school.[16]

What role architects had in designing these rows is undocumented and open to speculation. In these years there were two self-styled architects of prominence in Baltimore: gentleman-architect Colonel Nicholas Rogers designed the Palladian-style Assembly Rooms (also pictured on the 1801 map) and submitted a design for a temple form church building for the local Episcopal congregation. Robert Cary Long Sr., who began his career as a carpenter, became the chief builder of the Assembly Rooms (1797) and actually won the commission for St. Paul's Episcopal Church. He was responsible for the original Peale Museum building (1814) as well as the Pantheon-style School of Medicine of the University of Maryland (1812). Wealthy merchants *cum* land developers may have turned to these well-known local figures for design assistance, or they may simply have hired well-respected master builders to carry out their plans.[17]

Federal Rows for Ordinary People

Fashionable and grand rowhouses stood well beyond the reach of most eighteenth-century Baltimoreans. As the city's population doubled in one decade—swelling from 13,500 people in 1790 to 26,500 by 1800 (making it the third largest city in the U.S., after New York and Philadelphia)—there was a real need to provide housing for the new arrivals. These included middle-class craftsmen, merchants, and shopkeepers; ship builders and ship captains; "mechanics," brewers, building tradesmen and the like; and an even larger number of lower-income laborers, sailors, carters, and others who made up the majority of workers and who needed housing close to their workplaces.

Such construction fell under the purview of builders, not architects, and the structures they put up tended to be rowhouses, two-and-a-half stories tall. Although some of these ordinary houses had elegant fanlighted doorways and interior detailing, many more had simple rectangular transoms, and rather plain interior woodwork. All those built after 1799 were made of brick, as required by law, but until then about half the structures in the city had been woodframe and only a few of these survive.

The rowhouses that were home to most early-nineteenth-century Baltimoreans were similar in general design to those built in London: three bays wide and two rooms deep; two bays wide and two rooms deep; or, two bays wide and only one room deep. Most had back buildings, but, if not, the house sat on a high basement, which housed the kitchen. The largest of the three-bay versions measured between 18 feet and 23 feet wide and 30 feet to 40 feet deep in the main block, followed often by a narrow "pantry" no larger than 10 feet by 12 feet, and a kitchen wing of about 14 feet by 20 feet, or often smaller. A side hall extended the length of the main block, from which doors opened into the front and rear parlors. Stairs usually ran in a straight flight at the rear of the hall, with a second stair in the pantry. The back building normally contained two rooms, the family breakfast room and the kitchen. The second floor held three bedrooms in the main block and two more in the back building, the latter reached by the "Balcony."

For households further down the economic scale, two-bay-wide houses were most common. These had no side hall. Winder stairs to the second floor rose next to the partition wall separating the parlor and dining room; the kitchen was in a narrower rear addition. The interior millwork consisted of simple mantels, plain window and door casings, and an occasional chair rail. The low basement usually was accessed from within the house. Most houses had a one- or two-story back building no more than 9 feet by 12 feet in size with one room on each floor. The dormer story held a single room with a 7-foot ceiling at the center, sloping down to about three feet at the front and back of the house (FIGURE 9).

The most modest forms of rowhousing were built to house the city's poorest laboring population. The rapidly expanding city grew at a rate even builders had trouble keeping up with (the population rose by at least 20,000 people each decade early in the century); one solution was spare, multiple-dwelling housing, not unlike that found in British mill towns. In 1816 the trustees of the Methodist Episcopal Church directed the parish to build a structure 68 feet by 17-1/2 feet, "two stories, elevated," and "divided into four equal dwellings." Each unit was approximately 17 feet wide—one room per floor with basement kitchen and finished garret for extra sleeping quarters.[17] Many small rowhouses were built on the narrow streets, or alleys, that ran down the center of city blocks. These had such colorful names as Happy Alley, Apple Alley, Strawberry Alley, Bottle Alley, Cyder Alley, and Whiskey Alley. In the early nineteenth century some of these houses were quite small indeed—one-and-a-half-stories and only 10-1/2 feet to 12 feet wide, with or without a one-story kitchen addition. Most, however, were a full two-and-a-half stories in height, but they might be only one room deep under a steep gable roof, with kitchen in a back building (FIGURE 10).

The tiniest of the rowhouses often served as residences of the city's large free black population, as well as for the growing number of rurally owned slaves who had been sent to the city by their owners to work in wage-earning jobs, such as shipbuilding and brickmaking. These "urban slaves" enjoyed a large degree of freedom, living without masters, and rarely having to return to the plantation. (Frederick Douglass, for example, a Talbot County slave, was sent to Baltimore to work for shipbuilder Hugh Auld in 1825 and lived in several small rowhouses.) According to city directories, which after 1808 noted "colored residents" with a mark in the margin or listed them in a separate section of the book, the alley streets and other areas containing modest housing were remarkably integrated—with free black caulkers, mariners, laborers, draymen, and laundresses sharing blocks with whites who were in the same professions.

Constructing the First Rows

The rapid growth in the city's population from 1790 onward encouraged widespread building activity and, perhaps predictably, carpenters, painters, plasterers, glaziers, masons and other members of the building trades constituted a large percentage of the city's workforce. These craftsmen ultimately followed traditions established in Georgian England, both in terms of style and craftsmanship; however, in most cases the traditions were filtered through the lens of Philadelphia, the cultural and political center of the new nation. Indeed many of the building tradesmen in Baltimore hailed originally from Philadelphia, having moved on to Baltimore to take advantage of the prospering city's need for their skills.

Some of these craftsmen, especially the carpenters and masons, became speculative builders, as had their counterparts in London. They generally had been responsible for the lion's share of house construction, often assuming the role of "master builder" and subcontracting with the various other tradesmen—masons, plasterers, painters, glaziers, pavers, and plumbers—to finish the house. Given Baltimore's land rent system, the transition to speculative builder did not look to be a difficult step. Bricklayer James Mosher and carpenters Jacob Small and John Sinclair, who are credited with many prominent buildings erected in the early nineteenth century, epitomized these ambitious men.[19] They aspired to raise themselves socially and economically, to call themselves "architects," and as soon as they acquired capital, to begin building houses on speculation. The ground rent system allowed them to acquire the land on which to speculate for no cost, as the house could be under construction and already sold to an owner (who would then have some say in the finish details) before the first ground rent payment became due. These builders leased lots from either major landowners—such as John Eager Howard—or from smaller developers, who had acquired parcels from landowners like Howard.[20]

David Williamson was one such merchant-turned-developer, an entrepreneur who bought a two-block tract from Howard in Federal Hill in 1789 on which he laid out fifteen-foot-wide lots along Montgomery Street, a wide street just a block south of the basin. A few years later Williamson leased the lots to a variety of individuals subject to three-year building clauses, which specified that the buildings be made of brick (predating the 1799 city code that outlawed frame construction for all buildings except firehouses). Ford Barnes, a carter, hired craftsmen to build a pair of houses at 9 and 11 East Montgomery Street (FIGURE 11). He made his home in the three-bay-wide house at 9 Montgomery, and rented the adjoining two-bay-wide house. The pattern of building pairs of houses—one to live in, one on speculation to sell or rent—continued in Baltimore through the 1820s.[21]

Other speculators were drawn from the ranks of building materials suppliers, such as brickmaker John Cator, who in 1818 built not far from his brickyards in South Baltimore the first documented row of two-room deep, two-bay-wide, two-and-a-half-story houses to go up in Federal Hill: five along South Charles Street, and three around the corner on Henrietta Street. The houses demonstrate the ways in which builders adapted the features of high-style Federal townhouses to the more modest pocketbooks of average Baltimoreans (FIGURE 12). The rooms in the 11-foot-wide main block were 12 to 13 feet deep with ceiling heights of 8-1/2 feet on the first floor and 8 feet on the second. The front door opened directly into the parlor and the dining room beyond, reached through a 4-foot-wide opening. Tightly winding enclosed stairs rose just beyond the partition wall next to the dining room fireplace. One flight led down to the basement; the other, reached by a door set a few steps above floor level, to the second floor and dormer story. The four main rooms of the house had fireplaces. The two-story kitchen wing, measuring about 9 feet by 15 feet, had a wide cooking fireplace in the rear wall. The space above the kitchen provided extra sleeping space, though the ceiling height was less than 7 feet. Because the houses were built in rows, the kitchen wings were constructed in pairs, running back under a single gable roof set perpendicular to the street. The space between back buildings of neighboring houses formed a kind of rear courtyard or wide alleyway, which allowed light to enter the side windows of the wing. Rough frame privies were located at the rear of the 110-foot lots. Cator sold his houses for prices of $1,000 to $1,200, to the owner of an oil and paint store located on the newly built Light Street wharf facing the basin; the owner of a chair factory who used the rear part of his lot for his workshop; and to several different landlords who were investing in the property for its rental income.[22]

In many cases speculative building relied on the barter system, with various craftsmen exchanging their skills in building ventures, as each in turn undertook a construction project.[23] In 1822, for instance, Joshua Fort, a house carpenter responsible for one of the city's earliest long rows, advertised that he "would be willing to receive at least one half the amount of the sales of this property in any suitable articles of trade, or merchandize, or in several branches of mechanics' work, such as painting, carpenters'

23

work by the piece, etc." He further noted that he "continues to contract for and perform buildings in any articles of trade as above."[24] Especially for men in the building trades, there was great temptation to raise one's status from being a relatively low weekly wage earner, who might be employed only half the year, to a small-scale investment capitalist. A speculative venture that turned out well could substantially raise a craftsman's financial standing. Builders generally leased land at the beginning of the summer, obtained construction money by taking an advance mortgage from the landowner, and had the house(s) ready for sale by the next spring. If they had made judicious decisions—choosing a good location, building in a style and/or price range that had market appeal—speculative builders did well. If they misjudged the market and the house(s) failed to sell by the time the interest or principal of the advance mortgage came due, as well as the ground rent, the builder faced ruin.

To the Public
The subscriber some time since loaned a sum of money to a certain
HEZEKIAH REESE, house carpenter, about 5 feet 7 1-2 inches high, fair
complexion, light hair, rather portly made, and red face, with a stoop in
his shoulders—which money the said Reese has not repaid, but has
eloped or now skulks about the city. The subscriber therefore deems it a
duty to caution the citizens of the U. States, from being imposed upon
by such a swindler.

JOHN AYRES[25]

Many builders, after receiving on-the-job training in their youth, relied on builders' handbooks for a good deal of specific technical information as adults. There was no shortage of publications to choose from, for a boom had begun in 1678 with the issuing of John Moxon's *Meckanick Exercises*. In simple straightforward prose keyed to illustrations, Moxon explained the "art and mystery" of the building crafts—masonry, carpentry, plastering, and joinery. His how-to book was revolutionary. Instead of spending years as an apprentice and then a journeyman, Moxon maintained that one could learn the basics of construction in weeks. Moxon's book also encouraged practical men to understand the details of the other building trades. The approach caught on, and in the eighteenth century other authors followed his lead, notably Batty Langley, William Halfpenny, Francis Price, and William Salmon.[26]

Builders' handbooks published in England made their way across the Atlantic and became the primary source of construction training for local builders up and down the eastern seaboard. Indeed the rowhouses of early-nineteenth-century Baltimore suggest that builders followed Moxon's basic construction techniques: foundations were dug down to firm ground, and broad flat stones, two feet wider than the brick foundation wall, were used as footings. (Oak planks were used for footings as well, and when soil conditions were especially bad oak pilings were driven.) Joists were 7 inches by 3 inches, a size Moxon recommended, but were set on 20-inch centers rather than the 12-inch centers Moxon advocated. Mortise and tenon joints, a time-consuming carpentry method that required considerable skill, were routinely used. The ax and the adze were still the main tools for shaping joists and girders in the earliest of the rows. To be sure some changes did occur during the early nineteenth century. Square, rough-hewn logs were pit-sawn in lumberyards, a number of which were located on Baltimore's wharves. (A two-man, hand operation, pit sawing left the cross cut marks visible on the joists of a majority of early-nineteenth-century rowhouses.) This method was replaced in the 1830s by steam-powered perpendicular and circular saws that allowed lumber mills to produce upwards of 20,000 feet of plank per day. The invention of machine-made nails in 1795, and subsequent improvements in nail technology, made it possible to connect framing members by nailing, speeding up construction times and cutting labor costs so that ever longer rows could be built during the six to nine month construction cycle.[27]

Moxon had also emphasized the importance of wall thickness to building height, recommending a thickness of two bricks for the front and rear walls in a two-story building, and party walls one brick thick. Baltimore's speculative two-story rows follow these guidelines.[28] However, practical fears about fire even more directly influenced Baltimore building standards. In 1799 city leaders outlawed frame construction of new homes, and in 1826 the city passed an ordinance requiring that new buildings be finished with a parapet or fire walls on the gable ends and dividing walls between units, and that any reroofing be done with slate. Because rowhouse building was a speculative venture, builders were always trying to cut costs to increase profits and in many cases ignored the mandates. Thus if a fire started in one house, it quickly spread across the garrets of the rest of the row.[29]

Owing to the area's geological resources, with abundant amounts of high-quality clays for brickmaking in the soil, Baltimore became a city of brick after the passage of the 1799 ordinance outlawing frame construction.[30] A surprising number of the early frame buildings survived in the city until the Baltimore fire of 1904, and even today examples can be found in

Fells Point, Old Town, and Federal Hill. But beginning with the new century, the city's appearance began to change dramatically (FIGURE 13).

Early-nineteenth-century brickmaking remained a relatively small-scale operation, making use of hand methods of production that involved forcing wet clay into wooden molds. The result was an irregular-shaped brick that required a thick lime mortar bed to make up for its rough surfaces. On two- and three-and-a-half-story Federal style rowhouses, Flemish bond (an alternating pattern of headers and stretchers in each course) was used on façades until the mid-1820s, at which point it was supplanted by American common bond, which used a header row every five or seven courses. Common bond was already an established technique, used for the façades of the smallest houses as well as for nearly all cellars, rear walls, and party walls. Running bond (all stretchers facing front) began to be used on principal façades in the 1830s but aspects of the bonding were poor, leading to the bowing out of the front façades especially on many of the more inexpensively built rows.

For window and door lintels, bricklayers tended to use jack arches or segmental arches, though to save time and money many builders opted to put in simple wooden lintels. Sash windows, a Dutch invention that had supplanted the casement by the early 1700s, were generally set back from the plane of the front wall, as in England to reduce the risk of fire. Fireplaces, usually installed in all four principal rooms of a two-room-deep rowhouse, had openings that averaged 32 inches to 36 inches wide by 30 inches high, with depths around 14 inches; second-floor openings were as small as 24 inches by 22 inches. The flues came together in the third-floor garret, funneling into a single chimney on the party wall. Most fireplaces were jack arched and laid in a stretcher bond. Masons coated the interiors of fireplaces with cement to insulate the brick from excessive heat. The chimney remained unlined and the rough surface tended to build up creosote, a fire hazard. By law, chimneys had to be swept every four weeks. Chimneysweeps earned 8 cents for cleaning a one-story chimney, 12-$\frac{1}{2}$ cents for two stories, 15 cents for three, and 18 cents for a chimney of four stories or more.[31] While the English continued to use fireplaces as the main heat source for their homes, even long after most Europeans had switched to stoves, Americans gravitated to the newer utility of slow burning stoves, with their large heating surfaces.[32] By the late eighteenth century, many housebuilders recognized that coal was by far the most economical and efficient fuel: a coal-burning Franklin Stove provided thirty-seven hours of heat compared to ten hours for wood burning in an ordinary fireplace. Still, as one newspaper writer made clear in 1822, the technology of the day had its problems:

The defective and awkward manner which most grates for burning coals in, are constructed and fixed, not excepting such as are imported from England, and set up by European workman, has disappointed many persons, and prevented others from using coal fires, however safe, comfortable, or economical.

The author argued that the English grate created a draft that sucked all the heat out of the room and went on to praise the fireplace design of "our countryman Count Rumford" for being well adapted for burning coal, as long as the grate was properly constructed. (Rumford, a Massachusetts Tory who later worked in Munich, made a revolutionary improvement in 1796: by narrowing flues above the fire, providing a smoke shelf, decreasing the size of the front opening, and angling the sides of the firebox, his fireplace design increased radiant heat. Many of Baltimore's rowhouse fireplaces show the Rumford influence. In fact, users voiced complaints that too much heat was produced.) [33]

The number of U.S. patents for stove designs peaked during the 1830s and 1840s. Freestanding cast-iron stoves could be placed well into the room and needed only simple stovepipes. Base-burner stoves, designed to hold enough coal for ten to twelve hours of burning, were also popular among rowhouse owners. The coal was poured into a bin at the top of the stove; ashes fell into a second bin at the bottom (FIGURE 14).[34]

Attempts to Build an Infrastructure

As city lots filled up with new houses, Baltimore's municipal authorities became increasingly concerned about the effects of unregulated growth. Fire was perhaps their most constant concern and even before they took steps to prohibit frame construction they looked into providing firefighters with a continuous supply of water.

In 1792 the Maryland legislature created a fire insurance company and gave it the option of supplying the town with water for firefighting through a corporate body called the Baltimore Water Company; the insurance company chose not to exercise the option. As in many other cities, most notably Philadelphia, such reluctance to provide a public water supply was jolted into reality by a yellow fever epidemic in 1800. Because residents drew their drinking, cleaning, and cooking water from wells and springs, the mayor and city council had no choice but to create a water company to introduce water into the city. Finally in 1804, the Baltimore Water

Company took form through the creation of a joint stock company. Company directors included John Eager Howard, Samuel Smith, Alexander McKim, Thomas McElderry, and Robert Goodloe Harper, all of whom played a major role in the residential development of the city, as landowners, civic leaders, and speculators. They were well aware of how an improved infrastructure might raise land values.[35]

The company chose Jones Falls rather than Gwynns Falls as the main water source and in May 1807 channeled water to a reservoir on the southwest corner of Cathedral and Franklin Streets. They created a second reservoir east of Calvert Street, near Centre. The mains were 8-foot long hemlock logs, bored between 1-$\frac{1}{2}$ inches and 4 inches in diameter; the service pipes, 6-inch round cedar logs, had 1-inch bores. (Two-inch wrought-iron bands joined the logs.) From 1810 to 1821, residential development followed the path of the city's expanding water system.[36]

Most Baltimoreans drew water at a hand pump located somewhere along the block. Advertisements for houses often stipulated: "a pump of as good water as any at the door," or "several pumps of good water very convenient." Especially elegant houses always had their own "hydrant of water in the yard" (FIGURE 15). Not until the 1840s did publications extol the virtues of indoor plumbing systems and did architectural design books begin to explain how to install and use plumbing fixtures. It was rare in Baltimore and the rest of America prior to 1840 to have piped water inside the house.[37] Meanwhile housewives and servants emptied chamber pots daily and called upon night soil carters to empty out the privies. Given the city's sandy soil and steep grades, this method sufficed for awhile, but contagious waterborne and fatal diseases, such as typhoid and cholera, quite literally plagued the city from its beginnings. In 1817, recognizing the consequences of this primitive disposal system, the city prohibited residents and builders from sinking privy pits near the city springs (in the area bounded on the north by Franklin Street, on the west by Charles Street, the east by Calvert Street, and on the south by New Church Street, present-day Lexington). Existing privies remained and pollution of the ground water continued. Three years later another city ordinance called for the excrement from privies to be covered within five hours of deposit, subject to a $20 fine; dead horses had to be buried within five hours as well.[38]

With piped water available on a subscription basis, affluent citizens could install one of the myriad water closet designs and a few did so. All were based on John Bramah's design of 1778, which released water into the bowl to clean it out and featured a water-filled trap to seal the pipe and prevent odors. (Because of inadequate valve seals and poor flushing action, the water closet was constantly being redesigned.) No matter how elaborate bathrooms were, they emptied into cesspools or drained into the harbor. And, instead of being emptied, new cesspools were dug and old ones buried.[39]

City managers also tackled the thorny problem of planning early in the nineteenth century. Prior to the 1797 incorporation of Baltimore, planning had been handled in an ad hoc manner, with the result being that some additions to the town had no coherent relationship to the existing layout. Having decided that a matrix would facilitate future development, in 1811 the commissioners appointed Thomas H. Poppleton as chief surveyor but the War of 1812 derailed this effort. Contemplating an annexation in 1816, they decided to rehire Poppleton, who began the work in 1818 and completed the job in five years. Instead of resurveying the old part of the city, he left well enough alone and extended a matrix based on the original squares of one acre each comprising the original town of 1729 (FIGURE 16). Like that of most early-nineteenth-century surveyors, Poppleton's matrix was a grid. In America, William Penn had laid out Philadelphia on a grid plan; more recently most Midwestern towns were platted on the grid. In keeping with the times (and perhaps the instructions of the commissioners), Poppleton did not include any public squares in his design. Instead he applied a regular pattern of block after residential block. He also incorporated in the new areas the narrow alleys running down the centers of each block, already found in Fells Point, Howard's Addition, and Federal Hill. Although the alleys were intended to be used as service alleys for the houses located on the main streets, in Baltimore as in Philadelphia, the tradition already existed of building small dwellings on these narrow streets. Poppleton's plan legitimized this use for decades to come. (In contrast, New York's plan of 1811 eliminated service alleys and public squares entirely in its 2,000-block grid, so as to maximize developable land.) New York, and to a large extent Philadelphia, had flat terrains, for which gridiron plans were logical; Baltimore, like Boston, however, was punctuated by a series of hills, rising in grade from the harbor, as well as stream valleys to the east and west, so the gridiron proved cumbersome. One positive result of this superimposition of a gridiron plan on a hilly city is that when these streets filled with rowhouses, the city came to be characterized by picturesque vistas of ascending and descending rows of attached, repetitive houses.[40]

A New Fashion in Rowhousing

After the War of 1812 several of America's most prominent architects arrived in the city to design and oversee the building of monumental structures in newly opened areas of the city, many blocks removed from the harbor basin, merchant's wharves, and countinghouses. Benjamin Henry Latrobe, Maximilian Godefroy, and Robert Mills introduced the neoclassical style and in the process gave Baltimore a brief period of national architectural prominence. Influenced by the stripped-down neoclassicism of the British architect Sir John Soane and the French architect Nicholas Ledoux, Latrobe and Godefroy created works that emphasized interlocking volumetric forms of a spare, clean nature. Stone or stucco became the preferred building material (it seemed more monumental than brick and also created crisper lines), and in place of elaborate detail, architects manipulated the eye with subtle arched recesses, shallow, receding planes, and sharply cut window openings. In domestic architecture, windows were no longer placed in regular order across the façade; instead they might be paired or units could be joined together, perhaps under a shallow arched reveal.

Benjamin Henry Latrobe first used the new style in the monumental Roman Catholic Cathedral (built 1806–1821), and Merchant's Exchange (1816–1820). He limited his residential work to individual townhouses and for these designed severely classical exteriors with plain, smooth surfaces (usually stuccoed brick), sharply cut openings, plain deep cornices, and his trademark tripartite shallow-arched window reveals.

Robert Mills arrived in Baltimore in 1815 to supervise construction of the city's Washington Monument, for which he had won the design competition in 1814. The following year he designed a row of stylish classically inspired houses—Waterloo Row, close to both the monument and the cathedral. The row went up between 1817 and 1819 (FIGURE 17). Mills designed the row for the Baltimore Water Company, of which he was president, to be erected on land the company owned on North Calvert Street. A financial arrangement involving a consortium of building tradesmen and suppliers made erection of the row possible. Of the twelve houses in the block, Mills, as architect, received title to one; the water company, as owner of the land, retained two; six others went respectively to the bricklayer, the stonemason, two carpenters, the painter and glazer, and the plasterer; and the remaining three were parceled out to the suppliers of the brick, the lumber, and the hardware.[41] Mills charged $375 for "drawing of range of houses for Water company." The design much resembled his 1809 plan for Franklin Row in Philadelphia and made use of tripartite windows and recessed arches to articulate the façade. As in the Philadelphia project, the houses were three-and-a-half-stories high, two bays wide, and measured about 23 feet by 40 feet with an 8-foot-by-23-foot back building. The houses were valued at $8,000, making them the most expensive rowhouses erected in Baltimore to date. Their neoclassical style proclaimed them something entirely new in terms of Baltimore's residential architecture. No other rowhouses had such a sophisticated façade design, incorporating window openings of different sizes and shapes without traditional lintels and arranged in a less then perfectly symmetrical pattern. No other rowhouses had wide arched first floor door and window openings or tall English basements. And no other rowhouses had such low-pitched roofs, with those oddly shaped arched dormers.

Inside, the first-floor double parlors boasted elaborate woodwork, marble mantels, and plaster ceiling medallions. A spacious entrance hall led to stairs that were set beyond an arched opening at the rear of the house. The opening between the parlors was generous, creating a sense of a grand double room. (Demolished in 1970 as a result of urban renewal efforts, a first floor interior was reconstructed at the Baltimore Museum of Art, where it can be seen today.) Because the houses did not meet a ready sale and because there were legal problems involving some of the artisans, the water company received title to an additional four houses, which it insured in 1822, at which time the value of the individual houses had dropped to $5,100. (In these insurance policies it is amusing to note that the rear building is described as being "for stabling, carriage house, sitting rooms, and smoke house," giving yet another euphemism for the outdoor privy, which in all the original policies had been referred to as a "Necessary.")[42]

As the new streets in this section of the city were opened both speculators and individual homeowners rushed to lay claim to what they believed would be the most stylish neighborhood of the city. In 1817 a group of merchants and building tradesmen (including Thomas Towson, one of the two masons working on the nearby Washington Monument) joined to erect a monumental row of six four-and-a-half-story houses on the south side of Saratoga Street, just east of Baltimore's oldest and most fashionable Episcopal Church, St. Pauls. In the same year another group of building craftsman collaborated to erect a row of seven large and fashionable four-and-a-half-story houses just a block away, on the east side of St. Paul Street, south of Pleasant. These showed the influence of Mills by using recessed arches for the first floor windows, a belt course marking the ground floor level, and an elegant stone doorway. The joint speculators included John Sinclair—the carpenter-architect who owned the land and contracted with the other artisans; a bricklayer; a house carpenter and plasterer; two stonemasons; and a lumber merchant. They soon sold the houses they received as payment for their labors to wealthy merchants, including former mayor James Calhoun and Benjamin Chew Howard, son of John Eager Howard.[43]

On the western side of the city, on land belonging to his eighteenth-century estate, but bordering on the newly opened Lexington Market, Lewis Pascault, a Santo Dominguan refugee and prominent merchant erected an impressive row of eight three-and-a-half-story houses the same year (FIGURE 18). Eschewing the stylish neoclassical taste of Mills and Latrobe, Pascault retained traditional Adamesque federal forms and emphasized fine proportions, high quality brickwork, and a carefully detailed classical portico, with tall engaged columns flanking the doors. Elegant stone panels with an Adamesque oval set in relief, marked the façade between the second and third floors, indicating as well the high ceilings of this principal floor. These three-bay-wide, 28-foot-by-45-foot houses boasted a three-story pantry and a three-story back building. Pascault's partners in the project were carpenter and master builder Rezin Wight and merchant William Lorman, who lived nearby. Pascault initially insured the houses (a note on the insurance policy reads "having firewalls, but remote from Engines and water") in 1819 but sometime before 1828 transferred the policies to Wight and Lorman—an action that either reflects adherence to an earlier contract or Pascault's inability to sell the houses and pay off his building debts.[44] Lorman himself lived in a townhouse at the corner of Charles and Lexington that had been designed by Latrobe in 1816. It seems hardly a coincidence that the two most distinctive architectural features of Pascault Row—the stone panels with ovals in relief and the distyle-in-antis entryway—were elements Mills's mentor Latrobe had incorporated in Lorman's house.

Thomas W. Griffith, the first chronicler of early Baltimore, mentioned both Waterloo Row and Pascault's Row in *The Annals of Baltimore* (1833):

Among the unproductive expenditures referred to in the year 1819, of these Annals, might have been distinguished those twelve handsome buildings, erected by Messrs. Robert Mills, John Ready, James Hines and others, on grounds leased of the Water Company, at the intersection of Calvert and Monument Streets—and those eight commodious dwellings, erected on part of the grounds of Lewis Pascault, Esq., by that gentleman,

M. Rezin Wight and others, on Lexington near Pine Street; all of which, being considered too distant for men of business, as most all of our citizens are, would not command rent nearly equal to common legal interest.[45]

Regardless if Pascault Row sold well at the outset, its distinguished architecture and affluent residents merited it a named place on the map. Charles Varlé's *Complete View of Baltimore* of 1833, a pocket guidebook to the city's businesses, social, cultural, and educational institutions, and transportation facilities, included it—the only row noted on the map.

The influence of Mills and Latrobe did find their way into the townhouses and rowhouses designed by two local architects in the 1820s. Robert Cary Long Sr., adopted the design concepts of Waterloo Row when he built a group of five fashionable two-and-a-half-story houses with high English basements on Hamilton Street, a narrow street a block north of the cathedral (FIGURE 19). Although much more modest than Waterloo Row, the houses relied on similar neoclassical design precepts, including tripartite windows on the first and second floors and a smooth-surfaced (probably stuccoed) façade. Long formed a partnership with various building tradesmen to distribute the risk of speculative building. William Small, who had studied for two years under Latrobe, also used shallow-arched window reveals when he designed city homes for wealthy merchants in the late 1820s and early 1830s.

New Prosperity and a Taste for the Greek

The more archaeologically correct version of neoclassicism, the Greek Revival, arrived in Baltimore a few years later. James Stuart and Nicholas Revett's 1762 English publication *The Antiquities of Athens* had introduced specific elements of the Grecian style that some early-nineteenth-century American architects adopted. Robert Mills's 1814 design for Baltimore's Washington Monument was a distinctly Greek Doric column. William Strickland in 1818 designed the Second Bank of the United States in Philadelphia in the Greek Revival style; this building in turn inspired designers of schools, banks, and other institutional buildings to use ancient Greek forms. In New York the Greek Revival influence led to Doric-columned porches on fashionable rowhouses in the late 1820s. In 1832 Alexander Jackson Davis designed Colonnade Row, nine three-story three-bay wide rowhouses fronted by an imposing two-story Corinthian colonnade. Thirteen years later he designed London Terrace, with three-story pilasters that gave the effect of a colonnade, and to show it at best advantage set the row back thirty-five feet from the street and had gardens in front.[46] Philadelphia acquired its first grand, columned row in 1830 when John Haviland erected Colonnade Row on Chestnut Street; Greek Ionic columns ran the length of the ten-house unit. In the same year Thomas U. Walter offered Portico Row, a block-long group of sixteen three-and-a-half-story houses with doorways set beneath paired flat-roofed porticos supported by three Ionic columns. Asher Benjamin, whose pattern books influenced countless carpenters, was won over by the new enthusiasm and starting in 1826 began incorporating Grecian details in his designs. Minard Lafever followed suit and included Greek elements in his 1829 *The Young Builder's General Instructor*.

In Baltimore architect Robert Cary Long Jr., son of the designer of the Hamilton Street row, championed the Greek Revival taste. The younger Long had studied in New York and knew the local work of Ithiel Town and A. J. Davis. For the Patapsco Female Institute near Ellicott City, he offered a Greek temple design in 1834. Hired by Baltimore's most prominent merchants and emerging businessmen in the 1840s to build elaborate town houses in close proximity to Latrobe's Cathedral and Mills's just completed monument to George Washington, Long combined elements of neoclassical taste with Greek Revival decorative features. This section of the city—about a half-mile north of the harbor basin—had recently opened up for residential development. The Cathedral sat on very high ground overlooking the harbor, and just to the north, Belvidere, the grand country estate of John Eager Howard, stretched beyond the small plot of ground he had donated to the city for the building of the Washington Monument. Two blocks east, at the bottom of the hill where the land flattened to meet the Jones Falls, Mills had built the most expensive, and most fashionable, rowhouses Baltimore had yet seen.

In 1827 John Eager Howard died, leaving Belvidere (as well as his other vast real estate holdings to the west and south of the harbor) to his surviving children. Led by eldest son Charles they decided to turn the landed inheritance into cash—by leasing and selling house lots overlooking the monument on what they hoped would become Baltimore's most fashionable avenues. They asked Robert Mills to create a masterplan for residential development on this land. One of his schemes fit sixty-eight house lots into the four block area, with all the houses facing the north-south axes, but the design they accepted called for laying out small parks in the centers of the streets extending north, south, east, and west of the monument and siting the largest house lots along the east-west axis.[47] Dubbed

Mt. Vernon Place in honor of Washington's home, this gracious city square soon became Baltimore's finest address.

Charles Howard built the first house, on the northeast corner just opposite the monument (FIGURE 20). It may well have been designed by his brother William, a physician, artist, and engineer who was particularly enthusiastic about Greek designs. In the same year William designed for himself a monumental townhouse at the corner of Charles and Franklin Streets, directly across from Maximilian Godefroy's Unitarian Church. The tetrastyle Ionic portico, set in front of the five-bay façade, with its full height marble columns was modeled on the Erectheum. Howard frequently borrowed architectural books from the Baltimore Library Company, including Leoni's edition of Palladio, Peter Nicholson's *Principles of Architecture*, and Stuart and Revett's *Antiquities of Athens*. Charles Howard's house was more conservative, with Greek decorations limited to the Ionic portico. Two stories tall, the pitch of the gable roof was much lower than in typical Federal style buildings. Beneath the simple cornice, the architect set very narrow, decorative windows to provide light and ventilation to the attic, a style also used on a nearby house attributed to Latrobe. William Howard also designed Baltimore's first Greek temple building, the McKim Free School (1833), still standing in Old Town, modeling its hexastyle Doric front on the Theseum and may have collaborated with local architect William Small on the First English Lutheran Church (1825–1826, 1832), whose temple front was copied from Stuart's plates of the Ionic temple near the Illissus.[48]

Charles Howard's house set the style for fashionable Greek Revival townhouses in Baltimore. Its building coincided with the beginning of a new age of optimism and prosperity. Since the 1820s Baltimore had been making a shift from an economy based on maritime trade to one based on manufacturing. The Baltimore & Ohio Railroad, chartered in 1827, was at the heart of the new industrial activity. Its locomotive shops helped make the railroad a major employer in the city, and when the line reached Wheeling, West Virginia in 1853 new markets to the west of Maryland were opened to the city's manufacturers. A new group of wealthy and influential men—many associated with the railroad—became involved in city affairs and took their places in local society. New manufacturing enterprises sprang up to serve the railroad—machine works, foundries, and even bridge building—and construction of these new facilities alone provided considerable work for the local building industry. By the mid 1840s steam engine manufactories, glassmaking, paint and varnish factories, packing houses, and lumber mills shared the waterfront with the many shipbuilding yards. Their profits made it possible for affluent patrons to hire architects to build stylish houses in fashionable places. The success of their businesses fed demand by a growing workforce for other builders to erect hundreds of small vernacular houses.

A few years after Charles Howard built in the Greek style on Mt. Vernon Place, merchant (and later French consul) George C. Morton built a similar looking house two blocks west (FIGURE 21). Five bays wide, a spare box with crisply cut window openings, a stone portico supported by paired Ionic columns, elegant cast-iron window balconies marking the level of the principal floor, a very low-pitched gabled roof flanked by stepped brick parapets, and distinctive, small attic windows set in the frieze area of the simple cornice, the Morton house set a standard of Greek Revival elegance that would shape further development on the Howards' land near the monument. By 1840 other houses with similar features were going up around the square and all took familiar forms: smooth façades, usually painted a light color, severely cut window openings, a deep, plain cornice, and a columned portico. Most of these houses were only three bays wide—in typical Baltimore fashion, the wealthy tended to prefer putting their money into large country estates rather than city mansions—but seemed imposing nonetheless (FIGURE 22).

In 1840 John Hall, a Baltimore cabinetmaker and self-styled architect, published a book of twenty-four designs entitled *A Series of Select and Original Modern Designs for Dwelling Houses, for the use of Carpenters and Builders, adapted to the Style of Building in the United States.*[49] The plates illustrate Greek Revival designs, the majority of which, Hall claimed in his preface, "have been selected from the best examples of dwellings already finished, many of them during their erection, being under the author's immediate superintendence" in Philadelphia and Baltimore. Plate 8, a "three story house with an attic and back building" closely resembled houses built in the Mt. Vernon area (FIGURE 23). Three bays wide with a frontage of 25 feet, a depth of 42 feet, and a long back building extending back another 64 feet, the house had a low-pitched gable roof set behind a parapet above the elaborately ventilated attic story. All decorative details took Greek forms—Greek Ionic columns supporting the chaste portico set in front of paneled doors and sidelights; acanthus-leaf decorated consoles supporting the projecting window lintels; and attic-level ventilator panels designed with a distinctly Greek appearance. The double parlors in the main block were separated by pocket doors and wide openings, features first popularized in the neoclassical period. In more pretentious homes the parlor opening was marked by freestanding paired or single columns

1. LEFT   712 South Broadway, built 1805; purchased by Traugoth Singewald 1858 (J. Brough Schamp)

2. BOTTOM   Fells Point neighborhood of Traugoth Singewald, showing the Market in the center of Broadway and the small houses on Bethel Street to the rear of Singewald's block. Detail, E. Sachse & Co.'s *Bird's Eye View of the City of Baltimore*, 1869 (Maryland Historical Society)

3. TOP   Adelphi Terrace in London, by Robert and James Adam, 1769.
Published in R. Adam, *Works in Architecture*, 1778 (Winterthur Museum)

4. BOTTOM   B*altimore in 1752*. From a sketch made by John Moale, Esq.
Deceased, corrected by the late Daniel Bowley, Esq. Aquatint engraving by
William Strickland, 1817 (Maryland Historical Society)

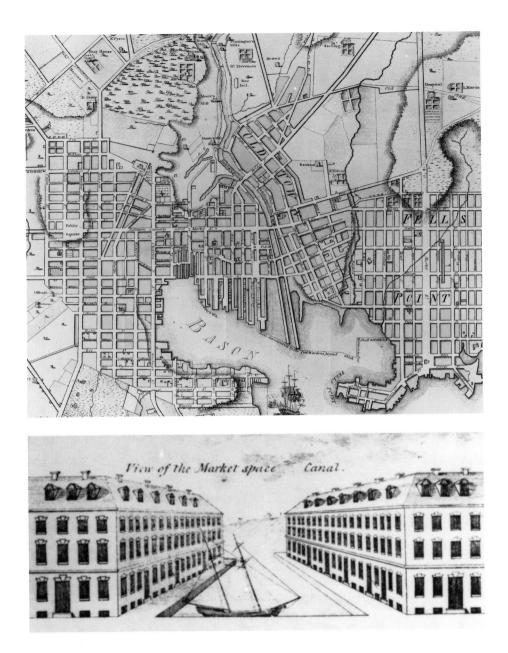

5. TOP Detail, *Warner & Hanna's Plan of the City and Environs of Baltimore*, 1801, showing the harbor basin, wharves, Old Town, Fells Point, and Federal Hill south of the basin; Cumberland Row is just to the north of Dugan's Wharf (Maryland Historical Society)

6. BOTTOM View of the Market Space—Canal, inset detail from *Warner & Hanna's Plan of the City and Environs of Baltimore*, 1801, showing three-and-a-half story rows built by Thomas McElderry and Cumberland Dugan in 1796 (Maryland Historical Society)

7. TOP   The sole survivor of Richard Caton's row of four, three-and-a-half story houses on the northwest corner of Lombard and Front Streets, 1796, now demolished (Historic American Buildings Survey)

8. BOTTOM   Dr. James McHenry's row of three-and-a-half story houses, built 1802 on the east side of what would become Monument Square. *Battle Monument, Baltimore*. Designed and published by W. H. Bartlett, H. Griffiths, London, 1838 (Maryland Historical Society)

9. TOP   1628–1632 Shakespeare Street, Fells Point around 1900; typical two-bay-wide, two-and-a-half-story house built in 1790s (Enoch Pratt Free Library)

10. BOTTOM   713–715 South Bethel Street, circa 1795, a one-room deep (with kitchen addition) Federal style rowhouse on an early "alley" street in Baltimore (J. Brough Schamp)

11. TOP 1–11 East Montgomery Street, 1800–1810. This group of early houses in Federal Hill, while not rowhouses, represents the modified form of Federal style detail used on modest, working-class houses in early-nineteenth-century Baltimore (Mary Ellen Hayward)

12. BOTTOM 821–829 South Charles Street, built by John Cator, 1818 (Steven Allan)

13. TOP   A mason points mortar joints from a scaffold, illustration in C. F. Partington, *The Builder's Complete Guide* (London, 1825), which was used by Baltimore builders; such manuals listed building rules, tables, and designs for carpenters and masons

14. BOTTOM   Advertisement for parlor stoves from the *Baltimore Biennial Advertiser*, a part of the 1831 city directory (Enoch Pratt Free Library)

15. RIGHT   Rowhouse builders bragged that their houses came with a "hydrant of water in the yard" or a "pump of good water at the door," as seen in this sketch of a Federal style house in *Harper's Weekly*, 1891

16. BOTTOM   Detail, *Plan of the City of Baltimore;* Thomas H. Poppleton, surveyor; Joseph Cone, engraver, 1823 (Maryland Historical Society)

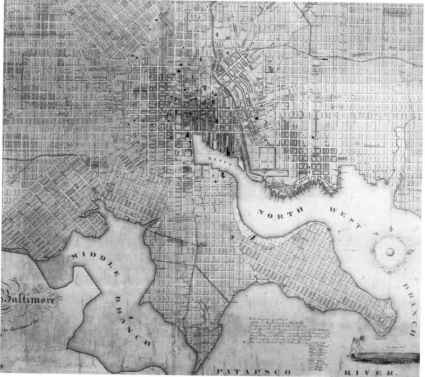

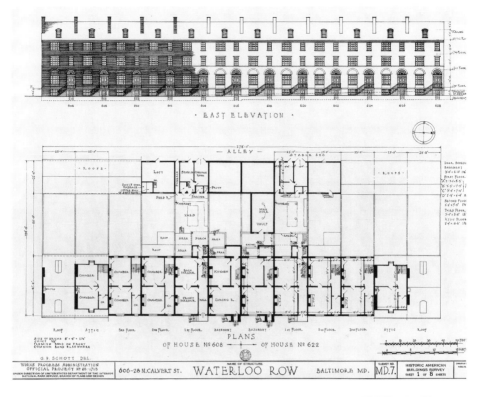

17. TOP   Waterloo Row, 200 block of North Calvert Street, elevation and plan, designed by Robert Mills, 1817–1819 (Historic American Buildings Survey)

18. BOTTOM   Pascault Row, 600 block of West Lexington Street, built 1819 by Lewis Pascault; restored in the 1980s by University of Maryland at Baltimore for offices and residences of medical and dental schools (Wayne Nield)

21. TOP   *The Dulin House*, anonymous, 1839. The squares laid out around the
Washington Monument would prove an attractive place for Baltimore's affluent
citizens to build Greek Revival townhouses, such as this five-bay, two-story-and-
attic house for merchant George C. Morton, 107 West Monument Street,
1836–1837. Beyond the dove gray mansion the dome and towers of Latrobe's
Cathedral loom; Godefroy's Unitarian Church rises in the middle distance, and
the Washington Monument is at the far left (Maryland Historical Society)

22. BOTTOM   *View of Baltimore City*, by E. Sachse, 1850. Three-bay Greek
Revival townhouses lined the blocks around the Washington Monument
(Maryland Historical Society)

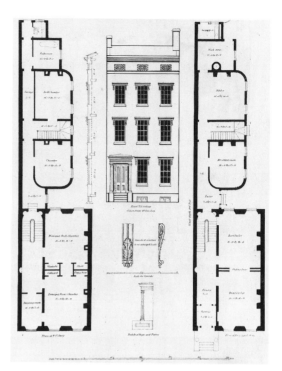

23. TOP   Three-story Greek Revival style townhouse, floor plan and elevation.
Plate 8 in John Hall, *A Series of Select and Original Modern Designs for the Use of
Carpenters and Builders Adapted to the Style of Building in the United States*, 1840
(Winterthur Museum)

24. BOTTOM   This row of three-and-a-half story houses on the north side of
Lexington Street at Calvert, just north of the Battle Monument, resembles the
type of rowhouse recorded by Hall as Plate 6, and the houses built for John
Hanson Thomas in the 500 block of Cathedral Street. Note the squat Doric
columns supporting the porches. Detail, *Baltimore, Md., U.S. Genl Hospital
Newton University*, lithograph by E. Sachse & Co., 1864 (Maryland Historical
Society)

25. TOP 601–607 North Charles Street, an elegant Greek Revival row built by Michael Roche, 1850 (J. Brough Schamp)

26. LEFT 8 East Hamilton Street, built by Michael Roche, circa 1850 for John Hanson Thomas, south of the three-story Greek Revival houses built facing Centre Street, just below Washington Place (J. Brough Schamp)

27. TOP LEFT 700 block McHenry Street, a row built to house Baltimore & Ohio Railroad workers, circa 1848 (Mary Ellen Hayward)

28. BOTTOM LEFT 27–37 East Hamburg Street, built by John S. Gittings, 1838–1840 (Steven Allen)

29. TOP 3–25 East Wheeling Street, built by John S. Gittings, 1845–1850 (Alain Jaramillo)

30. BOTTOM 206–208 East Montgomery Street, built by Samuel Bratt, circa 1853 (Mary Ellen Hayward)

31. TOP Two-story "alley" houses, built on either side of 600 block Dover Street in southwest Baltimore. Babe Ruth's boyhood home (now the Babe Ruth Museum) stands at the end of this block, on Emory Street (Steven Allan)

32. BOTTOM 10–16 West Cross Street, "half" houses built near the Cross Street Market in Federal Hill in 1852 (Steven Allan)

making use of Greek orders and interior door and window openings were framed with anthemion-decorated "eared" surrounds. The long back building contained a breakfast room, kitchen, and wash room on the first floor, two chambers and a bathroom above. Ceilings were high—13 feet on the first floor, 12 feet on the second, and 11 feet on the third; the attic ceiling was 8 feet or 9 feet high in the center, sloping down to 6 feet at the front and rear of the house.

Although many individual Greek Revival townhouses were built in the Mt. Vernon area, the sorts of block-long, high-style Greek Revival rows that went up in Boston, New York, and Philadelphia were not built in Baltimore. Land in the immediate Mt. Vernon area—Baltimore's first residential square to follow the English model—was developed primarily with individual townhouses. But a block or two south, landowners tried their hand at erecting more modest Greek Revival rows in the mid-1840s. To offer these homes at a reasonable cost, the developers eliminated expensive stone-columned Doric or Ionic entrance porticoes used on the large houses facing the square, replacing them with simple wooden Doric pilasters supporting a plain entablature. Often they enhanced the appearance of the façade by creating a rusticated basement of stone. One builder even tried using rows of projecting bricks to give the effect of a scored stone basement, bragging that no one could tell the difference between his technique and the real thing.[50] Another builder happened on a novel idea—he framed the doorways of his houses with wooden pilasters but supported the marble entrance porches with short, squat Doric stone columns (FIGURE 24).

A typical Greek Revival row rose a block north of the cathedral in 1847–48. The developer, George R. Gaither, a merchant, retained title to the houses as rental property for some years (he lived in one), but when he sold the first of the five houses in 1857 it brought the grand sum of $12,000; the second sold in 1865 for $16,000. Just over 22 feet wide, with lots running back a full 160 feet to the middle of the block, these extant houses are four stories with low-pitched roofs and simple modillion cornices, and a street level "English basement" created simply by marking the division between floors with a wide molding strip. The full-height windows of the principal floor have cast iron window balconies. The doorway entrances, though created in wood, are classic Doric pilasters supporting a deep entablature resting on a base of granite highlighted by wide marble steps. Double outside doors lead to a recessed vestibule with its own set of interior doors.[51] Directly across Cathedral Street, on land adjoining Robert Cary Long Sr.'s neoclassical row on Hamilton Street, John Hanson Thomas, a prominent banker, built a row of five similar houses on land he acquired in

1845, at about the same time he decided to build his own monumental townhouse on the southwest corner of Charles and Monument Streets, facing the Washington Monument. This row, too, had a wooden Doric-pilastered doorway set beneath a deep entablature, a recessed entrance, and marble steps. But here the builder retained the older, three-and-a-half story form, while at the same time adding a Greek touch by the use of short stone columns supporting the porch. Thomas sold one of the houses in March 1850 for $5,500, with a $120 ground rent.[52]

A more imposing Greek Revival row rose on the east side of Charles Street just south of the monument. In 1850 James H. Wilson, who now lived in Charles Howard's house overlooking the monument, hired local builder Michael Roche to erect a group of six four-story houses, four to face the east side of lower Washington Place, the grassy park extending south of the monument, and two to be located around the corner on Centre Street. Roche created a highly dignified composition, with a rusticated English basement faced in brownstone, a very low-pitched gable roof set behind a simple modillion cornice, end parapets, chaste window trim, and a long cast iron balcony running the full length of the façade at the level of the principal floor (FIGURE 25). The size of the houses (22 feet 8 inches frontage) and their prominent location were reflected in their cost. Like many of Baltimore's finer rowhouses of this period, the owner kept several as rental properties, charging his tenants $600 a year, payable quarterly. In an agreement that resembles today's rent-with-option-to-buy packages, the lessee could purchase the house outright anytime before 1861 for $10,000 in fee. For those dwellings sold soon after they were built, purchasers paid $13,250 in fee.[53]

A *Sun* reporter described these houses at length in a December 1850 article, also mentioning others in the block by Roche, built "on his own risk and responsibility." The group he built for Wilson on Washington Place had "basement fronts" of "the brown stone now so much favored for building purposes" and when completed "the whole exterior will be sanded and painted in imitation of this stone." In those houses with "what are styled basement fronts, the rooms on the first floor are suitable for offices or libraries, whilst the drawing and dining rooms are on the main or second floor." Three houses were built "on a somewhat new style, which is much favored in New York. The dining room is immediately in the rear of the parlors, and, divided from it only by sliding doors, the whole suite of rooms can, at any time when desired, be thrown into one." The five houses Roche built on his own account on the south side of Centre Street were occupied "by highly respectable tenants, the most of them being owned by their occupants; Mr. Roche himself occupying the easternmost one of the row." As soon as these were completed, the builder began another row of seven "elegant dwellings" across the street. These were finished "in different styles for those who now own and occupy them."[54]

At the southern end of the Centre Street parcel, Michael Roche erected another kind of Greek Revival house for a lower-income buyer (FIGURE 26). Only two stories high and two bays wide, these small, 14-foot-wide houses also had the signature attic windows associated with high-style Greek Revival townhouses. Called "two story and attic" houses by writers at that time, hundreds of these modest houses went up in working class areas of the city during the decade between 1845 and 1855. These neighborhoods included the maritime communities of Fells Point and Federal Hill; the country's first planned industrial development, at Canton, east of the harbor; and the area to the west surrounding the rapidly growing Baltimore & Ohio Railroad yards. The houses that Roche built facing Hamilton Street, a narrow, mid-block street, were finished to a higher level than most, with their pressed brick fronts, splayed brick lintels, marble sills, and steps. But they were there to provide housing for those who worked in this new neighborhood and who could not afford public transportation to get to their jobs. Although several lines of omnibuses were now running from downtown to Fells Point, and north, northeast, and west of the city, fares remained too expensive for average-income Baltimoreans. They would still have to live near their work.[55]

The new house type was dubbed a "two-story-and-attic" because builders had replaced the dormer story of the two-and-a-half-story Federal houses with a taller attic story set beneath a much lower-pitched roof, just as in the fashionable townhouses. Lighted by two small square windows set close to the floor at both the front and back of the house, this additional space under the roof allowed the third floor to be divided into two separate rooms, each with a ceiling height of about 7-1/2 feet in the center, sloping down to about 4-1/2 feet along the front and rear window wall. This additional chamber space on the third floor provided crucial extra living area for the large families that usually occupied these houses, many of whom had to rent to boarders to make ends meet. Beyond the changes in attic space, the floor plan of a two-story-and-attic house was almost identical to its Federal period predecessor: two rooms per floor with each room measuring about 11 feet wide by 12 feet deep, and 8-1/2 foot ceiling heights on the first floor and 8 feet on the second floor; enclosed narrow winder stairs rising from near the fireplace in the rear room; and a one-room deep kitchen addition, with a cooking fireplace located against the rear wall.

Interior decorative details remained simple—machine-cut beaded door and window frames, often with bull's-eye lintels, plain baseboards, and simple mantel shelves supported by flat Doric pilasters.

The attic story of these houses may have been a welcome practical feature for occupants, but its introduction owed less to functional considerations than to the design of the Greek Revival style. The earliest two-story-and-attic rows built near the B&O yards in the late 1840s had narrow attic windows simulating the decorated ventilator panels on the high-style versions. Soon, however, builders switched to larger and squarer attic windows, which were more practical, and by the early 1850s the façades had lost most of their original sense of style. The earliest Federal, two-and-a-half-story houses built for a working-class market were stripped of ornamentation for purposes of economy. On the Greek Revival façade, exigencies of economy and aesthetics complemented each other well: the rows of bare brick, with regular, well-proportioned fenestration patterns, simple lintels and sills, and plain door frames possessed a stylishness of which even their builders were not fully aware.

One of the first places in Baltimore where two-story-and-attic houses were built is in the area to the east and north of the B&O's Mt. Clare yards along west Pratt Street, about a mile west of downtown. In the mid-1840s this isolated corner of Baltimore quickly grew in population as the B&O expanded and hired more workers. Many were Irish immigrants and as the potato famine worsened, their numbers increased. Even by 1843 the Irish community of West Baltimore had grown to such an extent that a Catholic parish was founded, which hired Robert Cary Long Jr., to build an imposing temple front church. A decade later a group of Irish nuns—the Sisters of Mercy—relocated to the area to teach the children of the railroad workers and provide social services to low-income people and new arrivals.

Land in the area mostly belonged to the heirs of John Eager Howard and his brother-in-law James McHenry, whose country estate lay to the north. In the 1840s family members began selling off this land to local speculative builders who erected rows of small two-story-and-attic houses within walking distance of the B&O yards. One such buyer was Charles Shipley, a carpenter, who in 1848 built a row of ten houses along Lemmon Street, a narrow mid-block street just a half block north of the yards. Although only 10-1/2 feet wide and 24-1/2 feet deep, the tiny six-room houses (two small rooms in the attic story) featured four Doric fireplace mantels and beaded trim. They sold for $400 apiece to a variety of both Irish and German-born railroad workers, including a watchman, two firemen, a blacksmith, and several "laborers (FIGURE 27)."[56]

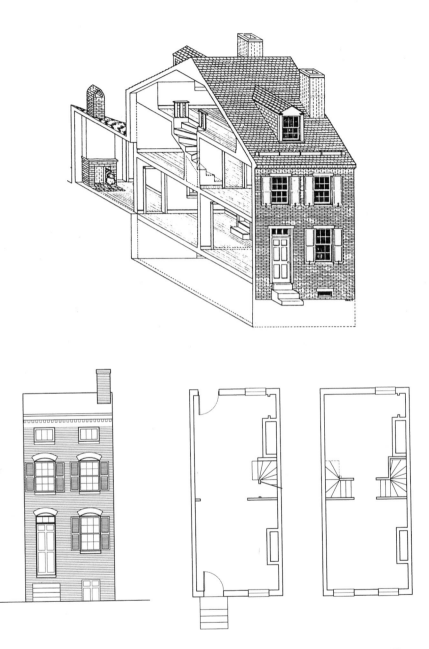

Typical of the early 1800s through the 1830s is the Federal Style two-bay two-and-a-half story rowhouse at 29 East Hamburg Street (top), built 1838. In the 1840s and early 1850s, Greek Revival two-story-and-attic houses, like 920 Lemmon Street (bottom) accomodated Baltimore's growing working-class population (Chester Design Associates, Gloria Mikolajczyk).

The Gentleman Developer

Banker and developer John S. Gittings came to be one of the most prolific builders of two-story-and-attic houses in the city. President of the Chesapeake Bank of Baltimore from 1836 until his death in 1879, Gittings began acquiring land in the Federal Hill area, south of the harbor basin, in the late 1830s. He first built rows of very plain two-and-a-half story late Federal style houses, which he sold for $700 to $900 (FIGURE 28). Since he was not a builder he either hired builders to construct the houses, leased lots to builders to build on their own account, sold lots in fee, or executed an arrangement that combined the three. On one block of East Hamburg Street, he leased two lots to Joseph Cassell, a carpenter, for $13 ground rents; sold two lots outright for $200 each; and built houses on two lots himself. Often, he offered advance mortgages to builders, such as the $300 he gave carpenter Joseph Stubbs to build on lots nearby. Considering the $500 to $600 sale price of similar houses in the next block, Stubbs's profit margin was considerable—if the advance mortgage covered the entire costs of construction, Stubbs could come close to doubling his investment for each unit constructed. A number of these two-and-a-half-story late Federal style houses were purchased by owner-occupants—a ship carpenter, a teamster, a mariner, and a watchman, among others—but most were bought by absentee landlords who invested in the property for its rental income.[57]

Beginning about 1845 Gittings began building long, continuous rows of two-story-and-attic houses on the north side of Hamburg Street (across from his 1839 two-and-a-half-story rows) and on the south side of nearby Wheeling Street (FIGURE 29). As did Charles Shipley on Lemmon Street, Gittings built these 11-foot wide houses as inexpensively as possible, with only single-brick-thick partitions between houses. For the interiors Gittings bought only the simplest machine-milled woodwork and put in mantels with plain Doric pilasters. Unlike Shipley's houses, Gittings's came with a one-story kitchen addition. Each house had a small privy located in the rear yard, but because of the shallow depth of the lot, it was offensively close to the house. There were no alleyways between the rear yards of the back-to-back properties and drainage was a problem. Gittings put similar rows on other streets of Federal Hill and built in Fells Point as well, but he did not limit himself to building for the working-class market. As affluent households moved to the Mt. Vernon area, he tried his hand there, building expensive Greek Revival style houses in a new neighborhood along West

Madison Avenue just at the edge of the city's northwestern development. It was possible for Gittings and other builders to gamble on speculative houses here because the area was being served by "Zimmerman & Co.'s new and splendid omnibuses" that "run within a square or two, arriving and departing every ten or fifteen minutes."[58] The first real form of public transportation, the omnibus, basically an urban stagecoach, was introduced to Baltimore in 1844. Owners of the few companies that offered service took pride in the elegant painted decorations of their coaches:

> A new and beautiful carriage has just been added to the line of coaches attached to Barnum & McLaughlin's Hotel, which, for excellence of design, beauty of finish and general comfort, is not surpassed by any similar conveyance in Baltimore. The body is of a rich cream color, the interior is supplied with velvet seats, whilst above the sash work, a talented artist has sketched a variety of interesting views, well worthy an examination. The panels outside are adorned with the picture of a steamer, "walking the waters like a thing of life".... The wheels and running gear are painted cream color, delicately striped in red and blue.[59]

The work of Gittings and such builders as Michael Roche characterized a new phase of building activity in Baltimore. Whereas in the 1810s major speculative rows like Waterloo Row were built by the risk being shared among landowners, building tradesmen, and materials suppliers, now in the 1840s and 1850s one builder took all the risk, and thus all the profits. He bought the land, built and sold the houses, *and* received the ground rents. Gittings was unusual among other builders, for he was a wealthy banker who had no previous connection to the building trades. Most risk-takers, like Roche and Charles Shipley, were men who had begun life in the construction trades. With the unlimited capital at his disposal, however, Gittings outbuilt them all. By the time he died in 1879 he had built 1,200 houses, a remarkable number for the era.[60]

Although the Greek Revival two-story-and-attic house was the most typical form built for Baltimore's expanding working classes during 1845–1855, three other vernacular forms of gable-roofed housing also date from this period. Of these, the most pervasive, found in all parts of the city, simply enlarged the two-story-and-attic type to a full three stories. Many three-story houses first appeared along commercial streets in areas like Fells Point, Federal Hill, and near the railroad yards, because the ground floor was occupied by shopfront space and the family lived above in the upper two stories. But soon builders began putting up two-bay-wide versions for residences; by raising the roof only slightly, the third story became much more spacious. The Canton Company built one such row for its Welsh copper workers in 1850, which soon acquired the nickname "Copper Row." Other builders used the form to provide houses for mill and factory supervisors. Samuel Bratt, owner of a steam engine manufacturing company located along the south side of the basin in Federal Hill, began building more spacious three-story gable-roofed houses in the mid-1850s along Montgomery Street, working his way east to Federal Hill (FIGURE 30).[61] Apart from the larger overall size, the most striking difference between these middle-class houses and the working-class rowhouses was the floor plan. Although many houses were still only two bays wide, they were designed with the stairs located in the rear "pantry" area, which also had its own separate entrance to the alleyway. This allowed space for a long front parlor (12 feet by 22 feet), which ran the length of the main block. The narrower pantry-stair area beyond connected to a two-story backbuilding containing the dining room and kitchen (10 feet by 14 feet each). The second floor contained four bedrooms, and the third floor had two. Three-bay-wide versions had essentially the same floor plan, with the addition of a side hall leading from the entrance back to the rear stair hall.

The façades of these middle-class three-story rowhouses were extremely simple. A few were decorated with the plain, flat wooden lintels and door surrounds that Gittings and other builders used on the working-class rows of two-story-and-attic houses. More had either splayed or segmentally arched brick lintels over the door and window openings. All the doorframes were quite simple and had plain rectangular transom lights as ornamentation.

At the opposite end of the spectrum, smaller houses than even the two-story-and-attics were built in lower income neighborhoods in the 1850s, usually along narrow, mid-block streets. These small two-bay-wide, two-story houses had low-pitched gabled roofs without dormers, and contained only four rooms, unless there was a one-story kitchen addition. Although these houses appeared astylar, they actually represented a late vernacular version of the popular two-and-a-half-story Federal style house built during the 1820s and 1830s. Because there was no dormer story, the pitch of the gable was lower on these later houses; otherwise the façade proportions and general design characteristics were identical to those of the rows of two-and-a-half-story houses built, for example, by John S. Gittings in Federal Hill. Façades were plain brick laid in common bond and had either flat wood or segmentally arched brick door and window lintels. The simplest moldings framed doors and windows, and the transom over the door held a single narrow pane of glass. The interiors had two small rooms on each floor, each only about 10 feet by 10 feet or 12 feet by 10 feet, depending on the width of the lot, with 8-foot ceilings. Both front and back rooms generally had fireplaces. Narrow, tightly winding stairs provided access to the second floor. The smallest version of this house type lacked a basement; the kitchen was located either in a small back building, or in the rear room of the house itself.

One such row of two-story houses was built along the west side of Patapsco Street in Federal Hill, just north of the Cross Street Market, perhaps by John S. Gittings, who had been responsible for the development of a large part of the adjacent block of South Charles Street. The tiny houses were usually crowded, with the families taking in boarders or newly arrived immigrant friends and relatives to help pay the rent. Once the residents had saved enough money to either rent or buy a larger house of their own, another group of newcomers replaced them. In Fells Point several different manufacturers built tightly packed rows of such houses within walking distance of their factories (FIGURE 31).[62]

An even smaller type of gable-roofed house also went up in the 1840s and 1850s, built to meet the housing needs of the lowest income residents. These houses were strictly rental housing and numbered far fewer than the others. It was called a "half house," because it represented only the front half of a two-story-and-attic house. The gable roof rose to the ridgepole and then abruptly ended, with the entire rear of the building closed in (FIGURE 32). Local tradition suggests that such houses were always meant to be finished, that the rear half would be eventually added. But scattered clusters still exist in Baltimore in their original one-room deep form and can be found in both Federal Hill and Fells Point. These tiny gable-roofed half houses were the last Federal style buildings to go up in the city.[63]

Times were changing, and advances in building technology were about to make possible a new fashion for houses and rowhouses. In cities across the nation, as the 1850s progressed, residents embraced romanticism and picturesque forms. Style-conscious suburbanites asked builders to erect Gothic cottages or Italianate villas, based upon the designs of fashionable architects. In the city architecture took Italianate forms—with public buildings modeled after Florentine palazzos, railroad stations modeled after Italian villas, and churches swathed with Gothic motifs. City dwellers that chose not to move to the new railroad suburbs would be able to choose Italianate rowhouses that were priced to meet a variety of budgets, from very large to quite modest.

CHAPTER 2

The Italianate Period:
1850–1890

As no city in the Union seems to have increased so rapidly in point of population as Baltimore, neither do any appear to have advanced so steadily.... Especially is this the case in regard to the design, erection, and completion of magnificent public and private buildings, which may now be seen from almost every point of observation.

Baltimore *Sun*, September 30, 1851

Bird's Eye View of Baltimore City, *lithograph by E. Sachse & Co., 1858 (Maryland Historical Society)*

BY THE 1870s every man in Baltimore needed a derby. It could be of any proportion of crown and brim, but a well-dressed man was not complete without one. Before the Civil War Paris had been the leader in fashion when it came to men's headgear, but after the war England set the standard—and the English were wearing derbies.

Traugoth Singewald had been in business as a hatter in Baltimore for nearly thirty years. He liked the city and he and his bother Gottlieb had been investing in Old Town and Fells Point real estate since the 1850s. By 1875 Traugoth had opened a new hat shop just a few blocks north on Broadway, which his oldest son Charles managed and lived above. The rest of the family still lived above their main store and manufactory in a commanding three-and-a-half story Federal style house on the main street of Fells Point, only a few blocks north of the harbor, but were increasingly aware that exciting developments were taking place in another part of town. West Baltimore beckoned middle-class residents and businesses alike. Already many prominent German-American families had moved there. In 1878 Traugoth decided to open a new store in this rapidly growing area of the city for his third son, John.

A new style of rowhouse lined the blocks of West Baltimore. Just as hat styles had changed in the 1850s, so had architectural design. The Italianate, an elaborate style that had made its first appearance in New York and Philadelphia in the 1840s, had supplanted the plain, Federal and Greek

Revival rowhouses of the previous decades. The new style featured ornate façades punctuated by bold, projecting cornices, tall, narrow windows, and a surfeit of applied architectural ornament.

Traugoth bought such a building, located on West Baltimore Street, the main commercial district, for his new store (FIGURE 33). Unlike in Fells Point, this building had been planned for commercial uses—the first floor consisted of an elegant storefront with plate-glass windows set within columnar supports, which allowed him to display all the latest hats for passers-by to see. The machine technology that had transformed American life at mid-century had produced almost every design feature on the façade of the new building. The same machine technology had also helped Singewald acquire the wherewithal to buy the new store. When he started in the hat business, making hats was extremely labor-intensive. The 1852 invention of the Wells Forming Machine allowed him to reduce his dependence upon skilled labor, and thus reduce his payroll. His willingness to introduce a new method of production made him successful; other Baltimore hatters who clung to the old methods could not compete and eventually failed.

At Traugoth's death in the early 1880s his sons continued the hat business. John, the third son, managed the new West Baltimore shop, selling "hats, caps, and umbrellas" from there for the next twenty-five years. Joseph, the second son, stayed at the Fells Point store living above it with his young family.[1]

In the early 1850s, as Traugoth took steps to modernize his business, Baltimore stood poised on the brink of a major industrial revolution. The economy of the city, previously tightly tied to the international maritime trade, was changing. The tracks of the Baltimore & Ohio Railroad (B&O) stretched to Wheeling, West Virginia, on the Ohio River in 1853, and six years later connected with lines that went on to Cincinnati, Ohio, and then St. Louis, Missouri. Baltimore business owners suddenly discovered that their city was the hub in a trading wheel of gigantic proportions. B&O freight cars brought coal from western Maryland to fuel the new steam-driven machines in numerous factories across the city. Transatlantic packets delivered cloth from Britain to the city's clothing manufacturers, who subsequently sent ready-to-wear garments south by ship and west by train. Farmers in southern Maryland consigned hogsheads of tobacco to Baltimore to be reshipped to Europe or turned into cigars at the city's many factories. The bounty of Chesapeake Bay—especially oysters, but varieties of local produce as well—arrived by boat at the city's several canneries and then left in tins aboard boats and trains, destined for markets throughout the U.S. Ships sailing to South America carried locally milled flour, and on their return passages brought back coffee (one of Baltimore's largest imports in this period), guano for the local fertilizer industry, iron ore, and copper. Other vessels sailed to Great Britain with locally grown grain (a change in Britain's grain laws in the 1840s reactivated a trade begun in the mid-eighteenth century), and came back with a hold full of immigrants eager for work as well as manufactured goods (FIGURE 34). The growing economy attracted more and more people looking for work. By 1860 the city's population had risen to over 212,000, double the figure of 1840.[2]

The Mount Clare shops of the B&O covered an area of thirty-four acres in West Baltimore and employed 800 men in preparation for the 1853 opening of the line to Wheeling. By the end of 1854 twenty-eight trains daily left Mount Clare for Wheeling, and a total of 208 cars were in use, all of which were serviced at the West Baltimore yard. Businesses throughout the city benefited, as the B&O contracted out many of the jobs to local machine shops and foundries. Monumental Locomotive Works and Hayward, Bartlett & Co., each employed 350 workers, Poole and Hunt 250, and the other foundries averaged between 100 and 150.[3] The growth of business also encouraged the iron foundries to develop technologies that could be used for products as diverse as bridges, stoves, storage tanks, store fronts, and decorative embellishments for rowhouses. By 1858, the ever optimistic *Sun* reported: "The iron business, in all its phases, has become a feature—and a commanding one—of our industry." Indeed the iron foundries had become the city's second largest employer, with 4,000 workers, one-quarter of the city's labor work force.[4]

Coal-fired steam engines also transformed the city and its manufacturing sector. In 1850 there were 110 factories, employing 4,300 people, which relied on steam-driven machinery. These included iron works, textile mills, flour mills, lumber mills, furniture factories, and tobacco works (FIGURE 35). Soon manufacturers found new uses for steam power, some of which revolutionized the look of buildings. Steam power ran brick molds, scroll saws, jigsaws, and sash-making tools, all of which brought rich architectural detail within economic reach of ordinary builders. Even the smallest alley house could have fine detailing on the façade.

When the Civil War broke out, Maryland, despite strong Southern sympathies, stayed in the Union. The B&O played an important role in the war, carrying supplies and Union Army troops, and because it had no competition made record profits. During Reconstruction in the 1870s Baltimore reestablished itself as an economic force in both foreign trade and domestic commerce. The *Sun* optimistically predicted: "With her perfected lines of foreign and coastwise steamships and her lines of railways reaching out in every direction under the influence of a proper enterprise of her merchants, a much larger growth and bright business future are promised to the city of Baltimore."[5] Baltimore's enduring ties to the South, despite the state's refusal to secede from the Union, put the city in a prime position to dominate markets in southern states for decades. The arrival of southern refugees, including blacks and whites, swelled the city's population.

Industries that existed before the war prospered afterwards. By 1873 the city's twenty-nine firms in the ready-to-wear clothing industry had 12,000 workers. The twenty-three boot and shoe factories employed 800 men and 700 women who turned out 8,000 pairs daily. The six piano factories had 500 workers and turned out fifty pianos a week. The sugar refining, cigar making, and fertilizer industries likewise expanded. But perhaps the greatest sustained growth occurred in the canning industry. By 1873 more than six million bushels of oysters from the Chesapeake and its tributaries arrived in Baltimore annually, carried by four hundred local vessels; fruits and vegetables in equal numbers were picked on local farms, often by the same workers who would later prepare, cook, and pack them. About 12,000 Baltimoreans worked in the dozen or so canneries in and around the city.[6] Many of the city's laborers also came from abroad, arriving on ships belonging to the North-German Lloyd line, out of Bremen. After watching the immigrants streaming through the port in the 1850s, Baltimore's John Work Garrett, president of the B&O, struck a deal with the steamship line in 1867; German steamship agents would sell Germans and Eastern Europeans tickets that would transport them to the port at Baltimore, and then on to the farmlands of the Midwest aboard B&O trains. In return Garrett would build a passenger terminal for the shipping line on Locust Point and make sure that the B&O tracks ran right up to the docks (FIGURE 37). After debarking their cargo of German and Eastern European immigrants, the ships would take on hogsheads of tobacco to bring back to Bremen, Europe's largest tobacco import center. New arrivals that chose to stay in Baltimore initially moved in with friends or rented a room and then found jobs. Between 1851 and 1860, 73,722 Germans came to Maryland. The war disrupted the flow but afterwards, almost all the immigrants passing through Baltimore were Germans, 12,000 arriving in 1868 alone.[7]

City administrators monitored the growth of the city carefully, well aware that expansion always seemed to prompt new demands for city services. Among the more pressing issues still facing them was the question of how best to ensure a constant water supply. At mid-century the city conceded that the water stored at the reservoirs was inadequate to supply the rapidly growing population. (Already there were signs of a much higher demand in the future, as builders were beginning to pipe water into the kitchens of the houses they were constructing for the well-to-do.) Hoping to solve the current problems and avert future ones, in 1854 the city purchased the Baltimore Water Company for $1.3 million and began constructing a four-hundred-million-gallon storage dam at Lake Roland, adding reservoirs in Hampden, Mount Royal, and Druid Lake. This sufficed for a while; however, during the post-Civil War years the rapid spread of indoor plumbing (for bathrooms as well as kitchens) in ever more houses put added strains on the water supply. The drought of 1869 finally convinced the city to begin construction of a system that would carry water drawn from the Jones Falls and the Gunpowder River through a tunnel to Lake Montebello, a reservoir in northeast Baltimore. Six years later this was in place, and served the city until 1915.[8]

Myriad issues involving development (and thus taxation) and transportation also kept the city officials occupied. To their chagrin, growth was proceeding unevenly. The northwestern and northeastern sections had developed rapidly but not the area in between, even though it was closer to the business center of Baltimore and adjacent to the most populous part of Baltimore County. Streams and rivers had impeded direct access and thus development came slowly. After debate the city agreed to fund the costly construction of a series of bridges over the Jones Falls, hoping that if the land could be developed in such a way that it extended the corridor of wealth northward from Mt. Vernon Place, the increased tax base of the properties would substantially add to city coffers and offset the costs of bridge construction. By the early 1880s the bridges had been built and development proceeded apace.

Concurrently with the demand for bridges came cries for the extension and paving of streets. Street openings were important news for they always foretold development, but the grading of proposed streets were enormous undertakings since steam-powered excavation equipment was rarely used. The city expected developers to pay for the grading: one land company's thirty-square-block parcel required 210,000 cubic yards to be removed, all by laborers shoveling earth onto horse carts that only had a two-cubic-yard capacity.[9]

Bridges, roads, and the construction thereof were also affected by demands to move people around the city. In 1844 a private company had established a line of omnibuses to transport people and goods across the city. To remain profitable, the omnibuses traveled along established routes that connected middle- and upper-class neighborhoods with the various business districts. The streets' rough surfaces, many cobblestoned, limited both the speed and capacity of the horse-drawn omnibuses and tended to make the rides rather noisy. The fares for riders were also costly, and well beyond the means of the average-income (let alone working-class) Baltimorean. In the late 1850s a new idea, horse-drawn cars that had iron wheels and ran on iron tracks similar to those used by the railroad, superseded these coaches. The iron wheels and track could be produced in the many foundries about the city. These new horse cars traveled twice as fast (six to eight miles per hour) and carried three times the number of passengers. A one-way fare was five cents, still beyond the reach of the working class, but affordable by many upper-middle- and middle-class residents.[10]

In 1858 City Passenger Railway petitioned city council for permission to lay tracks on city streets and laid claim to several routes, the first of which started at Baltimore and Sharp Streets on the west side of downtown and ran up Pennsylvania Avenue to the city's northern boundary. Soon afterwards competing lines received licenses to lay tracks, and horsecar service spread throughout much of the city. In 1867, after five years of consideration, cars were allowed to run on Sundays. In 1870 the United States Circuit Court ruled that the street railways had to offer accommodations for both blacks and whites on the same terms. When a system of separate cars was created, the court ruled in 1871 that there could be no discrimination between black and white citizens. From that time on, blacks and whites rode together.

From the city's point of view, the horse car offered a unique financial opportunity. Reformers and civic-minded groups had badgered city officials for more than a decade to provide open space for children, especially those from poor families. Various plans for parks and boulevards had been raised then abandoned. The city decided that its cut of the horsecar lines' proceeds should be twenty percent of gross receipts, or one cent out of every nickel fare, and this could be used to create a park system that served residents. In 1859 Baltimore had only two parks—Federal Hill and Patterson. The following year the city made its first two purchases using the horsecar tax money: twenty-nine acres to enlarge Patterson Park, and the five-hundred-acre Rogers estate, which became the main part of Druid Hill Park. Over the next fifty years, at which point the tax was eliminated, the city took in more than $9 million and added acres of parks and squares throughout the city.[11]

Romantic Architecture

Two significant and interrelated events opened the age of romantic architecture in Baltimore. In February 1843 architect Robert Cary Long Jr., who had made his name with Greek Revival designs, gave a lecture entitled, "The Beauties of Gothic Architecture," at the local Mechanic's Lyceum. Long gave his listeners "a more enlarged and just idea of the study of architectural design and beauty," detailing the essential tenets of what would come to be known as the romantic movement—an attraction to architectural styles of the distant past, asymmetry, irregular massing, dark colors, naturalistic forms, and motifs borrowed from exotic lands and far away places.[12] Just a few blocks away, Long's "Perpendicular style" Gothic church was rising at the corner of Park and Saratoga Streets, and it relied on the new structural material of cast iron. Used as a structural support in the nave, iron allowed a higher and lighter interior. It also proved suitable for use in the windows, outside moldings, and the elaborate sixty-foot spire. The façade was of brick, painted "a warm, rich stone color." The church, now known as St. Alphonsus, was built to serve German Catholics.[13]

Romanticism in design and cast iron in construction transformed the appearance of Baltimore and many other cities during the mid-nineteenth century. These two elements prompted a generation of Gothic, Egyptian, Italian, even Swiss and Moorish domestic and commercial buildings, explosively different from the severe classical forms that had gone before. New York inventor and engineer James Bogardus's design for the Sun Iron Building (1850–51), called for an all-iron skeleton with iron exterior cladding and drew national attention to the commercial applications of this new material. Architects quickly realized that a cast-iron structural frame would support buildings of five, six, and even eight stories, and it would also allow buildings to cover broad expanses of ground and still have large open spaces inside.[14]

Cast iron could also be used decoratively. On commercial buildings an entire four- or five-story façade could be elaborately embellished with iron columns and capitals, statuary, and window treatments—parts that could be cast at a single factory and partially assembled before shipping to the site. On houses some of the façade elements that had previously been laboriously handcarved of wood, such as lintels, window hoods, cornice parts, balconies, and stair railings, could be cast of iron, essentially stamped out and shipped ready-to-go. Nevertheless, cast-iron ornament remained the privilege of the well-to-do and only appeared on high-style rows.

Steam power also played an important role in the appearance of new romantic styles. Elaborate cornice brackets and decorative frieze panels could be rapidly fashioned at various woodworking shops, where relatively unskilled laborers used steam-powered scroll and band saws to cut a variety of stock patterns. Marble steps and marble lintels also were cut with steam saws.

The romantic style, based on both escapism and industrial prowess, appealed to members of the city's manufacturing elite who also loathed the growing congestion of the city. They no longer wished to live in the shadows of the mills and factories, amid a growing population that included Europeans who spoke little or no English. Life for them might be better if their families were removed from such potentially pernicious influences. They often rationalized the move by voicing concerns about health, but more than anything else they wanted to escape the chugging, smoke-belching factories and the cacophony of voices that were the lifeblood of the city. Their refuge was a pastoral home seemingly removed from city life. They sought to move to an exotically styled house set upon a lot in the country, or at least the suburbs. These picturesque houses represented a variety of influences, including Tuscan villas and quaint Gothic or Swiss cottages. Builders throughout America could copy such styles from popular design books such as Andrew Jackson Downing's 1842 *Cottage Residences* and 1850 *Architecture of Country Houses*.[15] Out of the plethora of available designs, the Italianate emerged as the most popular style for in-town and suburban residences.

In 1845 eminent New York architect Richard Upjohn had designed an Italianate villa for Edward King of Newport, Rhode Island, which his colleague Andrew Jackson Downing featured in his widely distributed *Architecture of Country Houses*. Downing waxed rhapsodic, pronouncing the villa "one of the most successful specimens of the Italian style in the United States.... The first impression that this villa makes on the mind is that of its being a gentleman's residence. There is dignity, refinement, and elegance, about all its leading features. It next indicated varied enjoyments, and a life of refined leisure—especially abounding as it does with evidences of love of social pleasures."[16] Should a house owner or builder want something slightly different, Downing also included designs for villas and cottages in the rural Gothic and Norman styles, but his Italianate designs seemed best adapted to the American climate. This in combination with the recent popularity of Italianate designs in England (Queen Victoria and her husband Albert had chosen an Italian style villa for their new summer home, *Osborne*) and the celebrity of Italy as a place for summer travel by

Americans promoted the style as one particularly suitable for both the country and urban residences of the well-to-do in the early 1850s.

Like wealthy families across the nation, affluent Baltimoreans who set out in the 1850s to build residences beyond the city's core, in what was then considered country, chose almost invariably, the style so befitting a "gentleman's residence." William Wyman consulted with Richard Upjohn on the design of *Homewood Villa* in north Baltimore in 1850, and then modeled it on the King house. Equally imposing and pretentious were the Italianate villa residences of the same decade built for Johns Hopkins, Thomas Winans, and A. S. Abell. Hopkins's *Clifton*, the only survivor, was created out of an earlier house on the site, transformed into an Italianate villa with bell tower and arcaded loggia by 1852. Winans's *Alexandroffsky* went up in west Baltimore in 1855 and was noted for its wide semi-circular conservatory and central tower; its owner made his fortune building railroads for the czar of Russia. *Guilford*, a fifty-two room Italianate villa belonging to A.S. Abell, founder of the Baltimore *Sun* was located in north Baltimore, not far from Wyman's villa. Other Italianate houses were built well outside the city, two of the most exotic being *Elmonte* and *Temora* in Howard County, which New York architect Nathan Starkweather designed.

The Italianate also became the preferred period style for such large public buildings as railroad stations and schools, and for shop fronts. Local architects J. Rudolph Niernsee and J. Crawford Neilson, the most prominent Italianate designers in Baltimore, met in the engineering department of the B&O Railroad, where in 1848–49 they designed the Italianate Calvert Street Station. About the same time, Niernsee and Neilson began receiving commissions to design elegant townhouses around Mt. Vernon Place for some of the city's wealthiest citizens, many of whom were also directors of the railroad. For their first major commission—a house for Dr. J. Hanson Thomas on a double lot opposite the Washington Monument—they added Italianate decorative touches (specifically, cast-iron window hoods), to an otherwise monumental Greek Revival design. A few years later they introduced brownstone to Baltimore architecture, using it on a Gothic style church just two blocks from the monument; this noteworthy building brought them commissions to design large brownstone townhouses on the few lots left available in Mt. Vernon Place.

Most of the architects working in America's cities based their Italianate designs on fifteenth-century urban palaces, or *palazzos*. Philadelphia architect John Notman, for example, adopted the Italianate style for the Athenaeum (1845–1847) on the east side of Philadelphia's Washington Square; the blocklike structure with rusticated basement, flat roof, and deep cornice was dressed with Italianate projecting window cornices, wide window surrounds, and a balustraded stone balcony across the front of the building. Baltimore was not to be outdone. In 1846 ground was broken for its Athenaeum, which, like Philadelphia's, had been founded to foster a love of learning, an interest in literature and the fine arts, exploration into scientific theory and inventions, and a deep interest in the past. Robert Cary Long Jr. designed a three-story, palazzo style building to house the Maryland Historical Society, the Library Company of Baltimore, and the Mercantile Library (FIGURE 36). The rusticated basement, pedimented and bracketed window cornices, deep modillion cornice, wide arched doorway, and window balconies made the decorative detail more elaborate than that of the Athenaeum in Philadelphia. And like many buildings previously erected in the Greek Revival style, the Athenaeum had its brick walls painted a light color to imitate stone.[17]

The Italianate style was also used for one of the most symbolically significant buildings of the era, the Maryland Institute for the Promotion of the Mechanic Arts, which opened in 1851 (FIGURE 37). This long, two-story hall with a tall Italianate tower replaced the old Centre Market, an established feature in the late-eighteenth-century city core. The institute's arcaded first story was still an open-air market, but the halls upstairs were planned for industrial exhibits that would promote the mechanic arts. Once built, the facility soon became the place to hold large events and meetings of any sort, and both Presidents Franklin Pierce and Millard Fillmore were nominated here.

Parks and Squares

The city's growth fed congestion, which in turn fed a wave of nostalgia for rural life. Baltimore, unlike Philadelphia or Savannah, Georgia, had no public squares. It had instead block after block of houses, expanding factories, and lines of warehouses, all gobbling up the undeveloped land that stood in their paths. Baltimoreans were not alone in their sense of loss. All across America intellectuals and reformers expressed concern over the loss of open land in the cities. One of the responses to this was the creation of the "rural cemetery." The first, Mt. Auburn, opened outside Boston in 1831; the country's fourth, Green Mount in Baltimore, opened in 1839, on the former estate of merchant Robert Oliver on the city's northern boundary. Here were reserved acres and acres of rolling, landscaped ground where visitors could stroll on Sundays, take in the air, and also contemplate the various meanings of mortality. A reporter for the *Sun* after passing through the cemetery's Gothic stone gates, found it "the most beautiful location for a 'city of silence' we have ever seen.... We found there a number of visitors, strangers in the city... viewing with a melancholy pleasure, the evidence there exhibited of the respect paid to poor frail mortality.... The feelings which crowd the mind while musing among the tombs, in any being, should deter him from destroying those beautiful tokens of friendship and love."[18]

One forty-acre cemetery, however, was insufficient to squelch the criticism about the lack of open space in the city itself. Baltimore's landowners and developers responded to such sentiment by establishing land for parks. Theirs were not altruistic decisions; they recognized a hidden opportunity. They understood that some wealthy citizens wanted to leave the noise and congestion of the city center but did not want to be beyond the reach of their businesses. They recognized that the wealthy wanted rural-like scenery but with urban amenities. To achieve this, shrewd developers in seven notable cases—four on the west side, three on the east—acquired a good-sized parcel, granted or sold a piece of the land in the parcel to the city, and stipulated the city use it to create a park. The public park, the open green space, thereby enhanced the value of the lots facing the new parks and elevated the value of those in the surrounding neighborhood. On the assorted lots, the developers and their builders erected a variety of three-story Italianate rowhouses. The heirs of builder John Eager Howard had pioneered the concept of improving the value of one's land by creating a park on their holdings when they developed the land around the Washington Monument in the 1830s. But initially few others had followed suit, although in 1839 the *Sun* publicly urged action:

> It is to be regretted that in the building of our city, so little regard is had to improvements of this description, for surely nothing contributes more largely to the beauty of a city, than handsome public walks and squares. On the score of health, too, it is an object; no one will deny that the free circulation of the air, will render a city more healthy, than where it is confined to narrow and dusty streets. Baltimore is eminently deficient in public walks and squares.... It was an unfortunate circumstance that more ground was not reserved around the Washington monument. There might a square have been made, which would have thrown in the shade any thing of a similar character in the country. The ground itself is finely elevated, and the view from the monument is such a one as the eye would at all times delight to feast upon.[19]

During the rest of the 1830s and into the 1850s parks remained a reform issue, a banner carried by those who also railed against the spread of disease. For decades Baltimore had endured recurrent yellow fever and cholera epidemics, and many believed that the crowding in the city had something to do with it. A writer for the new Baltimore *Sun* explained that in the city's narrow streets during times of "undue heat and vitiated atmosphere . . . the pavements and house-walls absorb the heat received from the mid-day sun, and retain it long after it has been lost by the walls and pavements of wider streets. . . . That the heat really is the cause of the diseases in question, no medical man with whom we have conversed on the subject, entertains a doubt. We allude particularly to the *summer disease*, and diseases generally affecting the bowels." He felt certain that "public squares distributed at proper intervals among the streets of a city, (and they should be numerous in exact proportion to the narrowness of the streets and height of houses) have a tendency to restore that equilibrium of heat which has become lost."

Exercise was another concern that reformers took up. They pointed to New York City's seventeen parks and Philadelphia's four, all of which youngsters used throughout the summer and all of which were a special boon to the poor who could not send their children away to the healthful countryside. One writer begged the city to pursue "the policy adopted by New York, Philadelphia, and other cities" of having public squares in different portions of the city, "at once ornaments, and promoters of health." A portion could be laid out in lots, and "a part enclosed in a neat fence to protect the growth of the natural verdure, and a few trees planted therein. What would have been the consequence? Why families of wealth and fashion would have selected such sites for the construction of a style of houses at once an ornament to the city, and a credit to the builder and proprietor. In time the vacant space would prove far more profitable than in an improved state, by the value it reflected upon adjacent lots—valuable from considerations of healthfulness, as well as beauty of location. . . . Thus, it is plain that the system of leaving squares would be far more advisable than the usual plan. . . . In view of our pride as a city and mere amusement, it is a shame we have no public squares to which we may point the curious stranger!" Another writer to the *Sun* complained that the city had failed to rein in the developers: "Baltimore has lost sight of her true interests," by allowing landholders to "go to work and lease hundreds and hundreds of parcels of ground, twelve or fifteen feet by fifty, or a hundred, at the low sum of *one dollar per foot*. On these, small tenements are hurried up soon to dilapidate. The aspect of sections thus *improved* (what a burlesque!) might be readily imagined, if the reader had not actual pictures to gaze upon in various portions of our own city. We could point to scores of such streets as have been opened and built up in this miserable manner."[20]

Such was the situation when in 1839 James and Samuel Canby for a consideration of $1 granted the mayor and city council the title to some two-and-a-half acres of land in West Baltimore, with the proviso that the area be kept as a public square forever. As successful speculators and builders in Wilmington, Delaware, the Canby brothers had acquired a thirty-two-acre tract in West Baltimore in 1835 from the heirs of Dr. James McHenry, whose country estate had been located along West Baltimore Street. The council accepted the gift and appropriated $2,550 to grade and fence what was to be called "Franklin Square," stipulating that whenever eight or more "three story brick houses, to cost at least $10,000 apiece," had been built on one side of the square, the city would improve that side of the square with a "handsome iron railing, six feet high," and a paved sidewalk outside the railing.[21] The Canbys, who still owned the land surrounding the new park, planned carefully and took their time. In the late 1840s they hired local architect Thomas Dixon to help them with the houses facing the square and also to design the first structure, reasoning that it would set the tone for the whole enterprise. That building was an Aged Women's Home for widows at the northwest corner. Dixon produced a romantic "Tudor gothic" stone building. Its entrance was through a wide and deep buttress; and "embattled parapets" capped the finely carved stone roofline. (The noble purpose of the Home was also a part of the high-toned sentiments of the age. Just west of it stood another benevolent institution, the Baltimore Orphan Asylum, completed in 1853. As the *Sun* noted, "The cause of the poor orphan cannot be too earnestly and frequently presented to the friendly regard of the community." The reporter assessed the "Roman style" design "as noble and commanding as the cause for which it is intended.")[22]

Franklin Square became a popular place for Baltimoreans to visit, even while construction was underway. On one spring Sunday in 1850, the keeper of the square noted that more than 3,300 persons had been by. "At almost every hour of the day, numbers may be seen promenading through the walks, the *Sun* reported. Two years later a "beautiful wrought iron railing," enclosed the square, its fountain, and seats, making it "the most inviting place of rural beauty in the city...attracting numerous companies of ladies and gentlemen to its pleasant walks and shady bowers."[23] Builder Charles Shipley managed construction of the houses around the square; in return, he received title to lots further removed from the square, on which he built houses on his own account. The first eight houses went up on the west side in the spring of 1850: elegant three-story units, "elaborately adorned with ornamental brickwork, with marble base and string courses, with vestibule entrances, and arched doorways of richly stained glass." They were built in pairs, each with a front of twenty-four feet on a forty-foot wide lot, "thus affording side yards and entrances whilst each front is beautified with grass plats extending the entire width, and twenty feet deep," surrounded by ornamental cast iron railings. Shipley and the Canbys made sure the houses were equipped with modern conveniences—gas lighting, central heating, "fine bathrooms, water closets, etc." The parlors had "beautiful cornices and centre pieces, finely carved marble mantels that were exquisite specimens of the art," and "boxing shutters, base boards, door and windows...painted with a refreshing lilac of various delicate tints, affording a grand *coup d'oeil* to the interior." The parlor windows extended to the floor, affording "full means for light and ventilation." The upstairs chambers were "models of what such apartments should be," with "lofty ceilings, colored marble mantels, and dressing or retiring rooms." The second floor also had "convenient rooms for libraries" and the upper stories were "devoted to apartments for children, nurseries, servants' bed rooms, &c." The back building contained the commodious dining room, and kitchens "supplied with every convenience for culinary purposes, with pantries adjoining." Each house's rear ell also contained "a reservoir containing a full supply of water for all purposes, and fine bath rooms, water closets, &c."[24] By the time the first eight were completed, foundations for the houses on Franklin Square's eastern and southern sides were being dug, and the "extensive lots completely fenced in." Eleven four-story rowhouses went up on the eastern side, and fifteen three-story rows on the southern.

As the grand row to the east neared completion in 1851, Baltimoreans took notice that something new was afoot. The *Sun* declared the row as "much handsomer than any yet finished in this city, and displaying the pure Italian style of architecture." Yet locals no doubt saw stylistic similarities between the Franklin Square row and the first palazzo built in the city in 1846, the Athenaeum by Robert Cary Long Jr. Named "Waverly Terrace" in honor of Sir Walter Scott's novels, the houses presented a unified block-long composition (FIGURE 38). The ground story was rusticated. A balcony of "highly ornamented cast iron" ran the entire length of the front at the level of the principal floor. The fronts were coated with "genuine mastic, the first ever done in this city." The full-height windows were "of the French casement style, filled with French plate glass, and dressed with architraves and cornices...admirably painted and sanded to represent brownstone." The "bold block cornice" consisted of a deeply projecting crown molding supported by scroll-sawn modillions set against a frieze. Fancy iron railings enclosed the ten-foot-deep terraced front yards; the fifteen-foot-wide sidewalk beyond was planted with a row of "handsome trees" to "enhance the attractions of the promenade." White marble steps led to a deep vestibule that opened into the sitting room and the dining room. The next floor up contained a forty-foot-deep double parlor decorated with marble mantels and plaster ceiling medallions, and paired fluted columns separating the front and back spaces (the last a remnant of Greek Revival taste). The two floors above offered six chambers with "spacious dressing closets." The back building boasted a kitchen "supplied with all the modern culinary improvements, including hot and cold water apparatus," and upstairs chambers for servants, water closets, bathrooms, and "a play-house for children."[25]

The *Sun* estimated the entire cost of the improvements at Waverly Terrace alone at $160,000. William G. Thomas, a commission merchant and investor in the enterprise, occupied the double house at the north end of the row. Builder Charles Shipley received title to the next four houses, three of which he sold to Thomas, and one of which he retained. The Canbys kept the six houses at the southern end of the row, offering them for rent, a common practice at the time. Thomas initially rented out the three units he acquired from Shipley, but by 1854 had sold them, two for $10,000 and one for $11,000, keeping the ground rents of $160 per lot. For two buyers he provided five-year mortgages of $5,000, to be paid back in $1,000 annual installments. The purchasers included the owner of a dry goods business, a clerk of the Circuit Court, and a wholesale dry goods dealer.[26]

Investor Thomas had played an active, but largely behind-the-scenes, role in the development of the Canby tract. Only a year after acquiring the thirty-two acres in the mid- 1830s, the Canbys began selling one-quarter- and one-half-block parcels to Thomas and his brothers Philip and Evan, who then leased lots to several different builders. This strategy enabled the Canbys to recoup their initial outlay of $52,400 (of which $15,000 was in cash and the remainder guaranteed by a three-year note). As the square became a public gathering place, the land escalated in value: in 1844 the Canbys received $10,000 for two quarter-block parcels and a half-block parcel; six years later a half-block parcel alone went for $15,000.[27]

As would be common throughout Baltimore's development history, these men made their money on the sale of the ground rents once buildings were finished. In 1850 the Canbys sold the ground rents for the six houses at the south end of Waverly Terrace for $16,000. A few years later the Thomases developed the eastern half of the same block by leasing land to two different builders. Builder William Woods constructed eight twenty-foot-wide houses on the southern portion of the parcel, facing Fayette Street, which he sold for $4,000 each, subject to $120 ground rents; James Broumel built five twenty-foot-wide houses on the lot to the north facing Lexington Street, which sold for $3,500 with $100 ground rents, and four fifteen-foot-wide houses on the east side of the parcel priced at only $2,200 with $66 ground rents. To aid Broumel in these endeavors the Thomases lent him $5,500 in the form of an advance mortgage.[28] The Thomases had paid $15,000 for the land in 1852; within two years, with houses built by Woods and Broumel, they sold the ground rents for $24,000.

If Waverly Terrace set the fashionable tone for the square, then the next major row to go up proved that Franklin Square was one of the most desirable places to live in Baltimore (FIGURE 39). In 1854 the Thomas brothers borrowed money from railroad car builder Thomas Winans to erect a row of six large brownstone-fronted houses on the south side of the square. Each unit carried an $8,000 price tag and a high ground rent of $300, an extraordinary sum in that day. The 24-1/2-foot-wide houses were smaller than those of Waverly Terrace, being only three stories in height, but the brownstone finish established them at the height of fashion, as did the elaborate door and window surrounds with flat projecting lintels supported by carved brownstone scrolls.[29] Thomas Dixon, now in partnership with his brother James, was probably the architect of the Franklin Square row; the brothers were working at the same time on another brownstone row in Madison Square, on the east side of town.

Despite brownstone's popularity in New York City, it enjoyed only passing notice in Baltimore, or even Philadelphia. Between 1848 and 1860 brownstone was used on only a handful of structures: two churches near the Washington Monument, several expensive town mansions in that vicinity, and three large-scale impressive rows. John R. Niernsee, the architect who introduced brownstone to the city in 1852 with his Grace and St. Peter's Church, garnered the lion's share of commissions for these brownstone *palazzos* in the Mt. Vernon area. Although each design is different, Niernsee used many of the same elements: windows framed by wide moldings, sometimes arched, and capped with flat pediments, usually supported by brackets; stone-columned balconies, supported by deep brackets, connecting the windows of the principal story; an occasional second floor bay window with its own piazza; broad, wide steps with stone railings leading to wide, often arched, front doors set beneath projecting pediments; and a deep modillion cornice. Local architect Louis Long preferred curved window hoods, which he used for a five-bay-wide townhouse on Monument Street, (FIGURE 40) as well as a speculative row he designed for Richard E. France, known as the "lottery king," on Mt. Vernon Place, east of the monument. In both designs the wide, arched doorway is set within a paneled entryway flanked by decorative moldings and capped by a projecting arched lintel supported by carved scrolls.

There were problems in working with brownstone, and these may have contributed to Baltimore builders being disinclined to use it. The invention of both steam-powered and pneumatic drills now made it possible for a single stonecutter to do in one day ten times the work of three hand borers at the quarry, and thus reduce the cost of the stone; but brownstone could delaminate. By the 1850s most architects knew that the brownstone on New York City's City Hall already had begun to deteriorate. Bedding planes, when cut or laid up as a veneer, had to be set parallel to the ground; if accidentally or deliberately set perpendicular, any water trapped in the stone deteriorated the structure during the next freeze and thaw cycle. Baltimore builders may well have felt that the skill necessary to lay up the stone correctly was just not available locally.[30]

Some builders did use brownstone to face the basement level or for decorative trim, but even more popular was imitation brownstone. In 1850 Michael Roche selected brownstone for the basements of his Washington Place row and finished the rest of the façades "in imitation of this stone." A year later Roche, using a design by Long, erected a row of four-story houses nearby "dressed with a rough-cast masticated imitation of Connecticut brownstone, the first stories being rusticated." Throughout the 1850s a number of different builders were putting up rows of houses with imitation brownstone fronts in the greater Mt. Vernon Place area, around Franklin Square, and facing another new square, Madison Square, located to the east of the city.[31] By the late 1850s, however, Baltimore's flirtation with brownstone had run its course. For the next thirty years builders opted for Italianate-style houses of fine pressed brick with white marble trim from nearby quarries (FIGURE 41). Used as sills, stringers, basement facings, and three or four steps, the marble gave Baltimore its lasting symbol of architectural identity.

Pressed brick became the material of choice for houses of affluent and middle-income residents in both Philadelphia and Baltimore. Its hard, smooth face and uniform red color and size—the result of the brick pressing machines—allowed for narrow, one-sixteenth-inch mortar joints, which gave façades the monolithic effect of stone to all but the close observer. Such work, though, was time-consuming and expensive. Thus a pressed brick façade cost about four times more than one of ordinary brick (and about the same as brownstone). Whereas a mason could lay up about 1,200 to 1,500 regular bricks a day for a wall, he could only lay 200 to 300 pressed bricks in the same time. Consequently pressed brick was used only on the front face of a house, and even then it was laid in front of a conventional, and structural, brick wall. Not everyone found pressed brick desirable. Some years later a writer for *American Architect and Buildings News*, a national trade journal, moaned that Flemish bond had been replaced by "the mere four inch thick pressed brick screen of the smoothest and reddest of bricks and the finest and whitest of mortar joints as a facing to a very poor wall behind it."[32]

Parks for the Rising Middle Class

Even before Baltimoreans judged Franklin Square a tremendous success, other developers were calculating how they too might donate land to the city for public spaces amid their landholdings. Southeast of Franklin Square sat Willowbrook, a magnificent Federal-period estate once part of acreage owned by the Donnell family. In 1847, at the death of their father, the two sons decided to "develop" the estate. They retained the main house and its grounds, and laid out building lots on the remaining acreage. Following the Canbys' model, they gave the city two-and-a-half acres surrounding a natural spring, stipulating it be kept as a public park, fenced and improved at city expense. The city agreed and by the early 1850s the spring, which had been turned into a drinking fountain, sported a Greek-style portico, the park's perimeter was fenced, and curving walkways wended their way through the plot, renamed Union Square (FIGURE 42).

Although the *Sun* predicted that "a square of enclosed ground in the city like this is always a nucleus around which improvements in the shape of handsome residences will cluster, and the establishment of such pleasure grounds is followed, without regard to location, by the improvement of the vicinity," Union Square never attained the social or architectural prominence that Franklin Square enjoyed. The houses overlooking Union Square, only slightly smaller than those at Franklin Square, sold for much less—$3,000 to $5,000—and carried ground rents of $100 to $150. The earliest ones, built on Stricker Street along the east side of the square in 1857–1858, resembled the three-story houses built along the secondary streets near Franklin Square, having pressed brick fronts, marble or

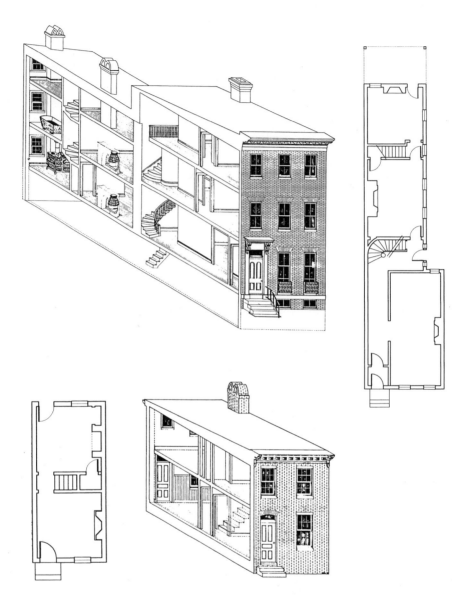

The three-story, three-bay rowhouse at 1412 Park Avenue in Bolton Hill (top) is typical of the elegant rows built around Harlem Park and Franklin, Madison, Union, and Lafayette Squares, 1850s–1880s. The 12 North Amity Street plan (bottom), circa 1870, is typical of Baltimore's smallest alley houses—two rooms deep, four rooms total, and measuring 11 to 12 feet wide and 25 to 30 feet deep. (Chester Design Associates, Gloria Mikolajczyk)

brownstone trim, and paired, pedimented doorways. They also bore something new—elaborate window lintels fashioned of cast iron, an embellishment that could be produced in a mold at a fraction of the cost of carving the same design in brownstone or marble (FIGURE 43). The twelve houses were built speculatively by builders who leased the lots and borrowed money from the Donnells to build the houses. John Mallonee constructed the eight houses at the north end of the block; George Bane the four at the south end. All the houses were 22 feet wide by 32 feet deep and had a 16-by-33-foot back building. A single long parlor ran the length of the main block, and the dining room and kitchen were located in the narrower back building.[33]

As was the case with the developers of the second-tier housing at Franklin Square, developers at Union Square did not feel the need to use architects, relying instead on builders with good experience and knowledge of the trade. Instead, many developers stipulated in their leases to builders specifications for the house's design and size. In the Donnells' leases to Mallonee and Bane, they added the clause: the houses should be "similar to houses on the south side of Hollins Street west of Fremont and on the south side of Fayette Street between Calhoun and Stricker built by said Maloney [sic]. They can have fronts of pressed brick or painted." Thus the three-story Italianate houses that filled these newly developing portions of the city looked remarkably alike. Contemporary writers called the narrower houses along the streets that did not face major squares, "second-class houses." Whereas the houses facing Franklin Square all had front footages of twenty-four feet to twenty-six feet, and the houses facing Union Square were twenty-two feet wide, houses built along the other sides of the same blocks only measured eighteen to twenty feet wide. A block or two away stood three-story, three-bay Italianate houses only sixteen to eighteen feet wide. Not only were they narrower, the main house was generally only one room deep (about thirty feet), containing a long parlor with bedrooms above. The dining room, kitchen, bathroom, and servants rooms were located in the back building, which also had a doorway opening into the rear areaway between houses, and a second set of stairs. The houses sold for about two-thirds the price of their first-class counterparts, yet still had embellishments such as scroll-sawn brackets supporting door and window cornices, full-height French parlor windows, and marble steps and basements. Such houses filled block after block of west and east Baltimore, before and after the Civil War (FIGURE 44).[34]

Rowhouse construction extended to the blocks around another newly created public park after the war, Lafayette Square, a few blocks north of

Franklin Square. The land developers of these parcels *sold* the future park-
land, two-and-a-half acres in northwest Baltimore, to the city in 1859 for
$15,000 (the purchase money being in exchange for paving the streets
"adjacent to the square and one-half of all the streets which bind on said
square"). For its part the city agreed to fence in each side of the square with
iron railings once six houses "of not less than twenty feet front" were built
on each side. The square was situated on "one of the highest locations near
the suburbs of the city" with fine views and a stand of "large and thriving
oak and other beautiful forest trees." Baltimoreans had come to believe
that amenities like this were important. One reporter observed:

> Attracted by the pleasant spring-like weather we walked out into the
> northwestern section of the city...we were both surprised and delighted
> at finding ourself...upon an elevated plateau of land, which appeared to
> have been especially designed by nature for the great Western lung or
> park of this extensive and growing metropolis of Maryland. We doubt
> whether the views from this sylvan spot, which has been patriotically
> entitled Lafayette Square, can be equaled for romantic beauty and exten-
> sive vistas of observation by any other section of this city. Standing upon
> its green fields, and surrounded by noble, majestic oaks, the wearied,
> toil-worn citizen, in the summer solstice, reclining upon the cool, green
> sward, and fanned by the cool breezes which prevail at this elevated spot,
> beholds before him a bold and glorious panorama of nature.[35]

Although the city looked forward to bringing the acres of land around
the square onto the tax roles, the outbreak of the Civil War halted all construction. Lafayette Square served as an army camp and barracks during the
war, and when peace returned the thriving oaks were gone, victim to the
heavy occupation. Undaunted, the city paid for curving walks and a fountain. By August 1867 upwards of eighty first-class dwellings were going up,
most of them ornate, three-story pressed-brick Italianate houses with
bracketed door and window cornices, deep bracketed roof cornices, and
marble sills, basements, and steps—much like the houses in the Franklin
Square neighborhood. The last square to be developed on Baltimore's west
side was Harlem Park, named in honor of the country estate it replaced
(FIGURE 45). Here, large three-story, three-bay-wide pressed-brick Italianates filled the streets bordering the square in the 1870s and 1880s. In
this later version of the style, bracketed cornices were more prominent
in the overall design, with very long and attenuated scroll-sawn brackets
supporting the modillioned cornices. Elaborate jig sawn or stamped metal

33. LEFT   Traugoth Singewald bought 1408 West Baltimore Street, built 1878, for his West Baltimore store (J. Brough Schamp)
BOTTOM   His son, Joseph T. Singewald Sr., took over his father's hat-making business in Fells Point around 1885 (Robert L. Tarring, Jr.)

34. FAR BOTTOM   Immigrants, Locust Point, circa 1910. After the North German Lloyd line established regular steamship service between Bremen and Baltimore in 1867, a steady inflow of German and Eastern European immigrants arrived in the city (Baltimore Neighborhood Heritage Project)

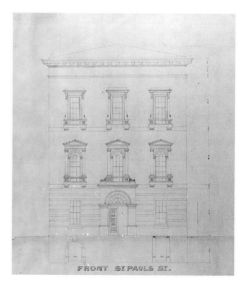

35. TOP   Wm. Maughlin &
Sons Steam Planing Mill, Sash
and Lumber Yard, circa 1870.
Steam-powered factories
mass-produced dressed lumber,
cornice parts, window frames,
sashes, shutters, and moldings, so
that inexpensive rowhouses could
afford to have such finishes.
Lithograph by A. Hoen
(Maryland Historical Society)

36. RIGHT   The Athenaeum,
designed by Robert Cary Long
Jr., 1846 (Maryland Historical
Society)

37. TOP   The Maryland Institute, one of Baltimore's most prominent Italianate buildings, built 1851; note the horsecar passing by in this 1863 view. Lithograph by E. Sachse & Co., *Illustrated Album of Baltimore City*, 1863 (Maryland Historical Society)

38. BOTTOM   Waverly Terrace, 101–123 North Carey Street, Franklin Square, designed by Thomas and James Dixon and built by Charles Shipley, 1850 (J. Brough Schamp)

39. TOP   1313–1323 West Fayette Street, Franklin Square, 1854 (J. Brough Schamp)

40. RIGHT   105 Monument Street, designed by Louis Long, circa 1853 (J. Brough Schamp)

41. TOP   The Beaver Dam marble quarries north of Baltimore supplied the marble for the city's famous white marble steps, window lintels, sills, basement facings, and parlor mantels. Marble was channeled out in blocks, five by nine by fifteen feet, which were lifted by derricks to a steam-powered sawing machine and cut into smaller pieces; the blocks were sent to the city via rail car for further dressing (author's collection)

42. RIGHT   Union Square, donated to the city in 1847 (Jane Webb Smith)

43. TOP 27–33 South Stricker Street, Union Square, built by John Mallonee and George Bane, 1857–1858; note the elaborate cast-iron window lintels (J. Brough Schamp)

44. BOTTOM 217–231 North Calhoun Street, built in 1859 by William Woods, an example of the second-class houses put up a block or two away from the more elegant squares (Steven Allan)

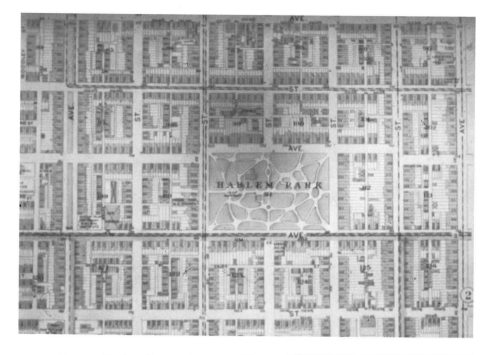

45. TOP Harlem Park, as it appeared in 1896. Developers laid out new Italianate style rowhouse neighborhoods on old estates, often around a central park. To insure the maximum return on investment *and* provide houses for local craftsmen and laborers, they laid out blocks with lots facing both the wide main streets and the narrow alley streets, which ran down the center of the block. From G. W. Bromley, *Atlas of Baltimore, Maryland*, 1896

46. RIGHT 1524 Hollins Street, Union Square, built by Jacob Saum, 1883. Henry Louis Mencken spent most of his life in this Italianate style house, which his parents had bought new (Jane Webb Smith)

47. TOP   Horsecar lines made it convenient for the residents of Baltimore's upper-middle-class squares to get downtown to work (Maryland Historical Society)

48. BOTTOM   1500 block West Lombard Street, built by Jacob Saum, 1874 (J. Brough Schamp)

49. TOP   1600 block Lemmon Street, built by Jacob Saum, 1871 (Steven Allan)

50. BOTTOM   Wagner's Point, south of the city on a branch of the Patapsco River, has two streets of two-story Italianate rowhouses built in the late 1880s by the owner of a cannery, who located his plant and worker housing away from the city to save on land cost; the cannery owner also helped his Polish-American workers obtain financing through several of the city's Polish building and loans (Jane Webb Smith)

51. TOP   *Baltimore Schuetzen-Park, Belair Road,* lithograph by E. Sachse, 1867, one of the shooting clubs and outdoor parks that working-class citizens traveled via horsecar (Maryland Historical Society)

52. BOTTOM   Two-bay-wide Italianate style rowhouses in northwest Baltimore, built circa 1885 (Baltimore Neighborhood Heritage Project)

53. TOP   The Odorless Excavating Apparatus, *Baltimore City Directory*, 1870

54. TOP RIGHT   1100 block of North Calhoun Street, sold in 1885 for only $700 (Jane Webb Smith)

55. BOTTOM RIGHT   Machine-sawn scroll cornice brackets, 1867, from George O. Stevens Co. *Illustrated Price List*, Baltimore

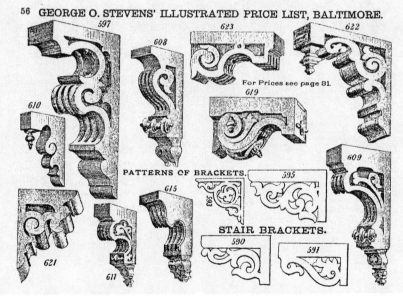

56 GEORGE O. STEVENS' ILLUSTRATED PRICE LIST, BALTIMORE.

597

608

623

622

For Prices see page 31.

610

619

PATTERNS OF BRACKETS.

595

609

593

STAIR BRACKETS.

590

591

621

615

611

56. TOP   600 North Calhoun Street, facing Harlem Park and built by Joseph Cone, 1876; traditional Italianate style houses with bracketed cornices and arched entranceway (Jane Webb Smith) RIGHT   In 1874 local photographer William H. Weaver captured this scene of rowhouses going up in the Maryland Avenue–Charles Street corridor, as new bridges spanned Jones Falls View. The view is from the First Presbyterian Church steeple, looking northeast (Baltimore City Life Collection, Maryland Historical Society)

57. TOP   900 block Fulton Avenue, built by Joseph Cone, 1878. Neo-grec door and window lintels update the otherwise traditional Italianate facades (Alain Jaramillo)

ventilator panels added distinction to the frieze and provided air to interior spaces under the roof. On these houses, Baltimore builders favored arched entrances and marked many of them with foliated keystones.

The four squares on Baltimore's west side—Franklin, Union, Lafayette, and Harlem–created a gracious milieu for members of the city's new middle class and the upper-middle class manufacturing elite. As production increased in the many factories lining the waterfront and located along major thoroughfares running out of the city, an increasing number of owners, managers, businessmen, and professionals gravitated toward the peaceful squares on the edge of the city. Situated on high ground, the houses offered splendid views of the harbor and surrounding countryside, gentle breezes on summer nights, an abundance of fresh produce from the nearby countryside, parks in which children could play and adults stroll, and large backyards for gardening and summer houses.

In the early 1880s a young Henry Louis Mencken, the future journalist and social critic, moved with his family to a typical new Italianate house facing Union Square (FIGURE 46). His father, August, owned a cigar factory downtown on Baltimore Street. Like many of the residents of west Baltimore, the Menckens were German-Americans and their parents still spoke German at home. In his autobiography, *Happy Days*, Mencken painted a vivid picture of life around Union Square in the 1880s. The neighborhood "was still almost rural, for there were plenty of vacant lots nearby, and the open country began only a few blocks away." The backyard had fruit trees, a grape arbor, and a summer house—"a rococo structure with a high pointed roof covered with tin, a wooden floor, an ornate railing, and jig-saw spirals wherever two of its members came together"—built by his maternal grandfather, "a very skillful cabinetmaker." The family used Latrobe stoves to supplement the hot air furnace; heat in the bathroom was supplied from the kitchen, "which meant that there was none at all until the hired girl began to function below." The outhouse at the end of the long yard was "for the accommodation of laundresses, whitewashers and other visiting members of the domestic faculty" and every spring an Odorless Excavating Apparatus pumped out and fumigated the shallow sink beneath it.[37] Mencken's father regularly hired German girls for domestic help at the "Norddeutscher-Lloyd pier at Locust Point," who tended to be "snatched away, after a year or so, by some amorous ice-man, beer-man or ash-man." Mencken's mother spoke German with these girls, as well as "with the German marketmen, plumbers, tinners, beermen and grocery boys who were always in and out (FIGURE 47)."[38]

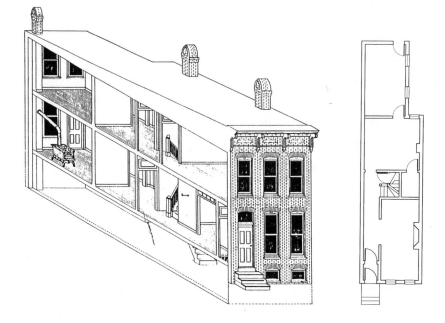

Modest two-story Italianate houses, similar to 1021 South Hanover Street in Federal Hill, went up in Baltimore's factory neighborhoods around the waterfront in the 1870s and 1880s. They had no indoor plumbing, but did include a vestibule and formal parlor (Chester Design Associates, Gloria Mikolajczyk)

Part and parcel of such new middle- and upper-middle-class rowhouse developments as that in which the Menckens lived was the traditional Baltimore alley house—a small, two-story house built along the narrow streets bisecting each block. Although middle-class residents could now commute to work via the new horsecar lines, laborers, mechanics, craftsmen, and those in the service sectors could not afford to do so. These people needed to live within walking distance of their jobs. Builders thus continued to erect small alley houses, which went at a fraction of the cost of the main street houses. By the 1870s the alley houses were miniature versions of the grand three-story Italianate houses, often put up by the same builders. Jacob Saum constructed the Menckens' house on Hollins Street in 1883, as part of a row running across the north side of Union Square. Twelve years earlier Saum, who then identified himself as a carpenter in the city directories, had developed part of the block at the south side of the square, building three-story Italianate houses along the east side of

Gilmor Street, the north side of Pratt, and the south side of Lombard (facing the square), as well as tiny two-story Italianates on Lemmon Street, the narrow street running down the center of the block. The 15-foot-wide houses on Gilmor Street sold for $2,000 with a $52.50 ground rent in 1871; the 14-foot-wide houses facing commercial Pratt Street went for $1,600 with a $36 ground rent, and the 11-foot 2-1/2-inch-wide houses on Lemmon Street could be had for only $700, with an $18 ground rent. Saum offered mortgages on all. Three years later Saum built 18-foot-wide houses facing the square, which he priced at $3,500 with a ground rent of $100 (FIGURE 48).[39]

The economies of machine-milled lumber allowed builders to give their alley houses a bit of stylistic flourish, usually bracketed cornices that were much simpler in design than those on their more expensive counterparts (FIGURE 49). The houses had limited amenities inside. Most had two small rooms per floor and a narrow central stair. There was no plumbing and the only heat came from stoves, one in the kitchen and one upstairs. In the predominantly German west Baltimore area, many of the houses on these narrow streets became the first residences of newly arrived immigrants, people like George Elsner, a laborer; Henry Grosbernd, a driver; John Munk, a quarryman, Herman Reich, a machinist; Jeremiah McCarthy, a laborer; and John A. Wallace, also a laborer. When McCarthy bought the house from Saum in early 1872, he and his wife put down $350, and Saum held the mortgage: $350 over three years, payable each month in amounts of not under $10. Many alley houses became rental properties. Bernard O'Neill, a stone worker, bought his first Lemmon Street house in 1874, bought another in 1877, and then three more in 1879.[40] He then rented them for about $6 a month to the wider market of renter who could not afford the high down payment of a house purchase.

Builder Saum's transactions with the Lombard, Gilmor, Pratt, and Lemmon Street properties demonstrated that speculative building had changed little during the past fifty years. The builder shared the risk with the various craftsmen working on the houses. Saum assigned the houses built on Lemmon and Pratt Streets to men in the building trades—painter Christian Buschmann, plasterers William L. Mallonee and Samuel Bilson, paperhangers Washington and Henry Head, gas fitter Robert J. Davidson, lumber dealer John Thomas Scharf, and lumber merchants George and Samuel Helfrich—who never took up residence. Some sold the houses immediately, but others retained them for rental income. That the resident-buyers of Saum's 18-foot-wide houses facing Union Square on Lombard Street included an owner of a lumber yard, a proprietor of a marble works, and a carpenter, suggests that members of the building trades were rising in status and income. Other purchasers included an attorney, a supplier of undertaker's trimmings, and a clerk. Around the corner on Gilmor Street, Saum sold two of the houses to men listed as "conductors," undoubtedly for the nearby B&O Railroad, a bookkeeper, a paperhanger, two merchant tailors, and a flour merchant. A policeman and a clerk named John Zugehov bought houses on Pratt Street.

Saum completed building on the south side of Union Square in 1877, and then continued to build in the immediate neighborhood before leasing more land from the Donnells on the north side of the square. The northern lots were a mix of 18-foot-wide and 17-foot-4-inches-wide, with ground rents of $81.00 and $76.50. August and Henry Mencken were the first to buy on the block, paying $2,900 for their 18-foot-wide houses. Their neighbors soon included a building materials' supplier, a grocery store owner, paperhangers, a commission merchant, a tailor, and the owner of an art gallery. All but the commission merchant and the paperhanger were German, and all operated their businesses on nearby West Baltimore Street, a block north of Hollins, where Traugoth Singewald's shop was located.[41]

East Baltimore experienced a similar pattern of park-centered housing development in the post–Civil War period. Madison Square opened in 1853; Johnson Square in 1878; and Collington Square in 1880. All three were soon lined with three-story, three-bay wide Italianate houses aimed at an upper-middle-class market and surrounded by narrow mid-block streets faced with rows of alley houses for local laborers and domestic workers. By the late 1870s some builders were beginning to offer plainer Italianate houses for a less affluent middle-class market on streets further removed from the prestigious squares. These three-story units stood only two bays wide, had the simplest of scroll-sawn cornices and plain door and window trim, and were priced accordingly, at less than $2,000.

Houses for Working-Class Families: Two-Story Italianates

Observers complained that the city had a glut of three-story houses and a dearth of houses affordable by the workingman. Some found it easy to blame the ground rent system and greedy developers. But the situation was more complex. The hierarchical system of building *had* made a variety of classes of houses available throughout the city, but those houses did not meet the needs of workingmen whose jobs were not in the immediate neighborhoods. For the almost countless men and women who spent ten hours a day laboring in factories near the harbor or in mills in the Jones Falls Valley, it was not economical to commute to a small house on a narrow mid-block street in a distant neighborhood. A five-cent, one-way horsecar fare amounted to a substantial expense, one best saved for an occasional splurge, such as a trip to a park that was well beyond walking distance. For one person to spend sixty cents a week on commuting back-and-forth to work was out of the question for someone earning only a few dollars a week. Baltimore was still a walking city, physically and economically. From that perspective, the city had a housing shortage.

Developers who heeded demands for working-class housing recognized that they had to eschew housing for multiple income levels (with its potentially higher ground rent returns) and instead build entire neighborhoods with houses designed for just one economic group: middle-income workers. Land for such lower cost development was still available near the factories, breweries, mills, and railroad yards. Here developers created yet another rowhouse type, the two-story Italianate. And even though the houses were small, the exterior decorations at least gave the appearance of stylishness. Although not living near a fashionable square, these working-men and their families could still partake of the rural qualities of life so important to the romantic movement, through public parks and German-sponsored Scheutzen Parks in their neighborhoods.

Almost identical in appearance to the three-story versions of the late 1870s and 1880s, two-story Italianate houses filled in the blocks on either side of the waterfront—in South Baltimore, Locust Point, and Canton; the low-lying land south of the B&O's Mt. Clare shops; land further west previously occupied by slaughter houses, a hair and brush manufactory, and tanneries; land in the northeast corridor where the breweries were located; and land to the north of the city that housed the region's important textile industry (FIGURE 50). Thanks to the efforts of the *Schuetzengesellschaft*, or shooting club, the Germans who worked in northeast Baltimore near the breweries could take pleasure in the nearby Schuetzen Park, which had acres of pleasure grounds, pavilions, bandstands, dance floors, bowling alleys, and target ranges for shooting matches; they could enjoy the healthful advantages of open space and exercise and then imbibe some of the beer that the breweries daily delivered to the park (FIGURE 51). To the southwest, along Frederick Road, the Wilkens curled hair factory hired hundreds of Germans and boasted, "You don't start to be an American till you've worked at the hair factory." Nearby, the Schuetzen association purchased land to build another working-class park and rows of two-story

Italianate houses on surrounding blocks. In South Baltimore, the Knabe Piano Factory offered employment to German craftsmen who could walk to work from their homes just a few blocks away and also relax in Riverside Park, a city park where two-story, three-bay Italianate houses flanked the square. The Knabe factory's annual picnic at Riverside Park took on the airs of a traditional German festival.[42]

One of the first builders to experiment with two-story Italianate houses was John S. Gittings, the prosperous banker who, in the early 1850s, had built two-story-and-attic working-class houses in Federal Hill and also tried his hand at architect-designed Italianate rows in Mt. Vernon Place. After the Civil War, Gittings resurfaced in South Baltimore, building two-story Italianate rows for workingmen. These small, two-bay wide houses carried ground rents that were less than one-tenth that of the three-story Italianate houses Gittings had built on Madison Avenue in 1851— $21 versus $250 for the large houses in a prestigious neighborhood.

Builders devised two versions of the working-class house, one two bays wide and the other three bays wide, ranging in width from about twelve to fourteen feet. Each of these had six rooms and most had a low basement. The three-bay-wide versions went up on the main streets, and the two-bay wide houses on the side streets. In the three-bay versions a tiled entrance vestibule led into a narrow hall, which opened into the front parlor (measuring about nine by twelve feet) and back to the stairs and the dining room. The kitchen was at the rear of the house, beyond the dining room. In a house so very narrow (some are only thirteen feet wide), it is telling that the builders crowded in an entrance vestibule, hall, and formal parlor, sacrificing crucial living space to preconceived notions of how life should be lived properly. The wide opening leading into the parlor from the hall was even framed by pilasters or marked by a set of pocket doors. In the two-bay-wide version they dispensed with the vestibule and hall and one entered the parlor directly. Such houses were built in long, continuous rows on shallow lots. The three-bay-wide houses generally sold to owner-occupants for $800 to $1,000; the two-bay-wide houses rented for $7 to $8 per month (FIGURE 52).[43]

The exterior designs adapted and simplified the highstyle Italianate house and relied almost entirely on machine-made decorative elements. Façades were plain brick with wood trim, although many of the three-bay-wide houses had a cut-stone facing at the basement level. Window and door openings, tall and narrow in proportion to the façade, had segmental-arched brick lintels, often with scroll-sawn wood tympanums. There was no doorway enframement, not even the simple arched molding used in middle-class Italianate houses. The main decorative feature of the façade was the roof cornice. The standard cornice was wood and consisted of a deeply projecting crown molding set above a frieze decorated with jig-sawn leaf and vine motifs or geometric figures. The carved areas served to ventilate the attic, but their primary function was decorative. Rows of machine-cut moldings, such as quarter rounds, scallops, or dentils, usually bordered the frieze. At each end of the façade an elaborately scroll-sawn bracket supported the cornice. All of the earlier classical forms used in the prototype Italianate cornice—modillions, dentils, plain friezes, egg-and-dart moldings—had been replaced by inexpensive sawn wood elements. By this means, economically built houses could afford to have decorative embellishments that echoed higher-cost fashions.

The interior arrangement and decoration of the two-story Italianate exhibited the same practical relationship between style and necessity as did the exterior. Interior elements manufactured by machine, such as turned balusters and newels, beaded door and window enframements, and scroll-sawn mantels, were common features, no matter how small the houses. Optional amenities included Franklin stoves and an indoor water supply, although outdoor privies were still the rule, emptied by the Odorless Excavating Apparatus (FIGURE 53). The floor plan, however, bore little relationship to the Italianate prototype, with its grand single or double parlor. In the more modest Italianate, the two-room deep designs resembled the floor plans of earlier two-and-a-half story and two-story-and-attic working-class houses in the area.

It is a striking reminder of the pervasive desire among all income levels of Baltimoreans to have style in their houses. Even in these smaller row-houses, such elements of the formal house as the tiled vestibule and the entrance hall with a pilastered opening into the "formal" parlor were scaled down and adapted to modest interiors. Builders realized that the people buying these houses, however modest their means, wanted such traditional amenities, as well as the exterior decorative embellishments that modern machine tools could provide in such quantity. Just as with more expensive houses, builders provided the amount of decoration the market could afford in order to make their houses more appealing to potential buyers.

Realtors aggressively marketed two-story Italianate rowhouses to investors, promising returns of 14 percent or more. In 1885 S. H. Hooper, a real estate agent, offered houses for sale to homeowners or investors: "Five new six-room DWELLINGS, one vacant, the other four rented; will pay 14 per cent; stoves in parlors, ranges, bath-room, hot and cold water, gas fixtures, etc.; nicely papered throughout; price only $700 each. Terms, $300 cash each, balance on each in half-yearly payments at 3 per cent interest, or all cash. Located on west side Calhoun street, the first five houses north of Mosher street; ground rent on each $60" (FIGURE 54). Some years later another realtor advertised, "FOR SALE—BATCH OF ALLEY HOUSES; always rented; nets 26 per cent."[44]

Changing Technologies

Although not all working-class families could afford to buy a house, several technological advances helped to contain the price of home construction during these decades. Indeed, no realm of housebuilding (except digging cellars) remained untouched by machine technology. Molding machines that relied on a plunger or piston and water or steam power replaced the practice of making bricks by hand. In the mid-1850s Chambers Bros. and Co., invented a steam-powered machine that mixed the clay, sand, and water, tempered it, and extruded it in a continuous ribbon that could be cut into individual bricks. These were sent through a drying tunnel and then fired in a kiln. Another technology advocated a machine to mold the brick and then compress it again. A number of inventors worked to improve the firing process, all in the interest of producing a better and cheaper brick.[45]

Woodworking shops likewise began churning out standardized components. The usual shop had a coal-fired steam engine at one end of the building, which powered a shaft that ran down the center of the shop at ceiling level. The shaft operated continuously and leather belts connected it to the individual machines; each operator (generally not a skilled laborer or artisan) activated his machine by throwing a lever once the wooden blank was positioned for cutting. When the piece was finished he shifted his machine into idle, measured or otherwise checked the piece to ensure it was cut to the exact dimension, and inserted a new blank for cutting.

Through the 1890s builders used a combination of hand-cut and machine-cut embellishments (FIGURE 55). A competent workman could fashion the elements of a typical Italianate cornice using just a few basic woodworking tools. A workman who followed a wood pattern could cut the curved brackets that supported the projecting cornice on a scroll saw. Sometimes the brackets were of one thickness of wood and other times they were built up out of three pieces with the middle piece recessed and decorated with balls or other shaped ornaments created by a shaper following a pattern. The cornice's main element, the crown molding, was achieved by pushing a long piece of wood through a die in which cutting knives were fixed. The ventilated frieze board with its myriad array of patterns began with a stenciled design that was first drilled, then cut by hand with a coping saw. These drill marks, which served as starter holes, can be seen on most Baltimore frieze boards. A lathe shaped the rope or egg-and-dart molding at the bottom of the frieze. A spindle molder produced the stair balusters inside the house. Though machines produced most of the artwork, an element of human labor was still involved in the cutting, assembling, and finishing. The entire cornice arrived at the site as one pre-fabricated unit or broken down into three or four components for easy application. As rows containing more and more houses began to be built, the construction work took on an assembly line quality. Nevertheless, designs throughout the city differ markedly and in most cases a builder's signature "style" can be identified.

The nearly flat, sloping roof that extended the length of the Italianate house behind the street-front cornice created concerns about water tight-ness, a challenge not found with traditional gable roofs. One clever Baltimore firm came up with a new system: "three thicknesses of woolen felt perfectly saturated with cement," covered with "one inch of cement in a heated state with heated pebbles," producing a roof, so the firm boasted, "likely to last as long as the building stands." The cement was a bitumen or tar-based liquid that remained the major component of built-up roofing membranes for the next century. A tin or zinc roof was used only on high style houses.[46]

The Development Process Changes

During the post-Civil War period rowhousing in Baltimore boomed along with the emergence of the middle class. The number of annual building permits nearly tripled in a span of four years, from 1,384 in 1866 to 3,630 in 1870. Even while the financial Panic of 1873, which depressed Baltimore as well as most cities and towns nationwide, slowed construction for a time, activity had reached high levels again by the late 1870s. The city's growth in these years accelerated the break-up of country estates surrounding the old city, especially those in the western section. Although most building was accomplished by fairly small-scale builders (in an 1869 *Sun* article on resi-dential development, for example, the 316 houses listed were put up by 70 different builders) real estate development practices were changing. The 1870s saw the beginning of the end of the small-scale builder.

The change began with the development of Harlem Park by several different land companies and builder Joseph Cone. Cone (1836–1905) became the largest-scale builder of his era, responsible for some 800 houses in thirty years. His methods initiated the move toward large-scale real estate development.[47] Harlem was a fifty-six acre estate in northwest Baltimore owned by Dr. Thomas Edmondson. At Edmondson's death in 1856, his estate was put in the hands of an executor who managed the property in trust for Edmondson's children. Twelve years later the trustees donated ten acres of land to the city as a public park—by then a tried-and-true development strategy—and sold a block of land east of the park to the Maryland Consolidated Land Company for $27,000. Covenants stipulated that construction was to begin by October 1, 1868, and that the houses be three stories high and at least sixteen feet wide. In return the estate agreed to pay for paving four hundred feet of street along the block. Maryland Consolidated promptly leased some of the land to builders and developed other parcels itself. The lease to carpenter John Cramblitt was typical of others. Cramblitt agreed to improve six lots "by erection of a brick dwelling house on each of said lots all to be built in a substantial and workmanlike manner." The company lent Cramblitt the money and gave him an advance mortgage, the terms of which stipulated that the rowhouses be sixteen feet wide and three stories high, with "fronts of good pressed brick costing not less than thirty-five dollars per thousand." It further stipulated that all the houses have "bath arrangements, hot and cold water and gas fixtures." Construction had to start by October 1, 1868, with the houses ready for occupancy within nine months, the following July. Maryland Consolidated would disburse the $9,600 loan to Cramblitt as he completed specified stages of construction. The term of the loan was indefinite, but half had to be repaid by April 1, 1870. The six percent interest was to be paid semi-annually, starting July 1, 1869, the same date the houses were to be finished, thus allowing Cramblitt interest-free use of the money while he was building the houses. The $64 ground rents, which were set by the land company, and the company's and builders' willingness to put up only sixteen-foot-wide houses indicates that no one involved in the project believed that Harlem Park was being built to compete for buyers of houses at Franklin or Union Square.

Carpenter Cramblitt built both on his own account as well as working as a hired carpenter on Maryland Consolidated houses going up just two blocks from the park. This was a common practice among small-scale builders; it guaranteed them a steady income in the event their own speculative venture failed. Cramblitt's agreement with the land company followed patterns set in Baltimore decades earlier: he built on land that he did not have to buy outright, he had access to working capital, and he had ample time to repay the loan. While Cramblitt built houses on only six lots in Harlem Park, the company had similar contracts with many other builders; the eastern section of the former estate developed quickly. The city began laying out and landscaping the park itself in 1874. Under the supervision of the commissioners of the square, now a city agency, the city built an oval marble basin on the Calhoun Street side in which a fountain, paid for by the adjacent property owners, was placed. The city built two smaller basins at the western edge of the park as well as an octagonal iron pagoda. Engineers re-routed two springs on the property to a new spring house. A reporter for the *Sun* predicted that "owing to its elevated and healthy position and natural abundance of shade trees, the park will be one of the most pleasant public resorts in the city." He also noted that the park improvements had given "great stimulus to building operations in the immediate vicinity," particularly mentioning J. M. Cone.

Joseph Cone was the major rowhouse developer of Harlem Park, as well as Baltimore's largest post-Civil War builder. Between 1865 and 1882 he built 500 houses and employed 75 men with a weekly payroll of $750. Cone played a pivotal role in the transition of small-scale real estate opera-tors (who would acquire a few lots at a time), to large-scale developers (who handled several-acre parcels). Cone specialized in rowhousing and rarely built anything else. Like his predecessors, he also experimented with the various ways the ground rent system could be manipulated. His objec-tive was to acquire increasingly larger parcels of land to develop at little or no cost, and to sell the land leases as soon as the houses were completed to avoid paying any ground rent. Throughout his career, he acquired land by a very economical and savvy method: he bought land from the heirs of great estate owners, land located at the outskirts of the city yet in the path of future development.

Cone began building in Harlem Park in 1874, leasing eight lots on Calhoun Street, across from the park, directly from the Edmondson heirs, who advanced him money to build (FIGURE 56). When the houses were under roof, the leases were executed, along with a deed in fee for the rear portion of the lots facing Woodyear Alley, his bonus for improving the main street lots. But Cone sold his interest in the alley lots to other builders, choosing not to build small houses. By the late 1870s Cone had accumulated enough capital, or had established good loan sources, to pur-chase lots outright and build on his own account. In some of these transac-tions, Cone bought land in fee, sold it for a small profit, then leased lots within the parcel from the new owner. For example, he purchased part of a block on Carey Street in Harlem Park for $6,250 with a purchase money mortgage held by the seller. A week later he sold the property for $1,000 and the new owner assumed the mortgage. He then leased five lots from the new owner at ground rents of $100, built and sold the houses before a ground rent payment came due, and made a clear $1,000 profit on the transaction over and above any profits he would make on the sale of houses he built. He acquired land to build without ever having to pay back any of the original $6,250.

By 1878 Cone had built 145 houses near Harlem Park. All were three-story Italianates, sixteen feet to eighteen feet wide, with pressed-brick façades, elaborately detailed bracketed cornices, and arched doorways. All had two- or three-story back buildings. Cone had purchased most of this land in fee simple and there were no restrictions on what he could build. At this point in his career, he was no innovator. His houses looked much like those of his competitors. And the houses he built facing directly on Harlem Park had no special design features befitting their premium location, an indication that he thought the opportunity to overlook a park and fountains was feature enough. A few years later Cone embellished his Italianate façades with such extra features as pedimented marble lintels with machine-cut, neo-Grec incised designs or marble keystones in jack arches (FIGURE 57). On one group of nine houses, a few blocks west of the park on Fulton Avenue, Cone tried something entirely new, replacing the second and third story windows with an elaborate oriel extending through both stories. Fulton Avenue, then the western boundary of the city's development, was a hundred-foot-wide boulevard with central grassy median. Two of Cone's competitors, Lucius Polk and R. E. Diffenderffer, were operating a stage coach line to run between Fulton Avenue and downtown, aimed at prospective rowhouse owners so they could commute to work until one of the city's horsecar lines extended service to the area.[48]

Cone was one of just a handful of builders able to obtain large amounts of capital for development in the post-Civil War period. (Most builders at the time could only secure $2,000 to $5,000 to erect three or four houses. Building permit notices and newspaper articles of the day reported on builders that would put up a few houses and then never be heard from again.) Cone, however, acquired land from sellers who would take back a mortgage on a portion of the purchase price, thus enabling him to undertake larger scale developments. For example, when he purchased a parcel near Druid Hill Park from the Sisters of Charity in 1884 for $125,000, he paid $20,000 in cash and they took back a mortgage for $105,000; installments of $70,000 and $35,000 were due in one year. Such favorable land financings enabled Cone to develop prime parcels, such as the large two-block area facing what was then the grandest street in Baltimore, Eutaw Place. In 1890 he helped incorporate the Builders' Exchange Company, a real estate development firm with assets of $250,000. Later in the 1890s he also built houses in the southwestern part of the city under the aegis of the Irvington Land Company.

By the 1880s well-capitalized land development corporations, such as Cone's, were becoming commonplace and the future of Baltimore's homebuilding industry was concentrated in the hands of a few men. They bought the land they would develop, subdivided it, built their own houses, and reaped all the profits. It was in this manner they were able to build on a scale unheard of in the early nineteenth century and amassed unprecedented real estate fortunes. Known as the "two story rowhouse kings," these men built exclusively (with one exception) for working-class residents. As the city's industrial base continued to grow, this would be the housing type most needed by Baltimore's citizens.

Joseph Cone's façade embellishments on his rows on Fulton Avenue gave a taste of what was to come in Baltimore's residential architecture. The very year these rows went up, a distinguished European architect visiting the city expressed his "surprise at the lack of architectural taste displayed in the construction of dwellings," noting that to his "artistic eye the uniformity, as seen in blocks upon blocks of dwellings built of brick, with unbroken fronts, was exceedingly unattractive." The problem was particularly acute in northwest Baltimore, he claimed, "where whole squares have been improved with dwellings precisely alike."[49] Even then, in 1878, some builders were experimenting with new approaches to dwelling-house architecture. A row on Edmondson Avenue just west of Harlem Park, the *Gazette* reported on October 1, 1878, was "at once unique and comfortable" with a continuous bay window projection extending from the ground to the fourth story and a small plot of grass in front of each house.[50] Architects and knowledgeable builders were beginning to offer wealthy clients a new taste in building styles. But for middle- and working-class clients, the vernacular Italianate remained the favored style among speculative builders well into the 1890s.

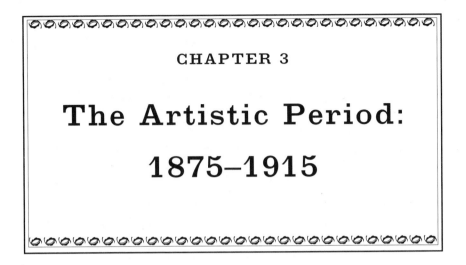

CHAPTER 3

The Artistic Period:
1875–1915

...the effect of the building is very striking as varying from the monotonous style of architecture so disagreeably prevalent in Baltimore.

Baltimore *Sun*, November 1877

Aerial view of Edward J. Gallagher's two-story rowhouses at Park Side, 1909–1912 (Maryland Historical Society)

IN 1912 FIFTY-YEAR-OLD Joseph Singewald decided that he no long-er had to live above his storefront hattery on South Broadway in Fells Point. Business was good. He could afford to move his wife, four sons, and daughter away from the bustle of a commercial street and the noise of the hatmaking machinery. Singewald chose to move northward, to a part of the city that had experienced dramatic growth over the last two decades. Following the completion of bridges across the Jones Falls in the mid-1880s, a building boom took place along the upper reaches of Maryland, Charles, St. Paul, Calvert, and Guilford Avenues. The stylish three-story rowhouses built along these streets were markedly different from the seemingly uniform Italianate rows that characterized city housing up until then. They were bold and enticed prospective buyers with imaginative details—details that might remind the well-read or well-traveled citizen of picturesque streets in Europe. Indeed a middle-class buyer had an array of creative rowhouse designs from which to choose. Singewald selected one in the Renaissance Revival style. This newly built three-story rowhouse had a gleaming golden-brown Roman brick façade, a bay window, white marble trim, white marble steps, and a small front yard (FIGURE 58). In 1912 it was the most fashionable rowhouse type available in Baltimore, executed in the last of the eclectic styles that had transformed the appear-ance of the city since the late 1870s. From his new house, Singewald could walk a block-and-a-half east to the St. Paul Street electric streetcar line, pay a nickel fare, and arrive at his Fells Point store fifteen minutes later. It was a small price to pay to live in a respectable neighborhood, a gracious environment in which his college-educated children could mix with others of a similar economic and social standing.

Singewald's move epitomizes the Baltimore rowhouse story during the so-called "artistic period." The years between 1875 and 1915 were a time of tremendous creativity in architectural design. This creativity was heightened by a technological development in transportation: the electric overhead trolley, which was introduced in Richmond, Virginia, in 1888. The electric trolley prompted a change in America's residential housing patterns by making it possible for urban dwellers to live substantial distances from their workplaces. Baltimore's first electric streetcar began operation in 1890. Within a few years the old horsecar companies had converted to all-electric systems; in 1899 they merged to create the United Railways & Electric Company, which quickly extended lines nine miles out from City Hall. Its cars traveled twice as fast as horsecars (ten to fifteen miles per hour) and carried three times as many passengers. Even while the electric cars and the power-generating plants that ran them, which were located in dispersed locations around the city, required a large investment, streetcars were less expensive to run per passenger mile than the slow-paced and labor-intensive horsecar. The electric trolley eliminated the costs of horses, stables, and cleaning up after 2,000 horses daily.[1]

Massive urbanization enabled by the streetcar was paralleled by rapid industrialization. In the post–Civil War period, technological advances transformed America from an agrarian nation into the world's leading industrial power. By 1913 the United States was producing a third of the world's goods. This growth brought prosperity, although at an uneven pace. Worst were the roller coaster business cycles. The national financial Panic of 1893 alone meant the loss of jobs for tens of thousands and bankruptcy for more than 200 railroads nationwide. In New York City, the 1893 panic was just one of many swings that hurt the economy. In that city the net value of production during the 1890s increased by only 21 percent; the preceding decade it had gone up 131 percent.

During these same decades the American corporation became the most influential business organization. Nationwide, local firms—from breweries to steel mills—were bought up by huge conglomerates. In many cases this move resulted in injections of capital that expanded production, but industrialization proved to be a double-edged sword. It produced the new machines that devalued skilled labor, thus displacing craftsmen with machine operators, but it also increased the production of goods and even lowered prices. The opening of new markets for mass-produced goods led to an increased demand for the goods and the need to hire more workers to meet that demand. This latter need was met by thousands of Eastern European immigrants and unprecedented numbers of rural Americans who resettled in cities in the late nineteenth century. They provided factories and shops with seemingly an unlimited supply of inexpensive labor. These workers all needed housing and every American city had its own form of low-income housing. By 1900 more than 80,000 tenements had been built in New York City, housing 2.3 million of the 3.4 million inhabitants. Because the city was surrounded on three sides by water, land was expensive: 50 percent of the cost of providing tenements lay in the cost of the land. Builders tried to maximize their investment, and so the tenement, a five- or six-story walk-up, usually occupied 90 percent of a 25-foot by 100-foot lot. On each floor the units were linked together like railroad cars, giving them the label "railroad flats."

The tenement problem did not exist in Baltimore, nor in most other cities. One- and two-family houses, rather than tenements, made up two-thirds of the housing built in America's cities between 1870 and 1930. The extent of multifamily housing varied from city to city. In Boston, Brooklyn, and Newark it constituted 15 to 25 percent of the city's housing stock in 1890. In Philadelphia and Washington it was slightly less than two percent; and in Baltimore, it was slightly more than two percent. America's cities also showed diversity in the architecture that housed the working class: brick rows in Philadelphia and Baltimore; wood-framed "triple deckers" in Boston; four- to six-room single-family houses for skilled workers and two-family houses for unskilled immigrants in Pittsburgh; and four-room flats in Chicago.[2]

At the outset of this period in the early 1870s, the leaders of Baltimore were trying to chart the city's economic future. After reviewing its progress as a mercantile center, they decided to encourage city businesses to shift toward manufacturing. Baltimore, they reasoned, had all the right prerequisites: rail and water access, a low-cost supply of raw materials arriving from around the country, capital for investment, and a growing pool of labor. In 1889 when a local lithographer published a contemporary bird's-eye view of the city, he depicted a prospering waterfront area lined with smoking factories and filled the harbor with steamships (FIGURE 59). Still, the change to a manufacturing base did not occur overnight. Baltimore held its own as a shipping center. The city rose from fifth in rank among American ports to third in 1900, with a four-fold increase in foreign trade value. More than $70 million in domestic raw materials traveled from Baltimore to South America and western Europe. Baltimore also shipped by rail to Southern ports large quantities of clothing, groceries, and durable goods, all of which gave credence to the civic boast that Baltimore was the "Gateway to the South." Indeed, Baltimore became a major financial resource to the post-Civil War South, with $40 million in capital invested there.

Industrial growth in Baltimore steadily attracted increasing numbers of people in search of jobs. Between 1880 and 1900 the population rose from 332,000 to 509,000 (a small part of that increase was due to the 1888 annexation of 18.8 square miles and its 39,000 residents). Unlike many other port cities, foreign immigrants constituted a small part of the population increase, between 5 and 7 percent. Most of the new residents came from rural Maryland, Virginia, and Pennsylvania. Soon a larger percentage of the city's population was engaged in manufacturing than any other sector. From 1880 to 1890, the number of manufacturing establishments increased by 40 percent and the number of workers by 50 percent (rising from 56,000 to 84,000). By 1895 Baltimore dominated the Southern states in the production of men's ready-to-wear clothing; by 1900 it ranked fourth in the nation. The garment industry was the city's largest employer, followed by the canneries, packing houses, canmaking establishments, and iron- and steelmaking and shipbuilding concerns. It was not long before Baltimore was known as a working-class city. At the turn of the century a man could earn $1.75 to $3.00 per ten-hour day for skilled work and $1.25 for unskilled. According to the Bureau of Industrial Statistics, "a typical workingman's family," relied on the earnings of three to five persons to attain an average income of slightly more than $600 a year. The success of Baltimore's manufactories made them attractive to outsiders. And, as in other American cities, many of Baltimore's largest firms went from local control to outside ownership, some of them being taken over by such trusts as Standard Oil and American Tobacco, which meant new capitalization and an expanded workforce—new customers for rowhouse builders.[3]

Between 1880 and 1900 the population increased by 53 percent, and the number of dwelling units increased by 76 percent. By 1890, 97.4 percent of the city's dwellings housed one or two families. But only 26 percent of houses were owner-occupied, the rest were rented. For $18 a month in 1892, a family could rent a nine-room house on a decent street; for $100 a month they could live at the best address on Eutaw Place, the city's finest boulevard. The *Daily Record* of 1891 stated, "Baltimore is becoming more and more, pre-eminently a city of homes and the apartment idea will never become popular with the masses of our people." The Baltimore *Sun* declared in 1907 that it was a "city of 100,000 homes and 149 apartments."

To rent in Baltimore meant to live in a rowhouse. The goal of many renters was to buy a modest rowhouse. City fathers and builders encouraged this aspiration.[4]

After the Baltimore fire of 1904 building proceeded on a scale unheard of in previous decades, in part because of the rise of rowhouse developers. These men had begun their careers working in the building trades as carpenters, stone masons, and bricklayers. From there they moved to small-scale building operations, first a few houses, then one side of a block, then a quarter of the whole city block, then half a block. The next step was a much bigger one: they tackled entire tracts of land that they subdivided into three, four, six, even ten city blocks, laying out the streets, grading, paving, and erecting fifty houses at a time. To ensure that their houses sold well, both builders and builder-developers mimicked stylistic features of high-style architect-designed houses going up in more affluent sections. The flat façade of the rowhouse enabled the builder to apply a variety of decorative features to the basic arrangement of door, windows, and cornice. Although it generally took about ten years for the highest of styles to filter down to more modest cost ranges, ultimately even much less expensive houses had many of the exterior features found on high-style models. The two-story, $1,500 East Baltimore rowhouse built for working-class households, was a simplified version of the $7,000 to $12,000 three-story rowhouse designed by a professional architect, such as the one Joseph Singewald purchased in 1912. The speculative builders also copied evolving high-style floor plans and methods of interior decoration in their ongoing efforts to give even the most inexpensively priced housing the touch of sophistication that would attract buyers.

Builders were able to imitate the design features of a $10,000 house in the $1,500 economy model because mass-production enabled suppliers to offer extensive product lines of up-to-the-minute architectural details. Supply houses, both in Baltimore and elsewhere, produced illustrated catalogs from which builders could order such diverse items as artistic tile for entrance vestibules; stained glass for door and window transoms, upper sash, and bathroom windows; metal cornices already stamped with classical details; tin ceilings for kitchens and hallways; newel posts, balusters, mantels and overmantels, fretwork grilles, freestanding columns, baseboards and crown moldings; an amazing variety of wallpapers; and even porcelain sinks, basins, tubs, and toilets. Thus the rows of two-story swell-front houses in west Baltimore in 1900, the stained-glass transom over the east Baltimore cannery worker's rowhouse of 1908, and Joseph Singewald's second-floor bay window, were all the result of a 30-year stylistic journey from the mid-1870s when the new picturesque styles first appeared in Baltimore buildings designed by professionally trained architects. That nationally popular architectural styles were adopted promptly by builders of expensive residential units is not surprising; yet the proliferation of simplified forms of these design motifs in the city's least expensive housing sheds new light on our understanding of how cities were built and what was important to the people who made their homes there.

A Palette of New Styles from Which to Choose

In 1878 the Baltimore *Sun* reporter covering "Local Matters" touted the new residences along the spacious streets north of Mt. Vernon Place:

> The variety and style of architecture observed in the erection of the dwellings is sufficient to avoid the monotony of unbroken similarity, which is so painfully apparent in some otherwise beautiful sections of the city. A block of marble fronts in one square makes a pleasing contrast to a block of pressed brick fronts in the next, and many of the houses have little plats of greensward in front of them, adorned by beds of flowers, fountains or other attractions.[5]

The refreshing variety in the architecture that the reporter observed in this fashionable section of the city was part of a larger trend, an international reaction against rigid, traditional classicism—Greek, Roman, and Italian Renaissance varieties—which for centuries had dominated urban architecture, first in Europe and later in America. One of the new styles, the Queen Anne, emerged in Great Britain. It began as a resurrection of sixteenth- and seventeenth-century English building materials (red brick), and traditional cottage-style forms (stucco and half-timbering). About the same time English ecclesiastical and public architecture came to be dominated by a second style—the "picturesque" (also called High Victorian Gothic), which encouraged a freer and more creative expression of traditional Gothic forms and often resulted in highly imaginative, colorful buildings marked by asymmetrical massing, polychromatic rock-faced stone façades, and picturesque roof lines. In Baltimore both styles were adapted to urban residential architecture and both began to share the upper-class neighborhood streetscapes during the late 1870s and 1880s. But in the 1890s classicism returned when the Renaissance Revival, a style that revived classical forms of the Italian Renaissance and included an admixture of American colonial elements, joined the scene.

Often referred to as the period of "creative eclecticism," by such historians as Henry Russell Hitchcock and Phoebe Stanton, the end of the nineteenth century was a time in which architects felt free to combine a wide array of historical details and styles in their buildings. In America this path was laid down by architects Charles Follen McKim, William Rutherford Mead, and Stanford White, whose New York firm of McKim, Mead & White was arguably the most influential in the country. The partners had become interested in colonial forms shortly after the 1876 Centennial Exposition in Philadelphia, and soon after they began studying the details on colonial houses in such places as Newport, Rhode Island, where they were designing summer homes for New York's elite. In the 1880s they also began experimenting with classical ideals.

Aiding the spread of design ideas was the move toward "professionalism" by architects across the nation. Baltimore's architects established their chapter of the American Institute of Architects (AIA) in 1870. It attracted to the city a number of professionally trained young architects. Many were college-educated and a few had studied at the Massachusetts Institute of Technology (MIT), the nation's first architectural school, or had spent time in Paris at the Ecole des Beaux Arts. Most, perhaps all, subscribed to architectural journals, such as *American Architect and Building News* (first issue, 1876) and the English *Building News*, both of which published articles on the latest styles being adopted in Great Britain, the Continent, and throughout the United States. These journals also played a critical role in the dissemination of the details and the appearance of historical architectural styles by publishing drawings of important buildings of the past—thus providing the fodder and inspiration for a wide variety of creative copies and amalgamations. Not all young architects could make a world tour, or even go to Paris, but they could enjoy the weekly offerings of such highly detailed plates as two-page spreads of "dormers," "oriels," and "bay windows," or order from the publisher one of the many special monographs filled with an amazing variety of carefully drawn details of European buildings. These were filed alongside every architect's drafting board.

The periodicals made it possible for architects to remain well apprised of the latest design trends. Consequently, American translations of the various stylistic elements did not lag far behind their English or European models. And at least in Baltimore, all three styles of eclectic rowhouses cost approximately the same amount to build—$7,000 to $8,000 for a three-story version and $10,000 to $12,000 for a corner townhouse. And whether

Queen Anne, Picturesque, or Renaissance Revival on the exterior, all three styles had similar floor plans and interior elements that were based on an amalgam of the popular precepts of the English Aesthetic Movement and the rising but romanticized interest in the American colonial past. (*American Architect* featured sketches and details of colonial buildings in its earliest issues and soon was publishing monographs on the subject. Colonial mantels, paneled dados, balusters, and newels—usually painted white—appeared in interiors designed by a wide range of architects and soon became an accepted part of the eclectic vocabulary.)

Queen Anne Rows: Redbrick and Sunflowers

In 1876 architectural critic Henry Hudson Holly announced that the Queen Anne style was "a delightful insurrection against the monotonous era of rectangular building" and thus the natural style for America: "the most simple mode of honest English building, worked out in an artistic and natural form...which expresses real domestic needs."[6] British architect Richard Norman Shaw was most influential in popularizing the return to redbrick cottage-style architecture in his country. His designs for great manor houses inspired American architects and led to the development of shingle style residences in America's suburbs. Shaw's design for the New Zealand Chambers (1871–72) became the model for many urban Queen Anne residences in America soon after it was published in *Building News* in 1873 (FIGURE 60).

Shaw, along with designer and craftsman William Morris, artist James McNeill Whistler, and architect R. A. Godwin, stood at the center of what they called the "aesthetic movement"—an outgrowth of Morris's well-known Arts and Crafts movement, which sought to purify the excesses of Victorian taste by returning to an ideal of craftsmanship and relying on natural forms for ornament. The movement touched all forms of art: painting, literature, architecture, and the decorative arts of household furnishings, textiles, wallpapers, and pottery. It prevailed among English tastemakers from the mid-1870s until the late 1880s. It was identified by such decorative symbols as the sunflower (strength), the lily (purity), and the peacock (Eastern exoticism and the beauties of intricate patterns). On new Queen Anne buildings decoration took the form of terra-cotta panels, molded and cut brick, colored glass set in multi-paned traditional sashes (reminiscent of old English building), and wrought-iron balconies. Many terra-cotta panels featured sunflowers, the two most popular motifs being a vase holding multiple, symmetrically arranged flowers and a stylized version of just the flower head. Lilies more often appeared on the interior, in the form of highly patterned wallpapers or as decorative carvings on architectural trim. The fascination with the jewel-like tones of the peacock's feathers was apparent in luminous stained glass.

Applying aesthetic design principles at Bedford Park, one of England's first garden suburbs, Shaw and Godwin designed some 490 cottages—each with a small yard—to attract members of the middle class with "advanced taste," who were interested in the cult of "the House Beautiful." In these houses they introduced a flowing and integrated approach to living spaces, one promptly adopted by other designers. Each house centered around a living hall, borrowed from Elizabethan traditions and furnished with an oversize fireplace and built-in seating, which served as an entrance hall and reception area. Stairs rose in two or three flights, separated by landings, and featured elaborate balusters and newels. In place of the highly elaborate and fussy Victorian interior, the designers sought simplicity and artistic feelings—achieved through soft, dark colors on the painted walls (green was a favorite), a paneled dado, an upper frieze featuring a popular William Morris wallpaper, and even Japanese embossed leathers for dados or wall panels in halls and stairways.[7]

Architect and native Baltimorean John Appleton Wilson brought the Queen Anne style to Baltimore. Wilson was both a member of a socially prominent local family and professionally trained at the prestigious MIT. After the requisite trip abroad, he joined the office of Francis Baldwin and Bruce Price as an apprentice in 1872. His first solo foray into house design in 1876, at the age of 25, was a bold Queen Anne townhouse for his cousin and later business partner, William T. Wilson. The house was located on the southeast corner of St. Paul and Biddle Streets, in the heart of Baltimore's most fashionable neighborhood, Mt. Vernon. A year later he designed a matching house on the northeast corner, which the *Sun* described at length. "The effect of the building is very striking." The exterior was of pressed brick, black mortar, some "black brick and tile,...a handsome wrought iron balcony," and a black slate roof with "bands of red." The interior had fireplaces with tile linings and glazed pictorial tile facings, richly carved hardwood mantels, "those in the first story having mirrors, shelving, etc.," an ash staircase, hall, and entrance doors, and throughout the house, plaster in "sand finish for decoration" (FIGURE 61).[8]

Wilson then set about designing a townhouse for Catherine L. McKim, a widow who had recently inherited Belvidere, the last five-and-a-half acres remaining of the large country estate originally owned by the

Howard family. She had decided to develop this valuable land, beginning with a house for herself. Wilson's design incorporated most features of the urban Queen Anne style that had been published in *Building News* and *American Architect*, as well as a design Godwin published in *The British Architect* in 1876 (FIGURE 62). Wilson then in 1879 designed Belvidere Terrace, a row of fourteen houses adjacent to Mrs. McKim's townhouse (FIGURE 63). On the opposite side of the street, another family member, the Rev. R. A. McKim, engaged the architectural firm of J. B. Noel Wyatt and Joseph Evans Sperry to design a facing row in the same style and of the same scale. Belvidere Terrace became the ultimate expression of the Queen Anne style in Baltimore. The Baltimore reporter for *American Architect* proclaimed it the "handsomest" square "architecturally of any in the city."[9] The overall design of both rows is masterful. The Wilsons created three different façade designs, one of which is carried out in white marble instead of brick, and arranged them in a 3-2-4-2-3 pattern, the four marble houses standing at the center of the composition. The three units on either end of the block feature the Dutch gable of the original design for Mrs. McKim's house and elaborate wrought-iron balconies. Carefully articulated triple and quadruple fenestration patterns add to the bold, overall rhythm of the design. Wyatt and Sperry's row has a richer combination of red brick and brownstone trim, arranged in a much more complicated pattern. That row of twenty-three houses is composed of no less than seven different façade designs: some with round-arched windows and doors; some with paired, gently arched windows and pedimented doors; others with round-arched windows and pedimented doors. Two units have a Dutch-gabled roof; the rest have their gable end to the street. Both rows have elaborate terra-cotta panels decorated with sunflowers, molded and cut brick, and multi-pane upper sash (FIGURE 64).

The floor plans of these houses also presented something new. Each house extended back its full width, instead of the earlier arrangements of a wider front building joined to a narrower back building (thus allowing light into all the rooms). This new plan, which came to be associated with artistic rowhouses, made use of Shaw's concept of the Elizabethan living hall. Instead of placing the staircase against one of the party walls, architects positioned the expanded stair area/reception room in the center of the house; the steps rose in two open flights, which ran parallel to the street and were separated by a comfortable landing. Often this stair hall area featured rich, dark paneling, built-in seating, and a mirrored coat and hat rack. The gracious dining room beyond had a bay window overlooking the garden and an adjoining servant's pantry equipped with dumbwaiter that went to the basement kitchen. On the second floor the center room often served as a library. A side hall led back to the bathroom outfitted with the latest flush water closet, porcelain fixtures, and stained-glass window.

Most other architects designing red brick, Queen Anne rows in Baltimore eschewed the use of curving Dutch gables in favor of a less expensive design: setting end gables into the steep mansard roof. By 1883–84 architects and builders knew ways to manipulate the roof line in a series of peaks in order to create the suggestion of pointed end gables, without having to build them at all. Six years later a Baltimore contributor to *American Architect* wryly observed: "There is still an unconquerable abhorrence of a straight sky-line under any circumstances, however small and square the building and flat the roof, pediments and pinnacles of all imaginable forms still break out at every point, even when their thin profiles often show there is nothing behind them or inside them."[10]

Among the finest Queen Anne rows in Baltimore are those created by Joseph Cone, the rowhouse specialist who was the city's largest rowhouse developer after the Civil War. In the mid-1880s, he took part in a four-block development adjacent to the grand Eutaw Place Boulevard, just south of what was then the city's northern boundary (now known as North Avenue). Only two blocks of these impressive houses survive; the rest were razed to create low-rise public housing in the 1950s (which in turn was razed in 1997). The design was so competent that Cone must have retained an architect. The houses were calculated to appeal to affluent buyers who had the "taste" to appreciate the stylistic package offered. The Robert Street façades are articulated with end gable motifs supported by brick piers resting on wide bases that suggest a slightly projecting bay (FIGURE 65). Large terra-cotta panels adorn the spaces between the piers and mark the gable, and smaller ones decorate the frieze area. Bands of fluted bricks mark each story. Red and blue etched glass panels frame the upper window panes. Instead of a mansard roof, the buildings have the earlier style Baltimore shed roof, but the cornice line is articulated with a deep and decorative row of stepped bricks. Priced for an upper-middle-class market, such houses sold for $12,000 in fee, which was less than half the $25,000 price of Wilson's Belvidere Terrace homes.

Around the corner, on Bolton Street, Cone built a more modest row of Queen Anne houses. These were a foot narrower, and in place of large terra-cotta panels he used small, square terra-cotta blocks decorated with sunflowers. To create the impression of the Robert Street round-arched door and window lintels with terra-cotta keystones, Cone used a slightly arched brick hood, a decorative feature that became one of the signature elements of his rowhouses. Further west in Harlem Park Cone was also building for another market (FIGURE 66). Here, his customers were mainly Germans who owned their own businesses or small manufacturing firms. For them Cone simply updated his earlier Italianate house, giving it a few Queen Anne touches: molded brickwork, cut-brick window lintels and door hoods, a more stylized cornice, and longer scroll-sawn brackets to frame the wooden friezes. Executed cheaply with a jigsaw, the frieze panels brought current fashion to even the simplest of houses. Some sport the hugely popular sunflower motif; others the Whistlerian butterfly or Japanese fan; and still others the scrolling tendrils and flower shape of the lily.

By the late 1880s a number of other Baltimore builders were putting up two-story Queen Anne houses, along the North Avenue corridor, on Broadway, and in the Eutaw Place neighborhood. The more adventurous made use of a cornice line punctuated by small gables to add a picturesque touch to the streetscape. Others followed Cone's Harlem Park model, using a traditional cornice but updating façades with paneled brickwork, rows of cut or molded bricks, small terra-cotta decorations, and stained glass. Invariably, their jig-sawn frieze panels sported sunflowers, butterflies, fans, or vine and lily-like shapes (FIGURE 67).

The Picturesque Rowhouse

In July 1886 the Baltimore *Sun*, ever interested in the architecture of the city, devoted a long column to Baltimore's residential architecture. Entitled "The Picturesque in Dwellings—Marble Fronts and Quaint Windows," the article described individual houses and impressive rows built over the last decade in the exclusive, stylish, and expensive Mt. Vernon district.[11] Architects locally tended to describe contemporary work as "picturesque," in opposition to the regular forms of traditional Greek, Roman, and Renaissance-inspired classical architecture. In England the term was applied to garden follies that looked like Gothic ruins, the fanciful Brighton Pavillion with its Oriental domes and Moorish arches, country houses that looked like Norman castles, single-towered Italian villas, or olde-English cottages—all of which had exotic and romantic or literary connotations that could inspire a sense of the far away or the distant past. A key feature was asymmetrical massing, often punctuated by round or square towers. Another was the reliance on rock-faced stone that enhanced the sculptural qualities of the building.[12]

In Baltimore as across America in the 1870s and 1880s, picturesque forms were enthusiastically adopted for churches, college buildings, schools, libraries, hospitals, asylums, orphans' homes, and other buildings that bespoke noble purposes and/or religious grounding. The picturesque style marked the early work of Henry Hobson Richardson, the first prominent American architect to design with polychromatic rock-faced stone—Trinity Church on Boston's Copley Square went up in the early 1870s—and published widely. For the detailing of the roof dormers Richardson borrowed from the French Gothic, the same source that influenced the use of steeply pitched mansard roofs and details such as trefoils and incised carving on many a Baltimore building. However, polychromy in architecture did not gain favor among Baltimore architects and builders. Instead they preferred to exploit the picturesque qualities of a readily available and reasonably inexpensive local building material—Beaver Dam marble. They designed marble-fronted houses that made use of many features of the Gothic vocabulary—carved stone rosettes, trefoils, incised scroll-work, stone columns with leafy medieval capitals, oriel windows, stone porches, and high mansard roofs punctuated with French Gothic-style dormers

Perhaps the earliest row was designed by a young Bruce Price and his partner E. Francis Baldwin just west of their new Christ Church (1872) on the northwest corner of St. Paul and Chase Streets (FIGURE 68). Price was born in Maryland and began his career in Baltimore. His Christ Church introduced picturesque French Gothic design to the city and was highlighted in *American Architect and Building News* in 1878. Like the church, the Price and Baldwin houses are replete with Gothic details—carved stone trefoils, pointed-arch doorways and window lintels, and pointed roof dormers set into the steep mansard.

A year later Hugh Sisson, owner of a marble yard, erected similar houses around the corner, on St. Paul Street. Responding to these residential designs, which must have appeared quite startling compared to the more subdued forms of earlier decades, the Baltimore *Sun* devoted a full column to the Sisson row: "Three fine dwelling houses in that beautiful and growing part of St. Paul Street…might with profit be examined by builders and housekeepers, as they are in many respects worthy of being considered models. Their fronts are all faced with fine marble ashlar for the whole height of the three stories, from pavement to cornice, with marble jambs, doorways, steps, and marble balconies to each house, with perforated marble railings of handsome design." The houses have "French attics," and bay windows at the side and rear. Each room has a fireplace and "handsome marble mantels, those of the parlor floor of very rich marble and design." All the first floor rooms boasted marble wainscoting in "variegated colors," a use that proved popular during the period, even when the houses were not built by the owner of a marble works.[13]

A few years later, A. S. Abell, owner of the Baltimore *Sun* commissioned Charles Cassell to design a group of ten very expensive Gothic styled houses for the southwest corner of Charles Street and Boundary (present-day North) Avenue. In October 1877 the *Sun* described these "marble front and French roof dwellings," on which "the cornice and moulding over outside doors and windows, and the entire dormer windows are of marble, with ornamental carving and heavy cresting on the mansard roofs . . . and a neat balcony at each of the first and second-story front windows." The "ornamental carving" included ferocious gargoyles, lions' heads, and stone capitals in the Romanesque manner. Priced at $15,000 to $20,000, the houses were among the most expensive rowhouses in the city.[14] Young Charles Carson also used the picturesque manner. Having designed one of the nation's first free public libraries for Baltimore philanthropist Enoch Pratt, Carson joined forces with older architect Thomas Dixon to design a row of three marble-fronted houses on St. Paul Street. These houses boasted steep mansard roofs, medieval-looking dormers, tall narrow windows, and distinctively Gothic incised decoration on the stone door and window lintels. Carved stone also decorated the undersides of window sills and was used for columns flanking the door.

As elaborate picturesque style houses became more popular in Baltimore's most affluent neighborhoods, a new type of rowhouse developer appeared, one who was willing to take full risk on building stylish and expensive houses—acquiring the land, hiring the architect, overseeing construction, and marketing and selling the houses. The few men who occupied this upper-end niche in the Baltimore real estate market did well, for they continued offering high-style rows at high prices until the elegant three-story rowhouse fell out of favor just before World War I.

One such man was George Blake, who, often working in partnership with his brothers Henry and Charles, built in the affluent stretches located north of Mt. Vernon Square. Although Blake catered to the carriage trade, his background was similar to most other rowhouse builders. Born in Ireland, he started work at age fifteen as a clerk for a Baltimore ship chandlery. Interested more in building and architecture, he soon moved on to an apprenticeship with a pair of builders, before opening his own firm at the age of twenty-two in 1860. By 1911 he had built between 200 to 300 residences in the city, including the 1883 McKim, Mead, & White-designed residence for Ross Winans on St. Paul Street (FIGURE 69). Blake hired the architectural firm of Dixon & Carson, and in 1877–78 they designed a row of eight marble-front houses for the 1200 block of St. Paul Street that Blake was developing, just one block north of the three very similar houses they had just designed. Two years later Blake commissioned them to design houses for a row one block west, on Charles Street on land Blake acquired through two deals: one with a railroad, and one with a private individual. He purchased the northern half of the lot for $34,000 from the Northern Central Railroad in the autumn of 1880. (The down payment was $4,200, with the balance due in two years, but Blake could begin building immediately.) On that portion Dixon & Carson designed four Gothic styled houses, very similar to their St. Paul Street row, but two were "of serpentine stone of a greenish color, from Chester, Pennsylvania," giving them a "novel and striking" appearance (FIGURE 70).[15] The first house sold in April 1881 for $16,000—a high sum for a speculatively built house. When two more sold a year later, Blake paid off the mortgage. The buyers were lawyers, bankers, and businessmen. Blake built the next group of four houses in 1883, retaining Charles Carson, who was now working alone and who continued his shift away from marble toward other colored stones. On these houses Carson used brownstone and a deep shade of green stone. When Blake sold the last of his first eight houses in the 1200 block of Charles Street, the price had risen to $19,000. (The purchaser of the last house put $9,000 down, with the balance payable to Blake in two years; typical terms at this time were one-half of the price paid in cash, with a two- or three-year mortgage.)

The construction costs Blake listed when he applied to the city for building permits for these houses suggested that he anticipated about a 10 percent profit on the development of this row, an average rate of return for the time. Like the builders of most expensive houses in the city, Blake sold his units in fee. Although the ground rent system served as the cornerstone of Baltimore's middle and working-class housing market, wealthier buyers generally preferred not to have the annual nuisance of paying ground rents. And they could afford to buy in fee. For Blake and builders like him, fee-simple sales meant that they could pay off their debts to landowners and materials' suppliers more quickly.

In December 1884 Blake purchased the southern half of the block for $39,500 from Dr. William A. Moale, a direct descendant of one of the first landowners of early Baltimore, the John Moale who first sketched the town in 1752. On this land Carson designed for Blake six houses of an even bolder character—they were to be executed in dark, rock-faced brownstone and the reddish seneca stone. The corner house, for Blake's own residence, even had a conical end bay capped with a tall turret. Both Blake's residence and a mid-block house featured wide, round-arched Roman-esque openings and naturalistically carved stonework panels. Carson's work for Blake in the 1200 block of Charles Street illustrates the evolution of the picturesque style in Baltimore during the 1880s. As the style took hold, darker stones replaced light-colored façades; oriels, bay windows, and stone porches appeared; and the façades were given an undulating charac-ter by the inclusion of rounded or squared bays, often capped by conical or polygonal turrets. This romantic architecture depended on individualism in design—ideally, no façade of a row group was the same—but still allowed designers to impose compositional balance to the overall row. Well into the 1890s this façade manipulation prevailed, adding a charming variety to the streetscape. Generally architects preferred rock-faced stone—serpentine, brownstone, granite, bluestone, red sandstone, and seneca—that added richness to the façade but remained in keeping with the tenets of the "brown decades." Some of their picturesque houses had Queen Anne stick-style upper porches; others had Moorish-arched or wide-arched Richardsonian openings. On some only the first story was faced with stone, the upper stories being faced with dark red or even brown brick. Most had elegant stained-glass windows set in wide-arched transoms over the door and large plate-glass windows.

Most of the city's leading picturesque-style architects adhered to these design precepts. In 1883 Charles Cassell designed for A. J. Gorter a row of nine "unique" houses in the "antique" style on Preston Street in upper Mt. Vernon (FIGURE 71).[16] Executed in rock-faced granite and Falls Road stone of a greenish-grey color, each house showcased different combinations of motifs—rounded or squared façades, oriels and porches, and a conical or polygonal turreted rooflines. Yet the overall composition was balanced, creating an undulating rhythm across the length of the façade. Cassell con-tinued designing for the same client around the corner on the 1300 block of Charles Street. On these units he opted for rock-faced brownstone artic-ulated with alternating round and polygonal bays, oriels, and wide-arched Moorish openings (FIGURE 76).

Just two blocks east, in the 1200 block of Calvert Street, another row-house developer repeated the formula in 1885. A Baltimore *Sun* reporter noted, he put up "three blocks of five houses each, separated by side yards. One row of Seneca stone, the second of Baltimore county marble, the third of Hummelstown brownstone. The houses are three stories with mansard roofs, swell fronts, with angular bay windows at the corners of the blocks and segment bays at the middle of the blocks."[17]

In the late 1880s and 1890s picturesque style houses began to line the fashionable streets near Druid Hill Park, along Mt. Royal Avenue, Eutaw Place, and Park Place (FIGURE 72). These houses, with an amazing richness and creativity of detail, provided living spaces for Baltimore's new mercantile Jewish elite, including department store owners and clothing manufacturers. Other versions went up along the boulevards of North Avenue and Broadway, where the buyers were wealthy German brewers, printers, merchants, and manufacturers.

As in other areas, the side streets of these affluent neighborhoods were given two-story versions of late picturesque-style houses; usually these were constructed by the same builders who had put up the three-story houses on the wider main streets (FIGURE 73). Whereas the Charles Street houses carried price tags of $13,500 to $20,000 and were designed by an architect, the side-street two-story versions sold for $3,000 to $4,000 and were either designed by the builder or by a lesser-grade architect. Thus, a measure of stylishness was available to solidly middle-class buyers. Men in the professions and owners of small businesses could afford a fashionable, "uptown" rock-faced stone dwelling that might have many of the same features as the three-story model—wide, arched openings, second-floor porches or bay windows, and stained-glass door and window transoms. Although not living in an expensive three-story house, these buyers were literally just around the corner from the people who did. Like Singewald, they were all living in new, fashionably appointed rowhouses in neighborhoods that were both removed from the city's growing industrial centers and near its latest amenities—the public parks, lakes and reservoirs, and grand boulevards that were making the city a more pleasant place to live.

Classical Rows

In 1890 the Renaissance Revival style arrived in Baltimore. McKim, Mead, & White designed a town mansion for John Goucher, the founder and president in 1885 of the new Woman's College, located next to White's monumental Richardsonian Romanesque Lovely Lane Methodist Church (1882). For the college, Dr. Goucher had commissioned a Romanesque design from a local architect, but for his residence he wanted something in the newest taste. The New York architects gave him a Renaissance city palazzo, a massive five-bay wide, three-story block of yellow Pompeian brick topped by a classical modillion cornice and stone balustrade. Like its Renaissance predecessors, the formidable structure sat on a heavy rusticated stone base and arched window openings pierced the flat façade. The house was strikingly different from the sculpted, rock-faced picturesque style of its neighbors.

McKim, Mead, & White had first ventured in this stylistic direction in 1883, with a commission for railway magnate Henry Villard in New York City. For Villard the firm designed a High Renaissance Italian palazzo, characterized by strict academic formalism and a classical vocabulary.[18] That same year, with the design for Louis Comfort Tiffany's house, McKim, Mead & White introduced a material that would come to dominate residential architecture in Baltimore for the next thirty-five years: light brown "Roman" brick, low and narrow, an archaeologically correct choice that had been used in the ancient Empire. About a decade later, the influential 1893 World's Columbian Exposition in Chicago revived interest in classical forms. Dubbed the "Great White City," because metal and glass exhibition buildings were almost completely concealed by elaborate columned, white plaster façades, the exposition left few Americans untouched by the academic revolution. But even before the fair, *American Architect* announced to its readers: "molded bricks and terra-cotta, galvanized iron and wood, most uncalled-for bits of glazed tile and stone carving are giving place to a certain amount of simplicity where plain surfaces and natural construction are allowed to take care of themselves."[19]

Many fashion-conscious Baltimore architects quickly adopted neoclassical stylings, abandoning the picturesque in favor of restrained, flat-roof, flat-façade, brown-brick rowhouses. Minimal ornamental detail and a strict color scheme of narrow brown Roman brick and white marble trim began to dominate rowhouse design, and residential design generally. One of the first architects to design in this style was J. Appleton Wilson. In 1890, directly across Maryland Avenue from a red brick Queen Anne row built a few years earlier, he designed for builder A. J. Gorter a row of light brown houses with columned doorways, arched and Palladian windows, a modillioned cornice set beneath the crown molding, a deep plain frieze, and in a nod to the neocolonial revival impulse, a pitched roof with Federal-period dormers. That same year Wilson designed for the 1100 block of Calvert Street an even more chastely academic row: flat roof, modillioned cornice, elegant balustrade, sharply cut window openings, splayed brick lintels, white marble horizontal bands at the second story and cornice level, round-arched doorway lintels, and two austere Palladian windows (FIGURE 74). In both designs, Wilson's aesthetic emphasis was on the flat, smooth, planar quality of the façade and the sharply picked-out classical details.

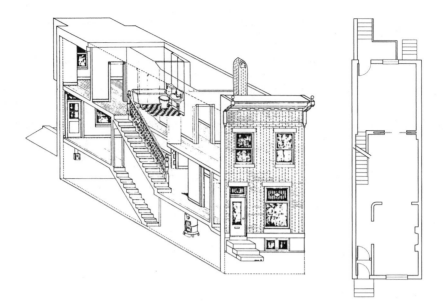

313 Luzerne Street is a two-story version of the rowhouse Joseph Singewald acquired in north Baltimore in 1912. Typical of the period between 1880 and 1915, rowhouse design reflected improved styling and technology. The interior plan opened up to allow for a more formal stair/reception hall, but also created windowless center rooms. The exterior was characterized by golden-brown Roman brick, larger windows with stained glass, white marble (or stone) trim and steps, and a sheet metal cornice. (Chester Design Associates, Gloria Mikolajczyk)

The McKim, Mead, & White and Wilson models set the standard for three-story Renaissance Revival rowhouses built along the eastern and western extensions of North Avenue and in areas bordering Druid Hill Park. Like Joseph Singewald's house on West 29th Street, built at the end of the decade, these were elegant units, with characteristic flat rooflines and classical cornices; deep frieze areas often decorated with delicate swags; and white marble trim in the form of flat lintels and sills, basement facings, stringers and steps. Molded and painted galvanized iron cornices were an important design feature associated with this style. The iron cornice had made its appearance on high-style rows as early as the 1880s, but in 1892 a new city building ordinance banned wooden cornices because they were fire hazards. At first the makers of metal cornices simply copied the forms of the old wooden cornices—long brackets shaped to look like the scroll-sawn versions, molded dentils or modillions, even pierced venti-lator panels. But by the late 1890s cornice manufacturers had adopted clas-sical motifs: stamped rosettes or acanthus leaves on the end brackets; egg-and-dart moldings, rope twists, and classical swags on the frieze. Next, the sheet metal fabricators came up with a new idea entirely—lightweight finials set above the end brackets to punctuate the long roofline with stac-cato rhythms of white balls floating above the white cornice (FIGURE 75).

As the 1890s progressed, McKim, Mead & White's influential work in the neocolonial revival, especially as seen in the pages of *American Architect & Building News* at this time, began to impact the interior detailing of Baltimore's Renaissance styled rowhouses. The parlor usually received the most up-to-date treatment: classical columns set in doorways, columned man-tels and overmantels decorated with swags and classical moldings, classical trim, and all painted white. The dining room and library still tended to show the influence of artistic precepts: in wallpapers, stained glass, hand-painted ceilings, and dark-stained mirrored overmantels (FIGURES 76 AND 77).

When speculative builders began offering the new Renaissance Revival rowhouses in a two-story version, they called them "marble houses" because of the rich use of marble trim on the façades. Builders rec-ognized Baltimoreans' long affection for the decorative use of white mar-ble on rowhouse façades and played up this particular feature of the new style houses in their advertisements. Several local variations on the flat-fronted Renaissance revival rowhouse gained popularity in Baltimore. One of the early ones echoed the undulating façades and roofline turrets of pic-turesque rows. These houses were called "swell-fronts" and had corner turrets and shallow curving bows that enhanced the rhythm of the streetscape; otherwise they resembled the details of flat-fronted Renais-sance Revival houses—brown brick and white marble trim, flat marble lin-tels and sills, marble basements or stringers, and flat rooflines with chaste classical cornices. Some rows of swell-fronts had the round and square bay combination of late picturesque style examples; others made use of pic-turesque style rock-faced stone for trim in place of the more academic pol-ished white marble. A number were built along North Avenue, extending east and west to the city's limits. Just north of the old city line, on tracts near Druid Hill Park, builders maximized the potential of Baltimore's gen-tly undulating terrain by siting block-long groupings of turret-capped swell-fronts along streets that gently rose and fell (FIGURE 78).

In all of these neighborhoods builders put up three-story swell fronts along main streets and two-story versions on streets running off of main thoroughfares. As builder George Spedden advertised in 1895:

FOR SALE—NORTH BALTIMORE—A row of two-story, Swelled Front, Marble-Trimmed HOUSES, situated on Twenty-Third street near Barclay. These houses have just the same conveniences as a three-story house— furnace, butler's pantry, cemented cellars and sewerage. Will sell on rea- sonable terms. Also have nice convenient three-story HOUSES on Twenty- second street, between Guilford avenue and Barclay street.[20]

By about 1905 a new element was added to the urban Renaissance Revival formula—an open front porch with classical columns. The open porch had been an integral part of Baltimore's suburban shingle-style houses in the 1890s. Baltimore's rowhouse builders finally got the message: to compete with the suburban market they would have to outfit their row- houses with a spacious front porch and a small green lawn. Labeled "Philadelphia porch-front houses," these also came with a second-story bay window, usually decorated with classical corner columns and swags. Porches and bay windows may have been nods to English Regency archi- tects' efforts to enliven the flat façades of Georgian rows, a step that also brought additional light and air into the house; however, and perhaps more important, in America the porch represented an extension of the rural ideal, the image of a family sitting on the porch and admiring the sur- rounding greenery. Baltimore builders advertised these expensive, three- story porch-front homes as "the city house with the suburban advantages." Between 1905 and 1915 most of the three-story rowhouses built in Balti- more had spacious front porches, bay windows, and small front lawns. Many went up around Druid Hill Park and in a new development known as Peabody Heights, a 400-acre tract originally laid out in the 1870s by one of Baltimore's first land development companies, near the new Johns Hopkins University campus along upper Charles Street Boulevard. The Peabody Heights Company also offered houses with exotic-looking Dutch gables and fancy, tiled roofs (FIGURE 79).[21]

Many of these houses were architect-designed, but the architects responsible for most rowhouses were not considered among the first tier of the profession locally. Architect John R. Forsythe designed Joseph Singe- wald's house on West 29th Street, and he was also responsible for other elegant Renaissance Revival rows along upper Charles and Calvert Streets. But perhaps the most prolific rowhouse architect was Jacob Gerwig, a favorite of the Peabody Heights Company. In the years 1905–1919 he designed some forty bay-window, porch front rows in Peabody Heights, both two and three stories high. The latter were always recognizable because of their fanciful tiled roof lines, with Dutch and Flemish gables and flamboyant finials. In the 1890s Gerwig designed two- and three-story swell-front rows near Druid Hill Park in a small development known as Auchentoroly Terrace. He even provided plans for the plainest of flat-fronted marble houses for builders in East Baltimore. Like other rowhouse architects he provided designs for a wide variety of clients. In 1911 alone, he worked on over twenty different projects, for as many builders and rarely repeated a design. Designers such as Gerwig had no formal architectural training; indeed, in the years immediately before he was mentioned in the *Sun's* real estate columns as an architect, he was listed in the city directories as a carpenter.[22]

The more characteristic form of the porch-front house in Baltimore was two stories and built primarily in the years 1910–1915. These rowhouses had all of the same stylistic features as the three-story versions: second-floor bay windows, usually trimmed with classical detailing, columned front porches, and small front lawns; however, they lacked any architect-designed extra touches, such as Dutch gables and tiled roofs (FIGURE 80). Rows and rows of these houses shared the streetscape with flat-fronted "marble" houses and brown-brick "swell-fronts," and all belonged equally to the Renaissance tradition. Their buyers were drawn primarily from the working class, and it is to them that we now turn.

The Rise of the Rowhouse Developer

In the early 1900s Baltimore's upper-middle-class and affluent residents were moving to eighth- or quarter-acre lots in garden suburbs (such as the Roland Park Company's developments, Chapter 4), where they commissioned architects to design shingle, neocolonial, Tudor, and Spanish colonial style houses. In the city the number of newly built three-story rowhouses was dwindling. Joseph Singewald's Renaissance Revival house was one of only 56 three-story rowhouses built in 1912; more than 2,000 two-story rowhouses went up that same year. Rowhouse builders were clearly catering to customers with modest budgets by constructing smaller units, which they could sell at lower, affordable prices; to make such lower cost construction feasible, they increased the scale of their operations. By World War I a number of these major "building-developers" had amassed the capital and labor force to develop multiple blocks at a time. Such economies of scale enabled them to offer stylistic amenities that made their houses more marketable, while keeping costs down. A concurrent expansion of the city's infrastructure also made it possible for builders of inexpensive rows to include features previously available to only the middle and upper classes—amenities such as indoor plumbing, gas, and electricity.

What is so fascinating about Baltimore rowhouse development from 1880 to 1915 is that even on the smallest, cheapest houses, Baltimore builders included fashionable, stylistic details—marble exterior trim, decorated cornices, fancy interior woodwork, and artistic wallpapers. How builders made these choices and how they were able to offer stylish yet inexpensive housing to the growing number of working-class home buyers in the newly industrial Baltimore is illustrated by the career of Edward J. Gallagher. The son of Irish immigrants, Gallagher (1864–1933) began building a few houses to sell on his own account in the late 1880s. Over the next 45 years he built more than 4,000 houses, primarily for the working class. Gallagher kept meticulous records of his building operations, and his extensive records, the only ones of their kind known to exist in Baltimore, make it possible to understand how builders were able to finance, construct, and market their own houses. Detailed itemization of all materials and costs in the construction of a particular style of house, when compared to the sales figures cited in advertisements and the cards Gallagher filled out for every house he sold, reveal the profit margins his operations generated.[23]

"Mr. Gallagher to Build"

In one of his scrapbooks, Edward J. Gallagher pasted the obituary of Lord Brassey, a good friend of King Edward VII. Brassey, the son of a bricklayer, amassed a great fortune through speculative building and received a peerage, but, as the article particularly noted, "others have done as much in a country where everyone has a chance." The similarity to his own life was most apparent. Gallagher was the son of an Irish laborer. Other clippings in the scrapbook attest to Gallagher's faith in the American dream—the idea that anyone who works hard and is determined can achieve success—such as the epigram Gallagher posted on another page: "Those who never do anymore than they are paid for never get paid for anymore than they do." Gallagher followed these precepts, even going so far as to attend law school classes at night to familiarize himself with building-related laws and make better decisions. As a self-made man Gallagher indeed represented a real-life Horatio Alger character. But Gallagher's is also the story of how a city was built.

Like most rowhouse builders before him, Edward J. Gallagher began his career in the building trades, working as a carpenter until he had saved enough money to strike out on his own and put up one or two houses. He first tried his hand in July 1888 by leasing two lots from the Canton Company, and following the long-established cost-saving procedure of building houses in less than six months, allowed himself a few months' time in which to sell them before ground-rent payments were due. Soon after their completion in October he sold the two 14-foot-wide, two-story Italianate rowhouses for $1,350, thereby pocketing about $500 for his four months' work. He had also secured the land to build on for no cost, and the new owners had the responsibility of making the annual ground rent payment to the Canton Company. A pleased Gallagher moved on to his next venture.

Leasing parcels from a large landowner like the Canton Company, which was eager to have its land developed, had been the easy part of the process. Finding the construction financing had been more of a challenge, especially for a young, unproven builder. But with his first two houses up, he was able to obtain a loan of $1,200 from a local building and loan to build three more houses, around the corner from the first two. When these sold, he was able to pay off that loan and pocket a few hundred dollars more. With this small success fueling his ambition, Gallagher behaved like the typical speculative builder he would become—he sought to achieve even greater profits by taking greater risks. His timing could not have been better. In 1890 Baltimore was well on its way to becoming the industrial center that city fathers had foreseen; its 5,265 manufactories employed 84,000 people.[24] Workers needed places to live, and Gallagher was there to build.

Gallagher next made a deal with the Pattersons, one of Baltimore's most prominent families. The Pattersons were descendants of William Patterson who had established a mercantile fortune in the decades after the Revolutionary War. (William's daughter, Betsy, gained international fame by marrying Jerome Bonaparte, younger brother of Napoleon. The Emperor had the marriage annulled and married Jerome off to an Austrian princess, but not before Betsy had borne him a son, who would later make his home in Baltimore.) A large landowner in East Baltimore, William Patterson had donated land to the city in 1827 to create Patterson Park east of Fells Point, on the high ground where Baltimore's defenders had stood off the British in 1814. By 1890 Patterson's grandchildren were in control of his vast landholdings, squabbling among themselves, and trying to convert the family's remaining acreage into a steady source of income for themselves and their heirs. Although from different social spheres, their interests directly coincided with Gallagher's—he needed land to build on, they needed someone to improve their land so they could receive the income from the ground rents created.

The land development agreements between Gallagher and the Pattersons typify the relationships between builders and estate owners in the late nineteenth century. In exchange for Gallagher's promise to build 19 houses on the northwest quarter of a city block north of Patterson Park, the Pattersons gave him fee simple title to 7 of the lots—3 on the lesser side street and 4 on the alley street running through the center of the block. The contract specified the overall ground rent he would owe the Pattersons for the 12 larger house lots, but if he could have the houses built and sold before the ground rents came due, the new owners would be the ones paying rent to the Pattersons. If he failed to have the houses ready for sale in eleven months, he would lose the right to retain the fee-simple title to the seven smaller lots. The Pattersons had retained the ground rents on the wide main street lots (those valued the highest) and had given up the lower-priced lesser-street ground rents to make the deal attractive to the young builder; Gallagher had the responsibility for building, marketing, and selling the houses. The builder took all the risks, but he and the Pattersons shared the rewards.

For this his first large-scale project, Gallagher opted for a tried-and-true product—a by then old-fashioned late-Italianate house with a scroll-sawn bracketed cornice, ornamental frieze, ventilator panels, and tall, narrow window and door openings capped with segmental-arched lintels and jigsawn tympanums. The twelve houses he built on Fayette Street were 14 feet wide, three bays, and three rooms deep; they carried ground rents of $35 and sold for $1,100. Those on the side street were 13 feet wide, two bays across, three rooms deep, carried ground rents of $32.50, and sold for $950. Those on the alley were 12-1/2 feet wide, two bays across, two rooms deep, had ground rents of $30, and sold for $500. The buyers of the more expensive houses were of both German and British descent and included two carpenters, a shoemaker, a cigar maker, a ship's carpenter, and a clerk. The side street houses sold to German-born craftsmen, including a cooper. The $500 alley houses went to Bohemian and German tailors, laborers, a cigar maker, and a porter.

Although many Baltimore builders retained ownership of the land they developed, earning income from the annual ground rent payments (as the Pattersons would), Gallagher chose to sell his leasehold interest in the seven lots he had acquired from the Pattersons. From the sale of these ground rents he netted $2,300, a tidy sum for his eleven-month commitment to the project. Because construction netted only about $50 to $100 for each house, Gallagher made more from the sale of the seven ground rents than he did from the sale of the 19 houses he had built.

In February 1891 the Patterson heirs entered into another building agreement with Gallagher, this time for part of the block to the south, prime land facing the park. Gallagher received title to seven more alley lots in exchange for building 16 houses on Baltimore Street, and, as was common with many landowners seeking to develop property, the Pattersons were willing to advance Gallagher construction money. In the contract they executed—an advance mortgage—the Pattersons specified the kind of houses they wanted to have built on the land: "similar in general appearance and architecture to certain houses lately erected by one Steptoe D. Hutt upon the north side of Federal Street west of Ann Street and to cost not less than the sum of $1,650." These houses were to have "white marble bases, stringers, lintels, and steps; pressed brick fronts and ornamental cornices with iron railings." The Pattersons' specifications, similar to many contracts of this kind in Baltimore, ensured that Gallagher would build houses worthy of commanding the high ground rents ($54) they wanted the lots to produce, thus guaranteeing the income potential of their land. Gallagher was also responsible for grading and paving to the middle of the street.[25]

Gallagher responded by building a row of quite elegant small houses (FIGURE 81). The short mansard roofs with iron cresting; the rock-faced marble basements, steps, and window sills; the stained-glass door transom; and the marble keystone in the door lintels, all gave a stylish appearance to what was otherwise an old-fashioned but classic late Italianate house, just like those Gallagher had built on Fayette Street a year earlier. From a grassy hill in the park it is possible to understand how Baltimore rowhouse builders translated recently fashionable styles into more affordable housing. There, built along Baltimore Street in the early 1890s, is the same combination of marble fronts and pressed brick fronts that a *Sun* reporter had lauded in 1878 when writing about the then fashionable district north of Mt. Vernon Place: a row of brick fronts, a row of marble fronts, another row of brick fronts, another of marble, another of brick—in two-story versions that were priced for people of moderate means.

As Gallagher's early building programs amply demonstrate, in Baltimore real estate, the long-term profits still came from the ground rents created, thus the usual notion of trying to keep construction costs down to maximize the profit on the sale of the house did not apply. The builder's goal was to construct a reasonably-priced house that would sell well, and thus ensure a perpetual, safe source of income for the landowner. The builder did not have to worry about cutting costs in the construction: as long as he could sell the house at cost he would derive profits from the sale of the ground rents to other investors. Consequently, he did not skimp on the details that would make the houses desirable, whether it be white marble trim, artistic wallpapers, or ornamental woodwork.

From his second deal with the Pattersons Gallagher cleared $5,800 in six months, exclusive of any profit he made on the sale of the houses. He sold the seven alley ground rents for $2,860, and received a premium of $2,940 from the Pattersons for developing the Baltimore Street lots (which represented the value the houses he had built had added to the lots). Everyone gained. By developing their land the Pattersons had made less than a half-acre worth more than $800 annually in well-secured perpetual income. Since ground rent investments paid 6 percent annual interest, the Pattersons' half-acre was now worth close to $13,500.

Gallagher entered into three more similar deals with the Patterson family, where he built and sold the houses for whatever profit he could make, and in return received title to lots on a street of lesser value. He then quickly sold these ground rents to obtain working capital for future ventures. It would always be the sale of the ground that would provide Gallagher with his annual profit margin. He had a ready market for the ground rents. Throughout the nineteenth century, ground rents provided one of the safest and highest-yielding investments in Baltimore. Compared to returns of 2 to 3 percent on savings accounts, or perhaps 4.5 percent for B&O Railroad bonds, the 6 percent dividend on ground-rent investments was attractive to many. Critics of the ground-rent system charged that this very reliability discouraged investors from putting their money into commercial or manufacturing enterprises, thus hindering the city's industrial growth. Because so much local capital ($60 million) was invested in ground rents, the argument went, Baltimore ranked only eighth among American cities in overall industrial growth in 1900. Nationally, the average capital investment in a manufacturing enterprise topped off at $25,760; in Baltimore the average investment amounted to only $18,000.[26]

The practice of obtaining and then selling ground rents made it possible for builders to increase their capital, enter into riskier (and therefore potentially more profitable) deals, and increase the scale of their operations. For Gallagher that came in 1893, then 27 years old, when the builder struck a sixth business deal with the Pattersons. Using $16,500 of his own capital, he bought outright from the family an entire half block (the eastern portion of the block where he had built his first houses), on which he built 59 houses. Apart from any profit he might have made on the construction, he cleared more than $7,500 from the sale of the ground rents alone.

Switching Markets

In 1895 Gallagher shifted his building operations to another part of the city. Gallagher's houses in East Baltimore were not selling. The national panic of 1893 had devastated Baltimore, and since January 1894, 30,000 (50 percent) of the industrial workers had been thrown out of work. Gallagher made a bold decision: to build three-story, fashionable houses around upper Eutaw Place, a grand boulevard that was attracting buyers from the city's newly rich Jewish mercantile elite—department store magnates, clothing manufacturers, and wholesalers. Since the late 1870s architects and builders had been filling these streets with delightful Queen Anne–style and picturesque-style marble-fronted houses, and Edward Gallagher decided he too would try his hand here. Although this venture was but a brief excursion from his usual working-class market, he learned three important lessons: 1) what it was like to work with a trained architect; 2) the importance of exterior details and interior fittings in marketing houses; and 3) the value of advertising brochures to help sell his product.

Gallagher leased eight lots on Robert Street, just north of North Avenue, from Frank Yewell, an established builder and developer. Yewell lent Gallagher $1,200 per lot to cover the costs of construction. According to the advance mortgage contract, the purpose of the loan was to ensure the completion of houses of a quality that would "render the ground rents reserved by the lease [$183] valuable and secure." Gallagher was granted the right to redeem the ground rents at 6 percent, which he promptly did, and to sell the houses in fee—the usual practice with expensive housing in Baltimore. His gambit worked. He had shifted his market to those in Baltimore least affected by the depression; all eight houses sold quickly for $7,000. Designed by a young architect, J. E. Laferty, the row featured a fashionable mix of round, square, and segmental bays, capped with stick-style porches, and first-floor façades of rusticated stone in a variety of colors. The buyers included Jacob Schoenemann, a major trousers manufacturer; Solomon Levi, the manager of a clothing business; and Julius Brafman, a large-scale clothing wholesaler. All three were among a group that had emigrated from Germany in the 1850s and had created the city's burgeoning garment industry. Edward J. Gallagher was building for the wealthy clothing manufacturers who probably employed the very tailors and seamstresses who lived in his East Baltimore houses.

Fueled by this success, Gallagher took an even bolder financial risk. He struck a second deal with Yewell, one for land in the 2400 block of Eutaw Place, just two blocks south of the entrance to Druid Hill Park. This time he bought the land, which had been laid out into ten lots. At a cost of more than $70,000, this purchase was a enormous investment for the young builder; he split the risk by offering half interest to a man he had done business with before, the treasurer of Baltimore's German American Bank. They obtained financing from the German Fire Insurance Company, a frequent lender to builders, and used Laferty again as architect. The houses Gallagher built in 1895–96 resembled those Laferty had designed on Robert Street, but were even more elaborate (FIGURE 82). The houses featured rock-faced marble, seneca, and brownstone façades; alternating round and squared bays capped with conical and polygonal turrets; third-story open stick-style or stone-balconied porches; arched and columned stone entrance porches; and elaborate stained-glass upper lights. Making use of the tried-and-true picturesque style of a decade earlier, Gallagher, like most builders, apparently felt safer with a proven seller. But to attract wealthy buyers, Anderson gave each house an individual look by varying façade details such as porches, oriels, and upper balconies, while keeping the overall composition harmonious. To effectively market these expensive houses (asking price of $14,000 in fee) Gallagher prepared an elaborate sales brochure, which showed floor plans and photographs of furnished rooms and described many artistic details and domestic refinements. The first house to sell fetched the asking price. The second purchaser preferred to buy his house subject to a ground rent, which reduced the price to $7,000 with an annual rent of $420. Over the next several years Gallagher sold the remaining eight houses to some of Baltimore's most prominent Jewish families, including department store owners like the Hutzlers and Hamburgers, clothing manufacturer Henry Sonneborn, and art dealer David Bendann.

Even as Gallagher was building the Eutaw Place houses, he had decided to return to the East Baltimore market. He realized that, in the long run, his greatest profits lay in the construction of modest two-story houses for the city's laboring classes. In 1895, with the city still suffering the effects of the depression of 1893, land prices were low and as one city councilman put it, "There never was a time in the history of Baltimore when persons were more justified in making investments in eligible building sites."[27] Gallagher bought a two-and-a-half block parcel of undeveloped land north of Patterson Park for $28,500, a bargain in comparison to the $16,500 he had paid for only half a block two years earlier. On it he laid out 73 lots but decided to wait until the real estate market improved before beginning to build.

In 1897 Gallagher began construction of two-story rows along Lakewood Avenue in East Baltimore, just north of Patterson Park, brick versions of what he had built in stone on Eutaw Place (FIGURE 83). Like the fashionable architect-designed rows, Gallagher designed the entire street front as a visual unit with an established rhythmic pattern of round and square bays, stick-style porches, roof gables, and turrets. He capped each corner house with a conical turret, and then established the rhythm within the row: a swell front, two square fronts followed by a signature house with an open stick-style porch at the second floor level of the square bay, which was capped by a distinctive polygonal turret with bold finial. Two more swells followed, then a square bay capped with a similar polygonal turret but no stick-style porch. The rhythm continues, two swells followed by a square bay with a turret, until the row is complete.

These were the only houses with swelled and squared fronts Gallagher ever built, perhaps because he decided that such stylistic extremes were unnecessary to attract working-class buyers. His competitors were offering simpler two-story houses with flat façades, a less expensive way to build. So, after this one attempt to provide stylishness to the working-class market, Gallagher returned to the flat façade of the Italianate rowhouse. What did emerge in his work after 1897 was a new fenestration pattern that gave the older-style, flat-fronted houses a new, modern look. Instead of tall, narrow windows, Gallagher and other builders of the period put in a wide plate-glass first-floor window with a stained-glass transom matching that over the front door. A wider first-floor window had become popular for expensive houses in the mid-1880s, when plate glass was first available at a reasonable cost (previously builders had offered a wider first floor window by pairing two vertical sashes under a single arched lintel). By the turn of the century, most builders' standard two-story rowhouses had a flat façade of red brick, marked by a wide first-floor window with stained-glass transom, marble steps and trim, and a white sheet-metal cornice with stamped neoclassical decoration and ball finials.

Gallagher continued building north of Patterson Park through 1900 but was already trying to assemble a much larger parcel. He wanted one large property bordering a park on which he could establish a project with a clear identity. It took several more years but he found what he was looking for in 1907: a six-block tract bordering three blocks on Patterson Park and three blocks south, which he bought in fee simple. With this project, Gallagher signaled an important change in real estate development in Baltimore. The era of the large-scale building developer had begun.

Homebuyers

In 1910 Bronislaw Wesolowski paid $750 for his brand-new, Gallagher-built, four-room house, within sight of Patterson Park. After being in America for six years, he no longer had to share a house with another family. He had his own front door, his own rear yard, and an indoor toilet, even if it was in the basement. He could sit out on his front stoop in the evenings and chat with his neighbors. He could walk just half a block north to Eastern Avenue to catch the streetcar that would take him west across town to Baltimore's busy garment district, where he worked as a journeyman tailor. One reason that Wesolowski could afford to own his own home was its low price. Another reason was the presence of ethnically based neighborhood building and loan associations. A third reason was that Baltimore's ground rent system enabled homebuyers to rent the land under their houses, instead of paying for it outright. As a result Baltimore had a nationally recognized high rate of homeownership.

Wesolowski's home was at 515 South Glover Street, in Park Side, Edward J. Gallagher's first multiblock development. The 1908–1914 Park Side development was a turning point for Gallagher's business; it represented the largest scale land acquisition he had ever made. Edward Gallagher, Builder, was transformed into the Edward J. Gallagher Realty Company.

Gallagher was one of a half dozen or so Baltimore builders who began to dominate rowhouse building in the early 1900s and by the end of World War I were clearly in charge of the city's housing market. (This continued through the early 1950s, creating whole neighborhoods that bore a builder's particular stamp.) Gallagher, and his fellow "building developers" were in business for the long term. By accumulating ground-rent profits and continually increasing the scale of operations to achieve maximum economies, they all became successful and wealthy men. What is most important, these builders linked their names in the public mind to well-built houses, thus ensuring a continuing market for their product. As each man became more successful, he was able to obtain increasingly larger amounts of capital from banks to continue large-scale development. The builders' track record of fast-selling quality houses added value to the undeveloped land they held, and this land became their collateral with lenders. At the height of their careers, each of these large builders lived in an imposing residence and maintained impressive real estate offices. Their posthumous legacy is that each built many thousands of homes, most of which stand occupied to this day.

Gallagher's Park Side project had two elements that developers to this day seek to achieve: a desirable location and easy access to transportation. Eastern Avenue was directly across from Patterson Park and had a streetcar line running by, which meant that Park Side's sales potential was strong. In making this deal, Gallagher did not stray far from familiar sources: he bought the western portion of the land from the Patterson heirs, and the eastern half from the Canton Company—both former development partners. The cost of the land—$128,700 in fee—and the capital needed to build the 416 houses that would go up—almost $600,000—represented a major investment. The former most likely came from his own pocket, since banks rarely lent money for the purchase of unimproved land. (This accumulation of capital came about directly from the creation and sale of ground rents in his previous building operations. According to the firm's ledger sheets, Gallagher had created and sold some $180,000 worth of ground rents to date.) For construction financing he obtained short-term loans from a variety of investment sources, loans made based on his ability to repay through the sales of the ground rents as each block face was developed and sold.

Drawing on his experience at Eutaw Place, Gallagher produced an elaborate marketing brochure for Park Side, complete with exterior photographs of all the block faces, detailed descriptions of the houses' attributes, information on how to get there, how to find the sales agent once on site, and how to get to work via streetcar lines (FIGURES 84 AND 85). He also outfitted a model house in the development and hired an "agent" to be "on the premises." His marketing brochures were available in the company's real estate office, in the furnished house, and distributed locally. To minimize his financial risk, Gallagher phased the project. He started with the three blocks bordering the park. He built one block face at a time, averaging about fifteen rowhouses every four months. These houses sold well and a little over a year later he moved to the next section. In the detailed expense sheets Gallagher kept for each phase of construction, he recorded the aggregate line item costs for various materials (see appendix). His approximate per-house cost for the initial phase was $1,300, and the profit and loss figures are typical of Gallagher's operations.

PARK SIDE – PHASE 1 – 202 HOUSES

GROUND RENT SALES	$139,663
LESS COST OF GROUND	$ 60,915
NET GAIN FROM GROUND RENT SALES	$ 78,748
SALE OF HOUSES	$250,229
COST OF ERECTION	$264,568
NET LOSS FROM HOUSES	($ 14,339)
TOTAL PROFIT	$ 64,408

The 20 percent overall profit from the development thus came entirely from the sale of the ground rents; otherwise, the project would have incurred a 23 percent loss. These statistics support the theory that Baltimore rowhouse builders were able to offer a more attractive product and more design features at a lower asking price than in other cities precisely because the builders were able to rely on the profits from the sales of ground rents—not from the development and sales of houses.

Gallagher's Park Side houses also represent the final stylistic evolution for the modest, two-story rowhouse in the artistic period. Built of brown, iron-spot brick, with white sheet metal cornices and white marble trim, they have both Renaissance and neocolonial detailing, motifs first used by architects on high-style rows in the early 1890s. Each house has a strictly classical flat-headed window capped with a striking white marble lintel. The stained-glass panel features simple geometrical forms (especially diamonds) and pale color schemes rather than the naturalistic and more richly colored designs of the picturesque style. Neocolonial-inspired white woodwork dominates the parlor, but "artistic" wallpaper and dark-stained mantels and overmantels hold sway in the dining room. The house extends back the full width of the lot and the stairs are located in a windowless center room, which is lit by electric lights.

At Park Side Gallagher initially followed the traditional practice of building much smaller houses along the narrow alley street running through the center of the block, which is where Wesolowski's house was located. Gallagher, like other developers, carefully had gauged the marketplace. As a savvy businessman, he was adapt at fitting the product to various economic levels of potential buyers. Since the basic Baltimore block was laid out with a narrower alley street running through the middle (either in a north-south or east-west direction), Gallagher had six block faces on which to build per block. On these he developed four differently priced categories of houses. Those along the street facing the park had the widest lots, the highest ground rents, and were the most elaborate. The streets running back on either side from the primary street became the secondary block faces; on these the lots were slightly less wide, carried lower ground rents, and the houses had fewer expensive finish details and interior fittings. A third price category of house was built on the street running across the bottom of the block. The least expensive houses of all—the kind of house that Wesolowski bought—were on the narrow, mid-block alleys.

The extent of the marble work and stained glass are the most obvious exterior features that distinguish Gallagher's classes of houses. The best and most expensive houses had a full marble basement and steps, marble lintels and sills, a wide plate-glass first-story window with stained glass and a stained-glass door transom. (A few also had second-floor bay windows.) The second-best houses had marble sills and steps but only a stringer course at basement level and segmental brick arches over the windows; there were still stained-glass transoms. The third-tier houses had marble stringers and steps, but no stained glass. The bottom-tier house had no marble at all and had simple wooden steps. Even though marble trim and stained glass added an important "touch of class" to Gallagher's houses, neither was particularly costly. Marble work on a main street house cost only about $65—for the basement facing, steps, and lintels. Marble stringers and steps cost only $25. The stained glass for a first-tier house cost only $60.

Gallagher designed the houses himself. That he was not a skilled draughtsman is clear from the drawing of a group of houses built in 1906. The 8-½-inch-by-11-inch linen is the quintessential builder's drawing: quick and not a line too many (FIGURE 86). Done with a ruling pen and black ink, the only information Gallagher offers is the overall width and depth, wall thicknesses, the size of window openings, and the layout and depth of the three rooms. Because of the repetitive nature of rowhouse building, Gallagher simply drew one end unit and noted, "two like this," and an interior unit with the note, "18 like this." The hasty quality indicates the builder did not believe this project warranted paying an architect $100, the standard fee paid to rowhouse designers. Because of the scale of the operation at Park Side, however, and the need for city building permits (required by law after the 1904 fire), Gallagher hired a draughtsman to execute plans from which blueprints could be made. This cost him $25—less than the cost of excavating one basement.[28]

About 1912, Gallagher's son and namesake Edward Jr., a recent graduate of the Maryland Institute College of Art's highly regarded architectural department, became the in-house architect. The younger Gallagher's drawings also are unmistakably builders' drawings—simple and to the point—but far more detailed and more competently drawn than his father's. Each design unit includes a complete set of plans—front and rear elevations, basement, first, and second floor plans, and sections. Since the Gallagher construction crews were well versed in rowhouse building, these drawings contained only minimal information—basic measurements, wall thicknesses, and room layouts. The building section called out lumber sizes and floor-to-floor heights and the basement plan indicated the method of heating and the placement of the flues. One set of drawings served as plans for rows built in many different neighborhoods. For this reason, actual house widths and specific addresses are omitted in many cases. Different locations and parcel sizes called for different solutions, or in Gallagher's lexicon, "Suitable Homes at Suitable Prices." The Gallaghers carefully laid out blocks to maximize profits and to fill streets with the correct price-range and size of house to sell in that location. The right fit maximized the source of profit: the ground rent leases.

Building Rowhouses

In addition to fashionability, Gallagher's homes also offered the working-man an affordable, generally maintenance-free product. Unlike the locally produced but softer red brick used throughout the nineteenth century, the iron-spot brick on his façades, as Gallagher's ads boasted, "need never be painted." It was not an empty claim, the mustard-colored brick still looks as it did in 1910. (And when the Formstone salesmen came to town in the 1950s, marketing their imitation stone, stucco-veneer products door to door, no one who owned a home built of iron-spot brick had it put up.) Composed of high-iron content fireclays from western Pennsylvania, the bricks were kiln-burned in such a way as to cause the iron particles in the clay to run and bleed out, creating the distinctive "iron spot" pattern. This brick had to be imported, and, although Gallagher's ability to buy in bulk lessened this expense, he had his bricklayers apply it only to the façade. There are about 1,400 iron spot bricks in each rowhouse and some 23,400 common red bricks, which composed the foundation walls, the rear wall, party walls, and the front wall to which the iron spot brick was applied like a veneer. (Gallagher's competitors also used iron-spot brick, but many chose a varying shade that would identify their rows.)

Although machine technology reduced the cost of rowhouse building materials—such as pressed brick, stamped sheet metal cornices, milled lumber, and windows—the basic construction process was what it had been a century before.[29] Day laborers still hand-dug the basements. A team of nine men, paid on average $1.25 a day, could accomplish the task in two days, thus costing Gallagher about $28 per house. The crew shoveled the dirt into a horse-drawn cart that held only two cubic yards. The excavation of one block of Park Side, which contained 90 house lots, yielded 7,000 cubic yards of earth—the equivalent of 3,000 horsecart loads. Gallagher had his own crew of carpenters, whom he paid about 50¢ an hour, but he subcontracted out the rest of the work (FIGURE 87). Bricklayers and plasterers earned the top hourly rate of 60¢; painters, 44¢; and common laborers, 33¢. For work on the average Park Side rowhouse, Gallagher paid carpenters $86, and bricklayers $95. According to construction costs attached to the 1909 building permits, Gallagher could build a 14-foot-wide, 1,200 square-foot house for around $1.18 per square foot. Frank Novak, his largest competitor, could put up a 12-foot-wide house for as low as 70¢ per square foot, but the average seems to have been $1.15 to $1.30 per square foot.

An additional cost that Gallagher and other builders had to bear was laying out the streets. They hired surveyors, who, following the street grid Thomas Poppleton had platted in 1823, laid a grid over the rolling acres of raw land. City ordinances regulated the actual opening of streets and developers had to follow procedures. The city would pave a street upon application of a majority of lot owners, but at the owners' expense. (If repaving were needed, the city paid a third of the expense.) Street paving costs were high—in 1891 it cost $7,750 to open eight blocks in East Baltimore—and there were constant discussions in the newspapers about who should bear the expense. Real estate men pointed out that in New York and Philadelphia the city provided this service, arguing that such municipal investments fostered development. They blamed Baltimore's backward attitude on the fact that "others whose wealth consists mainly of personal securities think that property owners should be made to bear the cost."[30]

Glover Street, where Wesolowski purchased his house, was one of the last narrow residential streets to be built on in the city. In 1908 Baltimore's City Council enacted a law forbidding building houses on streets less than 40-feet wide (Glover was only 15 feet, curb to curb). Only a year earlier, reformer Janet Kemp had published a searing study of Baltimore's overcrowded housing—complete with startling photographs of the squalid conditions of life in some of Baltimore's older districts in which newly arrived immigrant and poor black families lived sometimes twenty to a small house, with inadequate sanitary facilities, ventilation, and light.

Pressured by such reform tactics as well as newspaper articles quoting statistics of overcrowding, the city sought to eliminate these conditions by eliminating narrow alley housing, where many of these families lived. Thereafter, streets were to be wide enough so that adequate light and air were provided; interior rooms without windows—common to artistic period rowhouses—had to be ventilated by means of door transoms.[31]

In response to the new law, Gallagher chose to stop building the smallest houses he had offered and widened the mid-block streets in his parcels so they could be built up with second tier housing. In this way he was able to develop the whole block with a greater number of higher-priced houses (and higher-priced ground rents), thus increasing overall profits. Apart from the rows facing Patterson Park, Gallagher built long, continuous rows down each north-south street (including the widened alleys). He decided to build only two price categories of homes—the more expensive, clad in marble, faced the park; the cheaper houses with less marble and fewer interior features, faced secondary streets.

The neighborhoods of East Baltimore where Gallagher and other builders put up affordable rowhouses functioned as urban versions of traditional small villages. Although residents could hop on a streetcar to go to Baltimore's downtown shopping district, or to work at the Maryland Steel Company in Sparrows Point, daily needs were within walking distance. Most builders, including Gallagher, designed their working-class rowhouse units with a corner store at the end of the block. These might be operated as groceries, saloons, bakeries, or small repair shops by the family who made their home on the second floor. The neighborhood's main shopping district was usually located along a wide, through street that also served as a transportation route. Children could walk to the nearby primary schools, but most attended their local parish school, as in Wesolowski's Polish neighborhood.

Gallagher and his competitors literally worked next door to each other. Just to the east of Park Side John T. Donohue, another large-scale builder, erected eighty-nine houses quite similar to Gallagher's on land he leased from the Canton Company. And, like Gallagher, he relied on the sale of the ground rents for his profits, earning only modest sums on the sale of the houses. These builders felt sure that with the enormous industrial expansion taking place in Baltimore, there would always be more than enough workers looking for homes. In 1910 there was good reason to believe this. Of the 2,107 houses constructed in the city, only four percent remained unsold. The building boom continued for six more years, prompting the *Sun* to report, "In all sections of the city, rows of houses are being built in 'jig time.'"[32]

Gallagher depended on two basic forms of promoting his new development at Park Side: through a sign on the lot announcing new houses going up; or through brochures, the marketing vehicle Gallagher preferred. Brochures could be produced in great quantities, then either mailed or handed out to prospective buyers. "If you are not interested, do your neighbor or friend, who IS interested, a 'good turn' by handing him or her this circular." With photographic reproductions, Gallagher showed as many as six different rows in a single brochure. The text copy, "suitable homes at suitable prices," stressed affordability. Gallagher knew that his sales depended on the local building and loan associations, and he promoted them on the back of his brochures, pointing out the low weekly payment terms, which could be afforded with working-class wages. His later brochures featured interior shots showing the up-to-date kitchens with all their appliances as well as the interior detailing of living and dining rooms and entry halls (**FIGURES 88 AND 89**). About the time he was developing Park Side, Gallagher coined the slogan, "Lifetime Homes," featured in bold print at the top of every brochure. He was the only rowhouse builder consistently to identify his product with a corporate slogan.

Gallagher wanted his name to be synonymous with quality houses, and his brand identity became an important selling point in his advertising copy. Word-of-mouth also played an important role. If potential customers heard that a highly reputable builder like Gallagher had started a row, they might go out to see the new houses on a Sunday. As a builder of modestly priced homes, Gallagher identified his customers as employees of all the diverse manufacturing plants in Baltimore—canmakers, oyster and fruit packers, meatpackers, cigar makers, brewers, furniture and piano makers, shoemakers, glassmakers, shipbuilders, and iron and steel workers. He believed that these prospective buyers needed to know up front what his houses cost. He also specified the number of rooms and special features that each house offered, such as up-to-date bathrooms and cement yards, but he never noted the house's (narrow) width. A comparison of the advertised price and the final purchase price, as noted in the city's land records or in Gallagher's financial records, suggests that there was little negotiation. Gallagher held fast to his advertised price, but would add custom features for the buyer at extra cost, such as extra closets or an expanded kitchen. He averaged about ten sales a month with peak sales occurring in October.

By about 1910 most other builders were also beginning to promote their houses through illustrated brochures or paid advertising in newspapers and theater programs, a popular way to spread the word. Since the working-class houses all sold for about the same price ($1,000 to $1,500), marketing strategies focused on distinctive architectural or decorative features as well as the reputation of the builder. One major rowhouse builder, Walter Westphal, merged the working-class buyer's resentment of landlords with his dream of homeownership, coining the slogan, "It costs no more than rent." Using this phrase as the driving theme in his ads, he also offered his own financing plan, "the Westphal Plan."

Gallagher tended to use newspaper advertisements sparingly. He resorted to them when he needed to sell the last few houses in a development, stressing that the houses were going fast and prospective buyers must act immediately or lose out. He also reached recent immigrants by selectively advertising in the city's foreign-language newspapers (FIGURE 90). And he took out large advertisements when he opened a new development in a different part of the city. Mostly, though, he relied on brochures and word-of-mouth. Gallagher designed his brochures to appeal to buyers for whom such a purchase required careful planning and perhaps some sacrifice. For example, besides Bronislaw Wesolowski, five other purchasers of Gallagher's Glover Street houses were Polish immigrants who did piecework in the many factories that made up Baltimore's burgeoning clothing industry. All had initially settled in the Fells Point section. Similar to many immigrants they had a consuming desire to obtain property. As the newspaper had noted some fifteen years earlier, "One of the most certain things about these adopted citizens is their thrift and economy":

> By way of beginning to found a home, a small house is rented, probably containing four or five rooms. Two families often share the expense and divide the rooms. This makes the rent for each about three to five dollars. When the food and clothing are bought, and the rent, and, possibly the remainder is saved, and usually deposited with a building association. The fund grows rapidly and soon the family is able to make a beginning toward buying a $500 or $600 home. When this is paid for a larger venture is made, and in a surprisingly short period the fruit-parers are on the high road to a comfortable and comparatively luxurious existence.[33]

Making it possible for immigrants to buy a rowhouse was the next step (FIGURES 91 AND 92). Building and loan associations had been created for the purpose of lending money on real property. Members agreed to purchase shares and pay dues on a regular basis until their shares matured, the shares constantly accumulating dividends and interest. Generally, the terms required $1 a month per share to be paid in until a par value of $100 or $200 was reached. As fast as the money was paid in, it was lent out to other members in the form of mortgages. For a small down payment a member could borrow against the full value of his shares. In contrast, commercial institutions only offered loans based on 50 percent of the value of the house and the borrower had to pay off the mortgage in a lump sum at the end of a specified time period—usually only a few years—something out of the question for a workingman. As a writer for *Baltimore of To-Day* noted in 1915, "An essential element in the sale of the two-story dwelling is the easy payment plan which in Baltimore has been brought to unique perfection. Houses can be bought, as the saying is, for little more than rent. There is not much difference in the expenditure, but a world of difference in the ultimate result. In the easy payment plan, there are two factors, the ground rent system, and the building and loan association."[34]

Wesolowski went to the Kosciusko Permanent Building and Loan on August 23, 1910, and requested a $700 loan, 93 percent of the house's $750 value. A month later Kosciusko advanced him the full $700 on the seven shares he owned ($100 par value). Wesolowski's payment terms were typical: every Tuesday he paid $1.75 toward the $700 loan and a weekly interest charge, or "premium," of 12¢ per share, or 84¢ total. As each $100 of the loan was paid off, he was relieved of the burden of paying the 12¢ interest on that share, a practice resembling that of the later amortized mortgage. With an annual interest rate of just over 6 percent, Wesolowski could pay off his $700 loan in 7.7 years.[35]

Building and loans became the bastions of single-family housing in Baltimore and other American cities with financing especially tailored for low-budget families. Wesolowski—a piecework tailor—could make about $2.26 a day working six days a week, so the total amount of $2.59 that he owed each week constituted 22 percent of his weekly salary. Compared to the rule-of-thumb today that housing costs should not exceed 25 percent of one's gross income, this payment plan was realistic in terms of what a workingman brought home each week. A barber making $1.45 in a twelve-hour day or a cigarmaker making $2.22 a day could equally afford to purchase some house with the aid of a building and loan.[36]

For Wesolowski and other working-class Baltimoreans, the ground rent system proved an additional godsend. Faced with paying $1,450 for a house in fee or $750 with a $30 annual ground rent payment, there seemed only one choice for someone making but $13 a week. Wealthier individuals like Joseph Singewald might choose to buy their houses outright, but when this was the case, the house always cost about twice as much as it would if the purchase had been subject to a ground rent.

If propertied status represented the highest achievement to the immigrant, then losing one's home must have been the greatest humiliation. From the scant information available, building and loan associations almost never had to foreclose on customers. The Bohemian Building and Loan Association listed no foreclosures between 1900 and 1930. The building and loans also provided industry and management with a secure labor force. A 1915 publication encouraging industry to come to Baltimore noted that "the possibility of labor troubles is far removed, and strikes are not likely to occur in a city where a majority of its wage earners have obligated themselves to pay stipulated amounts weekly on homes in which they already own a large equity, as default in these payments would necessarily subject them to added distress, inconvenience and financial loss."[37]

The influence of the building and loans on Baltimore homeownership was enormous. More than 900 building associations were chartered in Baltimore between the Civil War and World War I. Most were neighborhood- and ethnically-based institutions, places immigrant workingmen felt comfortable going for help. Almost 87 percent of the loans made by the First Polish American Building Association and 79 percent of those of Kosciusko were confined to a twenty-eight-block portion of the surrounding neighborhood. A week before Wesolowski applied for his loan in 1910, sixty-three separate building and loans issued $85,000 worth of mortgages; trust companies and savings banks issued only $23,000. The building and loan's neighborhood roots gave substance to housing reformers' beliefs that urban life was enhanced through the creation of community. And some of the building and loans had greater ties to the community than others: 206 building and loans operated in East Baltimore between 1904 and 1914, but six of them provided over half the loans.

In order for Wesolowski to obtain his loan from Kosciusko, Gallagher had to act as his guarantor. Kosciusko gave one check directly to Gallagher for $600; Gallagher redeposited the other $100 check in the building and loan, to act as security for Wesolowski's loan. In order to help a buyer qualify for a loan, especially when the loan-to-value ratio was close to 100 percent, Gallagher would often take a part of the loan, up to $300 sometimes and deposit it in the building and loan. There it would sit accumulating dividends and interest. In the Park Side project, he guaranteed 16 houses; which cost him a total of $3,575. It was a way of securing a buyer for one of his houses and of earning interest on the purchase money. If the buyer failed to pay off the loan, Gallagher lost his guarantee. The records show that Gallagher guaranteed loans hundreds of times during his career. By the time of his death in 1933, the guarantee money that was deposited in nine different building and loans had earned him more than $61,000. More than forty different building and loans financed the purchases of Gallagher-built homes. For example, twelve different building and loans provided mortgages for the thirty-six houses he sold in the 500 block of N. Robinson Street in East Baltimore in 1915. Since less than five percent of all Gallagher customers paid in full for their homes, more than 95 percent relied on building and loans to make their dream of homeownership come true.

While Gallagher's market included immigrants from Eastern Europe, there was one segment of the population that was not included: Baltimore's black community. Jim Crow laws had restricted African-Americans to living in a twenty-six-block area in the northwest section of the city. Successful professional families made their homes in impressive three-story rows on upper Druid Hill Avenue but had to share their neighborhood with some of the city's poorest blacks who lived in Biddle Alley, just seven blocks to the south, which gained notoriety for its outbreaks of cholera, typhoid, and tuberculosis. Described by reformer Janet Kemp as "the lung block," this alley held some 400 residents in 1907.

As the black population in Baltimore increased from 54,000 in 1880 to 85,000 in 1910, many blacks tried to move out of crowded enclaves. Speculative builders, Gallagher included, felt threatened by this and feared the effect upon sales and prices. In 1909 the U. S. Supreme Court refused to review a case involving a restrictive covenant barring the sale of property to a black. The following year the city council passed a segregation ordinance, in response to a black family's purchase of a house on McCulloh Street, one block closer to the city's most fashionable neighborhood, Eutaw Place, than blacks had formerly been allowed to live. In essence the law said that no "Negro" could move onto a block in which more than half the residents were white and that no white could move into a block that was more than half black. A developer could not open a street without first declaring whether it was for white or black occupants.[38]

Builders of houses on "white" blocks were quick to cite "the safety" of their neighborhoods in advertisements. "Walbrook, 3000 block W. North Ave.," ran one ad of 1907, "Attractive Section, No Saloons, No Colored. Up-To-Date Three-Story Houses, Every Convenience." L. Irving German asked readers of the *Sun* to: Look at these fine two-story houses recently built in the 2000 block West Fayette Street, and see us at once about terms. We can make them very attractive to reliable men of character with small means. They are well built, contain six rooms, bath and pantry, are beautifully finished. Have sanitary plumbing, attractive wall paper and all conveniences. The NEIGHBORHOOD IS EXCELLENT, And no negroes are in the immediate vicinity."[39]

Even for blacks who could afford to own a house in these segregated neighborhoods, financing opportunities were limited. Just as Baltimore's immigrant population was shut out of traditional financing sources and had to create neighborhood-based building and loans, so too did blacks have to generate their own pool of capital. Just like the Polish-based Kosciusko Savings and Loan (which actually made several loans to African-Americans, probably a rare occurrence), the black business community organized at least eight separate building and loans to serve black home buyers. According to the *First Colored Directory of Baltimore City*, published beginning in 1913 as the community's business directory, most of these were located on Druid Hill Avenue, the most prestigious thoroughfare in the black community, and were headed by some of the most prominent black business leaders (FIGURES 93 AND 94). But Gallagher and the other large-scale building developers did not want to sell their new houses to African-Americans under any circumstances; they all continued to try to shape the character of the neighborhoods they built by selectively promoting and selling to only the people they deemed acceptable.[40]

Wesolowski was considered an acceptable buyer, and when he bought a house in East Baltimore from Gallagher in 1910, his life changed. The old garment district near which he had lived contained some of the city's most horrendous overcrowding. In 1899, for example, 228 people lived in seventeen rowhouses on a single street; another house was home to four families with 48 children. This he could leave behind. And from his new house, Wesolowski could walk out his front door, turn left and in less than a minute be at the stop for United Railway & Electric Company's Number 10 Eastern Avenue car, which ran every three minutes. The ride west to the clothing factory district took less than fifteen minutes (FIGURE 95).

Both rich and poor rode the streetcar, and Gallagher and other rowhouse builders understood the value of the streetcar to their business. Their ads always noted which streetcar lines ran near the new houses—to enable prospective buyers to come out and see them and also to emphasize the convenience of getting around the city once they moved there. Usually more than one line ran within walking distance, making it possible to travel quickly to various destinations. For example, Wesolowski could walk two blocks to the Fait Avenue car if he wished to go south to the waterfront. Gallagher's other Park Side customers could easily commute to work as well. Alex Morowsky, a meat packer, could take the Eastern Ave. car, with one transfer, to get to the A. Booth Packing Co. in Canton, in less than fifteen minutes. James Evers could get to his produce stall in the Fells Point Market in about five minutes.

In Baltimore, streetcar service was a prerequisite for rowhouse builders. Gallagher would not build in areas not served by a streetcar line: his buyers had to have easy access to inexpensive mass transportation. But streetcar service did not ensure a building boom. The 1906 atlas of Baltimore, for example, shows the Edmondson Avenue line stretching west into empty countryside; that land was not filled with rows until 1915. Sometimes land along the routes sat idle because private owners were not ready to sell; other times developers did not have the capital to build. The pattern of rowhouse development in the city always remained incremental, gradually extending block by block into vacant land—it was rare that an isolated development was built.[41]

After 1907 one of the most important selling points in advertisements for Baltimore's working-class rowhouses was the city's new sewer system (FIGURE 96). Baltimore was late in extending this modern convenience to its residents. With many streams to carry waste into the Chesapeake Bay and sandy soil easily absorbing sewage from cesspools, city fathers found little reason to invest in a complete sewerage system until the growing population and modern theories about disease made it absolute necessary. With increased water consumption from so many additional households, the sandy soil beneath Baltimore became thoroughly saturated. Sewage from surrounding cesspools seeped into basements on a regular basis, and the smell from the harbor became noxious during summer months.

Gallagher understood the importance of sewers to his customers in Park Side. The headline in his ad for Wesolowski's block of South Glover Street highlighted this: "It won't cost you an extra cent for the new sewer connection." For a city that had long relied on the most primitive waste disposal methods, the sewer connection was an important selling point. Until the construction of the sewerage system, which took the municipality ten years to complete, most working class homes used privies and still depended on night-soil removers, licensed scavengers driving wagons containing sealed barrels or a tank to pump out human waste at $2.50 a load. It was dumped outside the city or sold to farmers for fertilizer. The catalyst for a new sewer system was the great fire of 1904 which destroyed the central business district and which helped city fathers realize that their infrastructure was sadly out-of-date compared with other cities. A spirit of modernization literally took root overnight. With $10 million authorized by the Maryland legislature, work began in 1906 on a dual storm and sanitary system. More than 70,000 privies had been put out of business when the system was finished in 1916.[42]

The early twentieth century was a prosperous time for Gallagher. Between 1909 and 1914 the city's population increased by more than 75,000, and he built an average of 120 houses per year. In 1914 the outbreak of hostilities in Europe created an enormous industrial boom and this in turn drew thousands in search of work, all of whom had to be housed. Gallagher doubled his output of houses in the war years, and at the same time he greatly increased the sophistication of his building operations. He was beginning his final transition to becoming one of Baltimore's largest real estate developers.

These years also saw an acceleration of middle-class residents leaving their city rowhouses to live in freestanding shingle-style houses in the suburbs. Gallagher and the other rowhouse builders were steadily losing this market and had to change their designs in an attempt to stem the tide. The flat front rowhouse with marble trim had passed its peak on the fashion curve. Builders added front porches and radically altered the traditional rowhouse floor plan. The "daylight" rowhouse, so named because each room had a window, would fill up the next ring of city growth, in areas that could be reached by an entirely new form of transportation, the automobile.

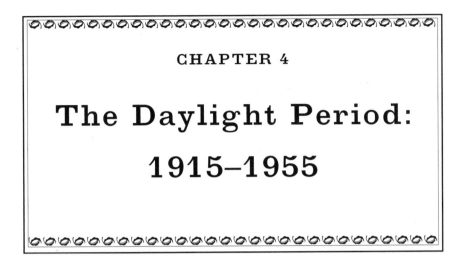

CHAPTER 4

The Daylight Period: 1915–1955

Why buy an old house with small dark and ill-ventilated rooms, when a house 20 feet wide, 7 rooms and bath, 1 square from the cars and 20 minutes from City Hall can be had for the same money?

Baltimore *Sun*, October 16, 1915

A bird's eye view of Edward L. Palmer's design for the "Meadow Block," Edgevale and Falls Roads, Roland Park, 1911; from Roland Park Review *(Enoch Pratt Free Library)*

HENRY ELMER SINGEWALD, the grandson of Traugoth Singewald, decided in 1919 it was time to get a place of his own. He was newly married and holding a good job. After receiving his law degree from the University of Maryland, he had secured a position as a trust clerk with the Fidelity Trust Company. His prior investment work included selling ground rents for the Edward J. Gallagher Realty Company and he was well aware of Gallagher's reputation as one of the city's best rowhouse builders. The builder had recently completed houses in the 2700 block of Howard Street, just two blocks away from the Singewald family home. So in 1919, continuing the family tradition of payment in full, Henry paid $3,850 in cash for the house at 2735 Howard Street and moved just 400 feet from his parents' home (FIGURE 97). The house, only two years old, was designed in the latest style—called the "Daylight " or "Sunlight" house by a rowhouse builder in 1913. Nearly every room (the bathroom being the general exception) had a window, which was achieved by widening the standard 12-foot- to 16-foot-wide rowhouse to 20 or 21 feet, and creating a two-room-wide, two-room-deep floor plan. Gallagher and other rowhouse builders were responding to fierce competition from suburban developers, who had successfully convinced a great many middle-class buyers to purchase detached houses outside the central city rather than rowhouses in town. Rowhouse developers studied the competing product—the suburban cottage, with deep front porches and lawns—and then reconfigured the rowhouse.[1]

Suburban cottages, which first appeared in Baltimore about twenty years before, appealed to families that wanted to live beyond the congestion of the city, in a quieter, landscaped neighborhood. In Baltimore as elsewhere in cities across the country, urban growth and foreign immigration that came with industrialization inspired a sentimental and backward-looking nationalism that celebrated a mythic rural ideal. Middle-class Americans also placed a growing emphasis on the sanctity of family; the phrase "hearth and home" became a shorthand reference to the desire to step away from what the middle class viewed as impersonalized and industrialized urban workplaces. (Affluent families had always been able to separate work and home; lower-class families never could, and indeed needed most members working in order to afford even a rental house.)

The popular shingle style arose during this time as an architectural panacea for such yearnings. Architectural historian Vincent Scully has called the shingle style "an architecture of suburban relaxation and country joys." Associated with the colonial revival because of its references to seventeenth-century colonial architecture, the shingle style was perhaps the first authentically American-born architectural style. It emphasized natural materials and siting sensitive to the surrounding landscape. The interiors, which opened to a large stair and living hall surrounded by suites of rooms through which space flowed freely, were well suited to a renewed interest in family life. Usually built with reference to Queen Anne styling—a corner turret or wraparound porch—the cottages appealed to those in the middle and upper-middle classes, who wanted to live away from the noise, heat, congestion, and smells of the city. At the turn of the century, rambling shingle-style houses arose on commodious tracts near the edges of cities and towns all around the country. The recent extension of electric streetcar lines actually made it possible for many men to resettle their families in new homes far removed from the workplace. In Baltimore shingle style houses could be found in planned suburbs such as Roland Park and Windsor Hills, and they in turn inspired the more modest frame cottages that became the hallmark of new suburbs.[2]

In early-twentieth-century Baltimore the shingle style was followed by various versions of the Renaissance and Colonial Revival styles, which the Roland Park Company used to fill the remaining lots on existing tracts.[3] In 1907 the company expanded its operations by purchasing *Guilford*, the country estate of A. S. Abell, publisher of the Baltimore *Sun*. Here, a half mile closer to the city than Roland Park, the company first built pairs of English Tudor style houses in 1913. The house style resembled that of the shopping center the firm built in 1894, but the choice of paired houses was unusual in this expensive neighborhood. Perhaps the company was being cautious. After all, Guilford was adjacent to the Wyman Park and Peabody Heights rowhouse communities, in which some of the city's most recent expensive rows had been built. The company's concerns were ill-placed: Guilford soon became the most affluent suburb in Baltimore, filled with impressive Georgian revival, Spanish colonial, and Jacobean revival mansions, making it *the* place to live in the city.[4]

In subsequent decades developers created many more single-family suburban neighborhoods; the Roland Park Company's 390-acre Homeland was the most important of these. The company again commissioned the Olmsted Brothers to create a site plan that capitalized on the natural beauty of the land (the firm had done the plans for the western section of Roland Park and Guilford), then began selling the lots to individual owners and contractors rather than taking on the construction itself. The new strategy worked well, within three years of purchasing the tract in 1924, 71 percent of the 564 lots had sold and expensive houses were going up.

Rowhouse builders closely tracked these changes in house design. Within a few years after neighborhoods began to fill with detached shingled cottages, they began experimenting with ways to open up the rowhouse to more light and flowing space inside. Singewald's Gallagher-built daylight house was typical of those constructed in the late teens and early twenties; it had a colonial-inspired façade and porch front, classical moldings, white-painted trim, a strictly colonial interior, and six-over-six windows in every room.

Another shift builders watched with concern was the move by some upper-middle-class residents into luxury apartments, a housing type new to Baltimore. In the first decade of the century the Marborough went up on Eutaw Place, one of the city's most prestigious neighborhoods. By 1910 luxury apartment houses were rising in other parts of downtown Baltimore and in Beulah Villas in Walbrook, which had earlier promoted the fact that it had no brick rows. Suburban neighborhoods that loathed the presence of rowhouses, welcomed luxury apartment houses. Architects who disdained taking on a rowhouse project eagerly accepted a commission to design an apartment house in which the units would rent for as much as $3,500 a year. In the 1920s a different type of apartment also made inroads into the domestic real estate market. High-style rowhouses, left vacant by middle-class residents moving to the suburbs, were being converted into "individual suites of 3, 4, 6 rooms for light housekeeping." The *Architects and Builders Journal* in 1901 predicted that once "people live in one of these apartment-houses with all the modern improvements," they'll never return

58. LEFT   17 West 29th Street, designed by John R. Forsythe for builder James R. Miller, 1911; purchased by Joseph T. Singewald Sr., 1912 (Steven Allan)

59. BOTTOM *Baltimore in 1889*; detail of bird's eye view drawn and published by Isaac Friedenwald (Maryland Historical Society)

60. TOP   New Zealand Chambers, Leadenhall Street, London, by Richard Norman Shaw, 1871–1872. *Building News*, 1873

61. RIGHT   George C. Wilkins house, northeast corner of St. Paul and Biddle Streets, designed by J. Appleton Wilson, 1876 (J. Appleton Wilson Collection, Maryland Historical Society)

62. RIGHT   McKim house, 1000 North Calvert Street, designed by J. Appleton Wilson, circa 1877; published in *American Architect & Building News*, 1879

63. BOTTOM Belvidere Terrace, 1000 block North Calvert Street, designed by J. Appleton Wilson, 1878 (J. Brough Schamp)

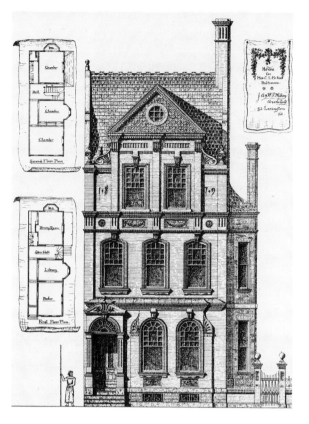

64. TOP   Detail of terra cotta sunflower panel, Belvidere Terrace, designed by J. Appleton Wilson, 1878 (J. Brough Schamp)

65. BOTTOM   200 block of Robert Street, built by Joseph M. Cone, 1885 (J. Brough Schamp)

66. RIGHT   1031 Harlem
Avenue, built by Joseph M.
Cone, 1883. Cone added
Queen Anne brickwork and
stained glass to Italianate
facades on many blocks he put
up in West Baltimore in the
early 1880s (Steven Allan)

67. BOTTOM   400 block East
North Avenue, 1888; Italianate
houses with Queen Anne window hoods and decorative sunflower panels over attic ventilator openings (Steven Allan)

68. TOP FAR RIGHT   12–16
East Chase Street, designed by
Bruce Price with E. Francis
Baldwin, 1872; the city's first
picturesque style houses
(J. Brough Schamp)

69. BOTTOM FAR RIGHT   1200
St. Paul Street, designed by
McKim, Mead & White for
Ross Winans, 1882; *American
Architect and Building News*,
1887 (Enoch Pratt Free Library)

70. TOP   1200 block of North Charles Street, designed by Dixon & Carson for George Blake, 1881–1885. The four units at the north end are the earliest, with marble and serpentine fronts; houses in the middle of the row have darker facades of brownstone and seneca stone; and the unit at the southern end is built of brownstone, topped by the then popular conical-roofed turreted end bay (J. Brough Schamp)

71. BOTTOM   Unit block of East Preston Street, designed by Charles Cassell for the builder A. J. Gorter, 1883–1885. Cassell introduced the design concept of the undulating facade to Baltimore residential architecture, which remained popular through the 1880s; note the rough-textured, rock-faced stone, another hallmark of the style (J. Brough Schamp)

72. LEFT 1500 block
Mt. Royal Terrace, an
elegant row of rock-
faced houses built
near Druid Hill Park
in the late 1880s
(J. Brough Schamp)

73. BOTTOM
2221–2239 Barclay
Street, two-story
picturesque style
houses built just
north of North
Avenue in 1892
(Steven Allan)

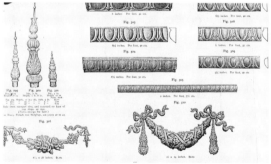

74. TOP   1100 block of North Calvert Street, designed by J. Appleton Wilson for builder A. J. Gorter, 1890 (J. Appleton Wilson Collection, Maryland Historical Society)

75. BOTTOM   Builders could buy a variety of classical sheet metal ornament for cornices, bay windows, and kitchen ceilings from catalogs. *Penn Metal Ceiling and Roofing Co., Ltd, Philadelphia*

76, 77. TOP Parlor and dining room, 2400 Eutaw Place, designed by J. E. Laferty for builder Edward J. Gallagher, 1895–96; neocolonial and aesthetic-period tastes merged in the interior decorations of Renaissance Revival rowhouses (author's collection)

78. BOTTOM LEFT   Blocks of both three-story and two-story "swell fronts" fanned out in every direction along the city's old boundary line, North Avenue, in the 1890s (Jane Webb Smith)

79. TOP LEFT   2700 block North Calvert Street, designed and built by Jacob Gerwig, 1905. Three-story porch fronts with imaginative rooflines, deep front porches, and yards were the last historic type of three-story rowhouse built in Baltimore (Steven Allan)

80. TOP   James Keelty offered two-story bay windowed porch fronts in the early 1900s in West Baltimore, where he was just getting started in the rowhouse building business (author's collection)

81. BOTTOM   Houses in the 2400 block East Baltimore Street, facing Patterson Park, part of row designed and built by Edward J. Gallagher, 1891 (Steven Allan)

82. TOP   2400 block Eutaw Place, designed by J. E. Laferty for Edward J. Gallagher, 1895–96 (author's collection)

83. BOTTOM   100 block Lakewood Avenue, designed and built by Edward J. Gallagher, 1897, following ideas he had learned on Eutaw Place (Steven Allan)

84. TOP   Edward J. Gallagher's advertising brochure for Park Side illustrated
each price category of house available in the community, listing respective features and costs; the row pictured on the cover was the most desirable, of course,
since it faced Patterson Park (E. J. Gallagher Collection, University of Baltimore
Archives)

85. BOTTOM   500 block Glover Street, where Wesolowski purchased his home
for $750; it had no marble trim and only plain wooden steps (E. J. Gallagher
Collection, University of Baltimore Archives)

86. RIGHT   Edward J. Gallagher drew these sketches for a row of 20 two-story houses he built in the 100 block of North Rose Street, East Baltimore, 1906 (author's collection)

87. BOTTOM   Edward J. Gallagher's construction crew, including his son, Edward Jr. (third from right, holding surveyor's transit) stands in front of a newly-built row in East Baltimore, 1907 (James Gallagher)

88, 89. TOP AND MIDDLE FAR RIGHT Elaborately furnished parlor and kitchen in Gallagher sales brochure; East Baltimore rowhouses, 1911–1913 (E. J. Gallagher Collection, University of Baltimore Archives)

90. BOTTOM FAR RIGHT   Gallagher advertised houses in the 600 block of South Glover Street in *Der Deutsche Correspondent*, the city's main German newspaper, to reach the large German-speaking populace; (Enoch Pratt Free Library).

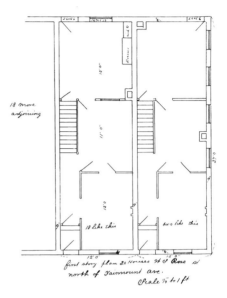

91. TOP LEFT   Mrs. J. Perontka's Northeastern Meat Market in East Baltimore, circa 1910. Wider corner rowhouses were often fitted out with storefront windows and occupied by family-owned businesses, the shop on the ground level, the residence above (John Dubas Collection, Maryland Historical Society)

92. BOTTOM LEFT   Photographer John Dubas's neighbors, Bohemian immigrants, on the front steps of their alley street rowhouse in East Baltimore, circa 1909. The redbrick houses had sheet-metal cornices; the basement was painted white to imitate the marble of expensive houses. This family earned its living repairing boots and shoes (John Dubas Collection, Maryland Historical Society)

93, 94. TOP   Citizens Realty and Investment Company of Baltimore City, Inc., advertised in Baltimore's *First Colored Directory*, 1915; the firm helped blacks purchase houses in northwest Baltimore. BOTTOM   Druid Hill Avenue was a very prestigious address (Philip Merrill; Baltimore Neighborhood Heritage Project)

95. RIGHT   The United Railways and Electric Company advertised its services to Baltimore riders, boasting that "They Don't Have To Live Near the Factory. Ride the Cars," in *Baltimore Sun*, May 17, 1926

96. BOTTOM   City officials toured the new 200-mile sewer system in 1909, which replaced 70,000 "earth closets"; builders advertised the sewer connections to new houses; in *Annual Report of the Sewerage Commission*, 1909

They Do Not Have To Live Near The Factory

Time was when the men and women who worked in the factories lived near the plant—ofttimes in houses owned by their employer, rarely out of sight of their work, and awakened by the whistle summoning them to their tasks in the building about which their homes clustered.

Now the factory is placed where it is most accessible to the railroads or docks to cut costs in receiving raw materials and shipping the finished product.

The workers find it convenient to live anywhere in the homes they themselves own, in the suburbs where the children have the green grass and the sunshine, or where they like.

The street cars make this possible.   At small cost and with increasing convenience they make the city possible for the worker and the country possible for his family.

The fact that the industrial plants usually close at the same time creates the Rush Hour, a difficult and expensive problem for the street car company, but that is part of our job and we are solving it day by day for the workers who

Ride the Cars

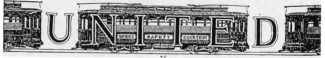

97. TOP   2735 North Howard Street, built by Edward J. Gallagher, 1917; purchased by Elmer Singewald, 1919 (Steven Allan)

98. BOTTOM   937–945 University Parkway, designed by Edward L. Palmer Jr., and built for the Roland Park Company, 1909; the first English style rowhouses to go up in Baltimore. Each house had the new "daylight" floor plan—two rooms wide and two rooms deep (Steven Allan)

99. TOP LEFT   Bretton Place, designed by Edward L. Palmer Jr., and built for the Roland Park Company in Guilford, 1914; one of the English style rows built for upper-middle-class Baltimoreans (Steven Allan)

100. BOTTOM LEFT   East 33rd Street at Alameda, typical daylight rowhouses built by the Frank Novak Realty Company, 1918 (Jane Webb Smith)

101. TOP   700 block East 33rd Street, built by Edward J. Gallagher, 1917 (Jane Webb Smith)

102. BOTTOM   Design for neocolonial daylight rowhouses on East 33rd Street by Edward J. Gallagher Jr., 1916–1917 (author's collection)

LIFETIME HOMES

103. TOP   Saint Clair, a development of both daylight and porchfront homes built by Edward J. Gallagher in the 2000–2200 blocks of Belair Road, opposite Clifton Park, 1919–1920 (E. J. Gallagher Collection, University of Baltimore Archives)

104. BOTTOM   Sunlight dayparlor houses on East 33rd Street, built by Edward J. Gallagher in the early 1920s (E. J. Gallagher Collection, University of Baltimore Archives)

105. TOP AND BOTTOM RIGHT   Advertising brochure for daylight rowhouses built by the Donohue Building Company, Monastery Avenue in West Baltimore in the early 1920s; note the white neocolonial woodwork in the living room, the "cream and green porcelain cabinet gas range," the basement garages, and the view of still undeveloped land out the kitchen window (author's collection)

Spacious Yards and Wide Cemented Driveways
Provide a Genuine Surburban Atmosphere

Even where outstanding differences are least expected the traditional Donohue thought for completeness is evident. Large, spacious yards, the largest in this section, cemented and sodded—hedges instead of unsightly fences—a large sleeping porch—doors weather stripped—all windows caulked. And just a peek into the cellar! American Heating Co. hot water heat—clean, smooth walls—gas hot water heater—and plenty of air and light!

BUILT-IN GARAGE

For a very small additional cost a built-in cement garage is available. And it's a real garage too! Full width and 18 feet long, it accommodates the largest car easily.

TWO IMPORTANT FEATURES

Location

With schools and churches nearby and directly adjoining the Monastery, these Donohue homes enjoy a most convenient location. Stores of every kind are conveniently accessible. The Frederick Road cars are but three squares away. Only twelve minutes is the usual running time to the downtown section.

Financing

We have a particularly attractive financing plan and many of the 5,000 Donohue home owners have enjoyed its advantages. The same convenient plan can be used in purchasing these Monastery Avenue Homes.

DONOHUE HOME BUILDING COMPANY
GILMOR 6459   CALVERT 1856

£OOK INTO THESE

DONOHUE HOMES
Monastery Avenue, · · · three blocks north of Frederick Road

for outstanding, amazing values

Note these features

$3990

With Garage $300 extra

Stone porch with concrete floor.
Modern iron spot brick front.
Spacious lawn ... well sodded.
Attractive shrubbery planted.
Through paved street...
...suburban walks.

Here is Modern Charm, Beauty and
Outstanding Convenience and Quality

Spaciousness and attention to detail is the most apparent note in these newest and most exceptional homes by Donohue. From the smooth finished walls in the bright cellars to the particularly appropriate wall decorations in the comfortable bedrooms, thoughtful planning is evident at every turn.

You will be delightfully surprised when you inspect these unusual homes, for here you will find convenience, quality, beauty and charm far beyond what could be expected at such modest prices.

A sample house is open from 9.00 A.M. to 9.00 P.M. and a thoroughly informed representative is present at all times. It will be well worth your time to inspect these modern, modestly priced homes.

Crystal chandelier and modern ceiling lighting fixtures.

Newest panelled walls.

⅞" Hardwood flooring over ⅞" subfloor.

Three coats of Barrelled Sunlight on all woodwork.

Double Electric outlets in every room.

Smooth finished cellar walls.

A Large, Airy, Bright Kitchen
That is truly Modern and Different

Like everything else in these Donohue homes the kitchen is a thing of striking difference—it is made as it should be made. There is no skimping of room or lack of any modern convenience.

The size alone prompts expressions of delight from every woman who has experienced the inconvenience and stuffiness of many present day "kitchenettes." There is ample room for everything and everything is there.

Adequate ventilation is another feature seldom found even in homes of much higher price. Here we have provided two large windows, a ventilating transom and a half glass door opening on a large rear porch. Bright, cool and airy, these are more than mere kitchens—they are cheerful, usable rooms.

High Grade cream and green porcelain cabinet gas range.

Built in cupboards and ironing board.

Armstrong's inlaid linoleum—cemented on felt.

Large, one piece, porcelain sink. Plenty of ventilation and light.

DONOHUE HOME BUILDING COMPANY
GILMOR 6459   Sample House Open 9 A.M. to 9 P.M.   CALVERT 1856

106. TOP   Aerial view of first blocks of Ednor Gardens and the Baltimore Stadium, 1928. Frank Novak's parcel, where he would build cottages, lies directly to the right of the stadium (Jacques Kelly)

107. TOP RIGHT   English style rows at Ednor Gardens, designed by Edward Gallagher Jr., 3600 block Rexmere Road, 1927 (Steven Allan)

108. BOTTOM RIGHT   Normandy style rowhouses at Ednor Gardens, designed by Edward Gallagher Jr., 3700 block Rexmere Road, 1929 (E. J. Gallagher Collection, University of Baltimore Archives)

109. TOP LEFT   Furnished neocolonial style living room in Gallagher's model "Bride's Cottage" in Ednor Gardens, 1936–1937 (E. J. Gallagher Collection, University of Baltimore Archives)

110. BOTTOM LEFT   Gallagher's brochures showcased the garage for the automobile, 1929 (E. J. Gallagher Collection, University of Baltimore Archives)

111. TOP   3900 block Cranston Avenue, built by James Keelty, 1931; Wildwood in West Baltimore (Jane Webb Smith)

112. BOTTOM   Continental Oil's gas station, near Ednor Gardens, 1931 (note the daylight house porchfronts in background (author's collection)

113. TOP 300 block Murdoch Street, neocolonials built by James Keelty in Rodgers Forge, a rowhouse community he built in the mid-1930s (Steven Allan)

114. BOTTOM 3700 block of Ednor Road, Ednor Gardens, built by Edward J. Gallagher Realty Co., 1940 (Steven Allan)

115. TOP RIGHT 1500 block Northwick Road, Northwood area, built by the Welsh Construction Company, 1940; Welsh advertised these houses at a low cost of $48 per month (Jane Webb Smith)

116. BOTTOM RIGHT Advertisement for new Northwood Shopping Center, from *Gardens, Homes and People*, the magazine of the Roland Park Company, 1940 (Enoch Pratt Free Library)

Announcing

THE OPENING OF THE

NORTHWOOD SHOPPING CENTER

ON OR ABOUT JULY 1ST, 1940

NORTHWOOD SHOPPING CENTER, Inc.

NORTHWOOD SHOPPING CENTER NEARING COMPLETION

•

OWNED AND OPERATED BY

THE ROLAND PARK COMPANY

CHARLES R. SCRIVENER CO., INC.
Builders

JOHN A. AHLERS
Architect

Assistance in the Securing of Leases
THE WHITE-MOWBRAY COMPANY

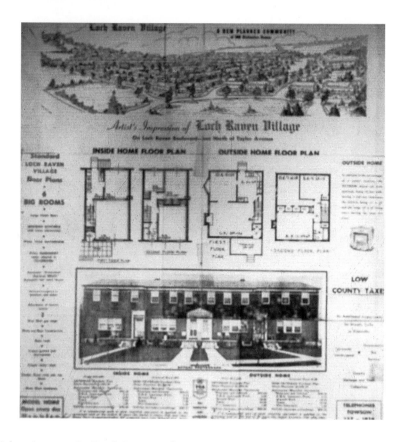

117.   Advertisement for Loch Raven Village, a community of neocolonial styled
rowhouses built in the early 1950s in northeast Baltimore (author's collection)

to the rowhouse. *The Daily Record*, the city's main business journal, disagreed: "Baltimore is a city of homes and will never embrace the idea of apartment living." In the long run the *Daily Record's* prediction proved to be more accurate.[5]

English Style Rows

Although the four-square suburban middle-class cottage was the most immediate antecedent of the daylight house, other important precedents existed. In the 1910s the very last expensive rowhouses in Baltimore arose along the fringes of Roland Park Company land. They were modeled after the English rural cottages popularized by the late-nineteenth- and early-twentieth-century Arts and Crafts and domestic revival movements. In the U. S., as in England, these movements were reactionary, proponents seeking an anti-urban architecture that defied machine-made furniture and crafts, which were made possible by industrialization. They looked to John Nash—designer of London's monumental Regents Park rows—who in 1811 had drawn heavily on traditional English cottage forms when he fashioned a series of houses at Blaise Hamlet in Bristol. Perhaps the best known of these men was architect C. F. A. Voysey who in the 1890s and early 1900s designed stone, stucco, and half-timbered cottages with sweeping hipped roofs, casement windows, and massive chimneys to exemplify "the sacred importance of the home." (Ironically, Voysey and other architects were designing the finest of cottages for upper-class clients whose wealth came from industry and trade.) Magazines like *Country Life* popularized these and other architect-designed cottages in the 1890s, and within a decade the middle and working classes were embracing cottage-style architecture as well, albeit in more modest forms. The designs, especially those inspired by Voysey, found their way into England's speculatively built cottage market, most particularly in the planned communities of Bournemouth, Port Sunlight, and Letchworth, and demonstrated that the rural cottage could be built in rows in the garden suburbs and thus give ordinary people the feeling of living in a traditional village.[6]

In like manner, Baltimore architects and developers quickly adopted the English rural cottage and added it to their offerings of the various revival styles popular early in the century. Edward L. Palmer, the architect of the Roland Park Company, found the style particularly suited for the rows he designed for company land.

Chartered in 1891, the Roland Park Company—a syndicate of London capitalists and their Kansas City agents—started out by purchasing some 550 acres directly north of Baltimore, built an electric streetcar line to provide transportation to the city, helped start a local private school, and constructed a few sample houses as well as a shopping center. By the late 1890s most of Plat 1 (east of Roland Avenue) had been developed; the partners turned their attention to Plat 2 (to the west). Edward H. Bouton, the leading force behind the company's activities, commissioned Frederick Law Olmsted Jr., to design the street layout and overall landscape plan. His father, now deceased, was already well known for his 1887 design of Sudbrook Park, a west Baltimore suburb. His son applied the same design concepts to the hilly site in Roland Park, laying out curving lanes that followed the contours of the steeply wooded hills.[7]

A decade or so later Olmsted laid out Guilford, the company's next suburban venture a mile to the east, on much flatter land. Olmsted executed what was becoming his trademark approach to suburban land use: all of the streets curved, and those on the outer edges of the tract were designed so that the house lots faced inward, toward a green or a cul-de-sac, thus ensuring the privacy of the new community. Bouton then went a step further. He decided to erect a series of very elegant "group homes"—otherwise known as rowhouses—on the outer fringes of the new development to insulate the expensive inner house lots from the "lesser" neighborhoods located to the north, east, and south. He directed company architect Edward L. Palmer to come up with a design for fashionable, highly attractive rows that would be appropriate to the elite suburb and that would provide an elegant housing choice for those persons who did not need the size or want the responsibility of maintaining a large house and yard, yet did not want to move into an apartment. As one advertisement boasted, "Here is an effort to provide HOMES distinctive and attractive in the best neighborhood with the care and trouble of living reduced to the minimum, as in an apartment house but with many more advantages."[8]

Palmer had been designing rowhouses for the company since 1909, his first effort being a Voyseyesque cottage design for a row of five houses on University Parkway. These he had fashioned of reinforced white-painted concrete with "exterior woodwork of rough-sawed lumber, stained, and red tile roofs." Setting them far back from the street, Palmer gave the houses expansive terraced front gardens and private gardens in the rear. He designed wide, covered, side porches for the two end houses and "summer houses in the gardens in the rear" for the central three. Indeed, it was this group of architect-designed rowhouses that introduced the four-square "daylight" floor plan to Baltimore (FIGURE 98) Two years later Palmer had again drawn on Voysey as he put together a village-like layout for a group of twenty-three semidetached houses to be built on a company parcel known as the Meadow Block. The stucco houses, "exceedingly picturesque, with low eaves and high-pointed gables ... [and] roofs ... of red shingles," he set around a central green, "tastefully planted" that doubled as a private park and children's playground.[9]

When Bouton requested a design for expensive rowhouses in Guilford, Palmer adopted other forms of English vernacular architecture that seemed to complement the Georgian-revival style houses being built on the interior lots—Tudor revival and colonial revival rowhouses, all with a daylight plan. The first went up in 1913. Arranged in an open-ended rectangle facing the street, the three groups of four houses each constituted York Court and shared a common front lawn as well as small back yards. As the *Sun* commented, "On the York road ... the company intends to build groups of houses in which each group will be treated as a single architectural unit—that is to say, will be given real architectural quality. These groups will be placed back from the street and will have trees and greenery about them. Thus, although they will be 'attached' houses and will be small, it is not intended that they shall bear any resemblance to the city blocks with which the Baltimorean is so unhappily familiar."[10]

That same year Palmer designed Bretton Place, freely combining Tudor half-timbering with elegant Flemish bond, herringbone, and diaper-pattern brickwork using glazed headers; steep, slate roofs with hipped and shed-roofed dormers; irregularly massed, oversize chimneys; multi-paned windows, double and triple sash; and a combination of round-arched and steeply pedimented craftsman entryways (FIGURE 99). The houses were put on the market the following summer, priced from $6,950 (in fee) for the seven-room version, to $9,875 for the ten-room version. They came with "Window Shades, Screens, Chambers' Fireless Cooking Gas Range, Laundry Stove, Gas Water Heater, Kitchen Cabinet, Folding Kitchen Table, Bath Rooms with tiled floors on second and third floors, well lighted Cellars—with Laundry, Servants' Toilet and Hot Water Heating Plant," and interior woodwork "all in white, except the doors, which are of birch with mahogany finish." The company offered to have a motorcar waiting at the entrance to Guilford (reached by streetcar line), or "better still, one of our salesmen (each having an automobile) will gladly call at any designated time, at your residence or office, and take you to Bretton Place."[11]

Just to the south of Bretton Place, on Newland Street, Palmer designed two groups of nine houses each, one for the Roland Park

Company and the other for a private builder. Each 24-foot-by-35-foot unit was designed on the daylight plan with eight rooms, two baths, and a selling price of $8,000. For the exterior he drew on elements he had used at York Court and Bretton Place, albeit in a different manner, and added new elements, including a second-story front porch just off the master bedroom. A deep, landscaped front lawn added a suitably picturesque rural flavor to the overall design; however, it was more for appearance than use, for as in traditional rowhouse neighborhoods, outdoor life was enjoyed in the backyard.[12]

The enthusiasm for expensive English-style group homes encouraged other builders to buy parcels on the fringes of Roland Park and Guilford and erect their own versions of the style. In 1914 Phillip C. Mueller, heretofore a builder of small, moderately-priced East Baltimore rowhouses, purchased Oakenshawe, a picturesque nine-and-a-half acre tract at the edge of Guilford "with many stately old trees" and "an artistic mansion" that was to be razed. Then Mueller, for the first time in his building career, hired an architectural firm, Flournoy and Flournoy, to design his rows. The architects drew their ideas from the cottages built in Bournemouth and Port Sunlight in England, all of which were heavily influenced by Voysey's work, and provided Mueller with a conservative and dignified design. Each group of seven houses followed the basic design principles Palmer had used a few blocks away on Newland Street: central and end units marked by cross gables and intervening units sporting traditional pitched roofs with shed dormers; brickwork laid in Flemish bond; and a front porch.[13]

Mueller continued building rowhouses at Oakenshawe through 1925, advertising them as offering "the man of moderate means the only opportunity in Baltimore to live in such a fashionable district...surrounded by the beautiful homes of Guilford, the University Parkway, etc." Pushing the point, he intoned: "living in one of these Mueller Built Homes, you will enjoy all of the refinements of the highly cultured community that it is. Your children will have the highest type of environment to mold their young characters in." Each daylight house had eight rooms, two baths, colonial stairways, a gas range, steam heat, hot water heater, and "linoleum on kitchen floor and pantry." Some of those built in 1920 came with the Gainaday Electric Washer & Wringer, "nationally famed and nationally advertised and endorsed by Good Housekeeping Institute....It can be safely said that the owners of these homes will not have to worry about washday."[14]

Another builder of expensive rowhouses was George R. Morris, whose distinguished University Homes went up in 1916–1917. The development consisted of several long blocks of semi-detached houses and rowhouses located, Morris pronounced, in a "section of Baltimore where values are beyond question." Transportation to and from the city was easy, for the houses were located just "one block from Charles Street and one from the Boulevard cars." More consciously English-looking in design than were the houses competitor Mueller was putting up at Oakenshawe, these red brick, stuccoed, and half-timbered designs featured stylish deep hooded and pedimented entryways, paired and triple sash, and wide, shed-roofed dormers set on the slate roof. Morris was also determined to offer houses that were as technologically up-to-date as possible. His was the first large group of houses ever heated by manufactured gas in Baltimore and in half-page newspaper advertisements Morris bragged "it is only necessary to light the gas once a year, set the thermostat at a certain temperature, and be comfortable." And the incinerator burned the garbage. Even more innovative was his offer to install "mechanical refrigeration when desired; so that the garbage cart, the ash cart, and the coal cart and the ice cart are all banished." He added one final bonus: "these houses are provided with fireproof garages having heat, light and water, under the sun parlor, so that the owner can at any time go down-stairs and drive out over the smooth road at the rear."[15]

The design endured. Nearly a century later Morris's University Homes and other similar English style rowhouses remain very appealing and saleable. Their gables and porches break up the façades and give the illusion that each house is different. Instead of continuous rows, groupings of three to nine houses give blocks a residential scale, an important attribute considering their proximity to suburban developments. The heavily landscaped front yards buffered the houses from the street. Most important, residents of Guilford and Roland Park accepted the structures because the units in them were affordable only to people of about their own income level and because the group houses screened them from the rows in which lower-income people lived. Suburban group houses were as expensive as many single-family houses selling from $16,000 to $20,000 each in the 1920s.

Daylight rowhouses began to be built in Baltimore around 1915, characterized by two-room-deep, two-room-wide floor plans that allowed sunlight to enter every room. Builders advertised the porchfront houses as "the city house with the suburban advantages," competing for buyers who were drawn to new suburban neighborhoods. (Chester Design Associates, Gloria Mikolajczyk)

Daylight Rows

Daylight rows came quickly on the heels of the upscale group houses. On January 29, 1913, a building permit listing appeared in the *Sun*, announcing that the Alconde Realty Company planned to build eleven, two-story houses in West Baltimore. This was nothing out of the ordinary except for the dimensions, noted as 20 feet wide and 36 feet deep. Fifteen months later, an advertisement for the same houses described them as seven-room "daylight" houses. This was the first time the term *daylight* had been used in a Baltimore real estate listing, and it marked the beginning of a rapid shift in rowhouse design. The new floor plan also ushered in other new features that allowed the ideals of the suburban movement to enter into vernacular rowhouse design.[16]

As with the more expensive precedents, these daylight rowhouses were shallower, so they could be set back from the street, which gave them a small front yard, allowing the novelty of grass, shrubs, and flowers in modest-priced housing. The houses also had a deep front porch, similar to suburban residences. The four-square plan allowed daylight and fresh air to reach *every* main room. Moreover, the majority of daylight houses were actually built beyond the central city in Baltimore's newly annexed suburban areas, on large tracts of land at the end of streetcar lines. (Today, this aspect of the daylight house has been lost, because the city limits now extend well past these 1920s pockets of development.) Finally, many of the houses had a rear garage, or the space in which to build one. The people who purchased daylight rowhouses knew they would be living differently than they had in their street-locked long, narrow traditional rowhouses. For those who did not immediately discern the difference, the builders were there to drive home the point: "These houses are something different; they carry that air of beauty and refinement that becomes the high-price homes of Guilford and Roland Park."[17]

The first vernacular daylight houses closely resembled the brown-brick "marble" houses of the late nineteenth century, albeit with a white columned porch and small front yard. But as the stylistic influence of the imposing Georgian revival suburban homes pervaded the market, many rowhouse builders switched to a neocolonial combination: red brick, white trim, multi-pane sash, and porches with classical columns and balustrades. They also gave the rooflines an unusual treatment that soon became a signature design element of daylight rowhouses—short, mock mansards carried out in slate, shingles, or green tile (FIGURE 100). (The early and more expensive versions of these vernacular rowhouses also had shed-roof dormers mildly reminiscent of the pitched roofs with shed dormers on the group houses at Oakenshawe and University Homes). On the vast majority the mansard roof is a totally false front, a parapet placed atop the traditional flat roof. The green Spanish tile, inspired by the terra cotta tiles used on the mansard roof of the much publicized California building at the 1915 Panama Pacific Exposition in San Francisco as well as Spanish colonial revival buildings generally, is also artificial; it is actually galvanized sheet metal. (The fair garnered extensive press coverage, and the tile proved to be a design feature easily translated into much less costly sheet metal. Thus, the new rooflines became another inexpensive addition to the kit of embellishments for rowhouse façades.)

By 1917 daylight rowhouses were solidly established, but materials shortages following the entry of the United States into World War I prevented builders from constructing large-scale daylight developments until the 1920s. Meanwhile, four major developers vied to dominate Baltimore homebuilding: Frank Novak, James Keelty, Ephraim Macht, and Edward Gallagher. In the 1910s and 1920s each builder kept pace with the others, incorporating the latest style changes and offering buyers the latest in heating equipment, kitchen appliances, and the like. They provided inexpensive, well-built houses that could be bought easily on liberal financing terms, and because these developers, like their predecessors, made their money on ground rents, they still sold the houses at close to cost. Their "easy terms" of small cash down payments, with the "balance like rent" in weekly installments of $5 to $10 gave people of moderate means the chance to become homeowners.

Frank Novak (1877–1945), the first of the four to buy up individual tracts of suburban land on which to build large-scale, moderately priced daylight rowhouses, was the son of Bohemian immigrants. He began his building career at the age of thirteen as a carpenter's apprentice and at the height of his career was called the "Two Story King of East Baltimore." Whole neighborhoods of daylight houses mark his developments and fill large sections of east and northeast Baltimore. Many of his customers were first- and second-generation Czechs and Poles, whom he reached in the city's foreign language newspapers as well as the Baltimore *Sun* and *American.*

Irish-born James Keelty (1870–1944) came to Baltimore as a child. He began his career as a stonemason in the old Irish Tenth Ward (in East Baltimore) but later concentrated his building operations on the west side of the city. Keelty acquired large tracts of land in the late 1910s and early 1920s and developed Wildwood on the hills south of Gwynns Falls Park. In the 1930s he built Rodgers Forge, an upscale Baltimore County rowhouse community.

Ephraim Macht (1866–1944), the first Jewish real estate broker who operated on a large scale in Baltimore, founded Welsh Construction Company in 1911, naming it after John Welsh, an Irish clerk in the office, so his business would not be weakened by Baltimore's pervasive anti-Semitism. He began building in West Baltimore, but by the late 1920s had moved his building operations to northeast Baltimore.

Edward J. Gallagher (1864–1933), discussed in Chapter 3, built daylight houses in both the northern and eastern sections of the city.

These four large-scale builders prospered from the economic boom that began in 1912 and accelerated in 1914 as the United States became a major supplier of munitions and war materials for the Allies already at war in Europe. During these years industries in and around Baltimore increased their manufacturing capacity, and also increased the size of their workforces. The newly hired workers, most new arrivals, needed places to live, and the builders knew those places would be rowhouses. (City coffers grew as real estate taxes, a major source of city revenue, rose. Much of the money went back into infrastructure projects, especially road building and paving.) The nation's entry into the war in 1917 brought housing starts to

an abrupt halt, a hiatus followed around 1920 by a postwar boom and infla-
tion. The price of building materials doubled and tripled from 1915 to
1921: bricks went from $7 per 1,000 to $21; nails from $2 a pound to
$5.75; and two-by-fours from $27 to $60 per thousand board feet. Labor
rates more than doubled as well: a bricklayer's wages went from $3 a day to
$7; a common laborer's wages rose from $2 per day to $4.50. Thus, a typi-
cal rowhouse that sold for $1,500 before the war went for $3,000 after the
war. (Henry Singewald's house when new in 1917 sold for $1,900.) Rents
that had been $12 a month climbed to $20. Between 1914 and 1920 the
cost of living in Baltimore increased 114 percent.[18]

Gallagher the Builder of Lifetime Homes

In 1914 Gallagher sold 120 houses, the number he typically sold in a year's
time; then between 1915 and 1917 sales shot up to an average of 170 a year.
When sales picked up again in 1922–23, Gallagher reached a peak of 246
houses. The war had given him and his sons, Norman and Edward Jr., time
to consider their building strategy and they decided to expand their product line, which would enable them to reach other markets, specifically the
middle-class, in addition to building homes for workingmen's families.

In the 1920s the elder Gallagher set up one of his several building
operations on the fringes of the Guilford-Charles Street-University
Parkway area, where he had built his own suburban villa at the corner of
Charles and 39th Streets in 1911. To attract middle-class buyers, the conservative builder changed his rowhouse design. He did so by adding a
porch to the design he had used for houses facing the park at Park Side just
two years earlier, with its shallow second-floor bay window. He chose not
to set the houses back from the street to create a front lawn; after all,
Wyman Park was just a block away and he had paid good money for this
land. When he advertised these new porch-front houses, Gallagher took
aim at the perceived competition, asking, "Why Live in an Apartment?"
Other developers had built luxury apartment buildings in the immediate
area and had succeeded in attracting upper-middle-class families. In his
advertising materials Gallagher prominently featured his sylvan "view from
the porch" and a site plan that illustrated the proximity of the houses to the
park, the new Charles Street Boulevard, and the new Johns Hopkins
University campus. So far so good. But fashion-conscious buyers who
looked at the other images, most particularly the "combination parlor &
living room," recognized that Gallagher was still building a turn-of-

century house: the dark-stained wooden panels with grillwork separating the rooms, mirrored overmantels, hand-painted ceilings, and shower lights all belonged to an earlier age.[19]

Next Gallagher began purchasing land nearer Guilford, hoping to attract those middle-class buyers who wanted a stylish address. In 1915, when land bordering the grand East 33rd Street boulevard (connecting Wyman Park to Clifton Park) became available following the death of estate owner August Hoen, Gallagher acquired ten acres of the property along both sides of the street for $50,000. He now had the financial resources to "land bank" property—to buy undeveloped land when it was still cheap and hold it for future development. He had a short wait. He began construction a year later.[20] The 33rd Street houses represented a quantum leap for Gallagher—his first daylight houses (FIGURES 101 AND 102). Designed by his son Edward Jr., the company's architect, the houses were a full 21 feet wide. "These beautiful Sunlight Homes contain 8 rooms, bath and kitchenette and individual front porches," his brochure touted. And they each had a front yard. Gallagher had created a more sophisticated product. It was not a change in design philosophy, but a marketing choice.

Gallagher's first daylight houses were conservative in design when compared to the architect-designed English style rows in nearby Guilford. They represented an evolution of his traditional brown brick porch front homes near Wyman Park, and before that his marble houses in East Baltimore. He still relied on brown, iron-spot Roman brick for the façade; however, at the roofline he put a short, shingled mansard with shed-roof attic dormers. The rest of his stylistic vocabulary became strictly colonial: Georgian keystone marble lintels, a deep modillion cornice, a plain classical frieze band, traditional eight over eight sash and simple doorways set beneath the classically columned and balustraded porches. Advertising copy boasted that the living room had a "colonial mantel and gas log heater" and that "the papering and decorating of these beautiful homes are of the very latest designs." These houses sold for considerably more— $4,950—than any houses Gallagher had previously offered. As he had hoped, the location attracted a different class of buyer: salesmen, a civil engineer, an accountant, managers, business owners, and even Gallagher's own son Norman moved there. And many of these buyers were buying up, moving to a better class of rowhouse than the house they had lived in before. For example, accountant Percy Shores had been living in a 14-foot row at 217 North Linwood Avenue in East Baltimore. But like the working-class buyers, many of the white-collar buyers needed help from building and loans: 90 percent of them took out mortgages. As in East Baltimore, Gallagher posted a bond to secure the loan when a buyer's loan-to-value ratio was high.

Such was the case when Henry Singewald bought a Gallagher home on Howard Street in 1919 for $3,850. But Singewald's daylight house did not have a front yard and it was mixed in with other two-bay wide houses with the older three-room-deep floor plan of earlier decades. Gallagher retained this cautious pattern of development—mixing true daylight houses with those of more traditional plan—in the several other areas around the city where he built blocks of homes in the late teens. Each of these parcels faced along a wide main road near a park, and it was on that face Gallagher constructed the 20-foot-wide new daylight houses.

In a small development facing Clifton Park, Gallagher experimented with six 20-foot-wide daylight homes priced at $2,650 each in 1916, while the 157 other houses, which sold for $1,700, were traditional 13-foot-wide, three-room-deep houses. In Henry Singewald's development on Howard Street, out of the 38 houses built between 1917 and 1919, only twelve were true daylights; the remainder, at 14 feet wide, sold for only $2,400. At St. Clair, located along the Belair Road near Clifton Park, Gallagher built 18 daylight houses in 1919 and 1920, ranging in cost from $4,500 to $5,500; he priced the remaining 107 houses that were only 13 feet and 14 feet wide at $3,400 to $4,400. Workingmen purchased these more modest houses—brakemen, electricians, machinists, paperhangers, and policemen—many of whom were moving up from less affluent neighborhoods in East Baltimore. For them, a move directly north above North Avenue was a definite improvement in status even though the new location was still a working-class neighborhood (FIGURE 103).

In these developments, Gallagher initially used iron-spot brown brick for all the façades and put traditional white columns on the front porches. The houses he situated on the side streets retained all of the stylistic characteristics of his traditional artistic-period rows—simple flat lintels, stained-glass panels over the wide first-floor window and door, one-over-one sash, and sheet-metal cornices. Interiors looked exactly the same as in the much earlier Park Side rows: "Mantel Mirror in Parlor, and Mantel Mirror with Bookcase built-in in Library [the center stair hall area]; Shower Gas and Electric Light Fixtures; Hand Decorated Ceilings; and Beautiful Colonnade and Grille between Parlor and Library." Gallagher wanted them to appeal to the buyers of his earlier flat-fronted East Baltimore rowhouses, buyers who were ready to move up to a better neighborhood further away from the central city. Electric streetcar lines served all these new developments, which Gallagher made a point of noting in his advertisements.

On the remainder of the ten-acre 33rd Street parcel, Gallagher built red brick daylight houses with green-tile mansard roofs. For these houses he also added an exciting new feature, "the latest conservatory front architecture" otherwise known as a sun parlor (FIGURE 104). Although he and his sons had studied competitors' rows in Baltimore, Philadelphia, and Washington, their inspiration may have come from closer to home. In Guilford stood a large four-square red brick dwelling capped by a prominent hipped, green-tile roof, and with casement-windowed sunporches, each with their own green-tiled roof, extending out from three sides of the house. Gallagher's versions, the sunporch rowhouses along 33rd Street and those he built in a smaller development in northwest Baltimore, are simply miniature versions of this Guilford prototype.

As a builder of speculative housing for a much less affluent market, Gallagher made modifications that he felt were important to his prospective buyers. Although he switched to red brick, he used "tapestry bricks," a textured brick that "need never be painted," the brochure claimed. The galvanized sheets of metal used to create the Spanish-style tile roofs cost less than slates used earlier. His sun parlors were heated, connected to the living room by french doors, and had multi-pane sash windows.

Gallagher was still convinced that it was good marketing to offer differently priced houses within the same development. In the 1920s he offered true 20-foot to 22-foot-wide daylight houses on the wider streets, and narrower and less expensive versions of the same house on the lesser streets. Although only 16 feet to 18 feet wide, Gallagher forced a daylight configuration into these narrower houses by eliminating one of the front bedrooms and replacing it with the bath. Whereas a 21-foot-wide house on 33rd Street sold for $7,800 in 1922, a 17-$\frac{1}{2}$-foot-wide house two blocks north could be had for only $5,600 in the same year. Gallagher believed in the correlation between rowhouse width and purchasing power of a particular segment of the buyer market. In his sunporch houses in northwest Baltimore on Reisterstown Road near the older suburbs of Forest Park and Arlington, Gallagher offered 21-foot-wide houses in 1923 for $7,800 and 17-foot versions for $5,200, exactly the same prices as on 33rd Street. These buyers came from white-collar occupations—salesmen, clerks, and a corporate treasurer (FIGURE 105).

The English Village in the City

With the economy moving along in high gear and with profits from his earlier developments (including the completely built Hoen tract on 33rd Street), Gallagher looked north to another tract of land—the southern section of Montebello, part of the estate of the Garrett family. Gallagher had started his building career working with the Pattersons, who had made their fortune early in the nineteenth century, and now he was about to collaborate with the richest and most powerful Baltimore family of the post-Civil War era. The seller was Mary Sloan Frick Garrett Jacobs. Gallagher was wealthy, but he was not part of Mrs. Jacobs' circle, which centered around her home in Mt. Vernon Place: a monumental brownstone rowhouse designed by Stanford White for her father-in-law and enlarged by John Russell Pope.

In 1872 the popular Mary Sloan Frick had married Robert Garrett, the son of Baltimore and Ohio Railroad president John Work Garrett. The railroad had made Baltimore a major commercial city on the east coast, and the Garrett family wielded enormous influence in business, society, and the arts. In 1884 Robert succeeded his father as president of the B&O, and Mary assumed the role of leader of Baltimore Society. In addition to their city residence, the couple enjoyed a country home outside Baltimore, and a mansion-sized cottage in Newport, Rhode Island. Health problems caused Garrett to withdraw from business and his wife asked Henry Barton Jacobs, then on the medical staff of Johns Hopkins, to be her husband's personal physician. Garrett died at the age of forty-nine in 1896, leaving considerable property to his widow. Six years later Dr. Jacobs and Mary Garrett married. With residential development expanding above East 33rd Street in the early 1920s, Mary Garrett Jacobs decided it was time to sell off her land holdings

At that time commercial banks rarely lent money for the acquisition of unimproved land. As a result, many estate owners offered developers what was called a "purchase money mortgage"—the seller financed the sale and received incremental mortgage payments from the buyer, with the balance due in a few years. On June 21, 1923, Gallagher bought a 48.4-acre parcel (known as tract #1) from Mrs. Jacobs for $146,299; he made a down payment of only $5,000. The next payment of $31,332 was due in January 1924. The balance was to be paid in three installments of $35,824.75, each over the next three years. Interest on the unpaid principal was 5 percent, payable semiannually. In return for the initial $31,000 payment, Gallagher would get a deed that held a vendor's lien for the deferred payments. This meant that Gallagher did not have to wait until the next $35,000 installment had been paid to get portions of land released to him. Mrs. Jacobs released one acre with every $4,000 of principal Gallagher paid.[21] Gallagher then sought construction financing from his bank; it would not lend money against land that the developer did not own free and clear. Since banks did not want to take a subordinate position behind the landowner, they often requested that the landowner take a second position on the loan, so that the bank could lend the developer the funds needed to build. In many cases landowners agreed, since they realized that without construction financing, developers could not build and sell houses and thus repay the original loan. Mrs. Jacobs was unwilling to do this. Instead, she allowed Gallagher to buy the land in increments. With each acre paid off and in his name, the bank would be willing to lend construction funds. At this time Gallagher also took an option on the remaining forty-three acres of the estate, which he purchased less than a year later for close to $130,000 on almost exactly the same terms. Gallagher rounded out the parcel by buying a six-acre piece from Ida Hoen, the daughter of August Hoen, from whom he had purchased the East 33rd Street tract in 1915.

The original 1,400-acre Jacobs estate had been thickly wooded, and Gallagher faced huge site development costs (FIGURE 106). Clearing and grading totaled more than $106,000. The expense dramatically reduced the amount of capital he had left for construction, so he asked Mrs. Jacobs to cut his yearly mortgage payments in half and extend the payment period. She refused, explaining that she was counting on Gallagher's payments to satisfy other business commitments. In December 1925, Gallagher asked her to settle early. "We contemplate developing a large portion of Tract Number One during the coming year which will require considerable capital; we would prefer to have the Tract free of all liens." He paid off the balance on January 1, 1926, obtained further construction financing, and moved ahead with the project.

At the time of the initial purchase in 1923, the *Sun* reported, "Mr. Gallagher has not definitely decided upon the type of home he intends to build on the new tract. It is his desire to build something a little out of the ordinary but within the limit of the average homeseeker's pocketbook." Gallagher named the new development Ednor Gardens, in honor of his sons Edward and Norman (combining the first syllables of their names), who developed a radically different design for these houses.[22] The Gallaghers decided to emulate the high-style English houses found in Baltimore's wealthier suburbs, but to do so in smaller versions that would only cost half as much; their English-style rows would be affordable.

Edward Gallagher Jr., came up with a number of daring ideas that went well beyond those of the more expensive group homes, only a few of which in the greater Guilford area had followed the English tradition of combining brick, stucco, and half timbering. Young Gallagher's bold designs called for various combinations of materials, picturesque rooflines, prominent chimneys, sunporches, and a heavy reliance on stone (found on the site), with the result that his rows had an especially English feel. The firm's advertising brochures made the most of this romantic appeal: "With the atmosphere of old England in their architecture, this group of English type homes bids you most cordially to consider a home in Ednor Gardens."

The first row of houses in Ednor Gardens opened in 1925 at the height of the housing boom. It went up along East 36th Street opposite Venable Park, and represented the most conservative houses in the development—random ashlar brownstone, low shingled mansards intersected by occasional cross-gables and a bold chimney stack, wide sunporches, and arched entryways. The extensive blasting required to remove the ledges during the grading and foundation work had produced both a black and a tan stone, and the Gallaghers decided to use this for foundations, first-floor walls, and the retaining walls that created the terraced lawn effect.

Taking cues from some of the Roland Park and Guilford houses, and because of the rocky terrain, the Gallaghers sited the first Ednor Gardens rows seven to ten feet above grade, creating landscaped terraces extending down to the sidewalk, with "artistically planted shrubbery" (FIGURE 107). This feature gave the rows a prominence most others in Baltimore lacked, and the lush landscaping added to the picturesque qualities. The higher grade also made possible a walkout basement at the rear of the houses and a single-bay garage. There had been a few built-in garages in some of the English-style rows at the edge of Roland Park but Gallagher was probably the first to introduce them on a large scale. More common were detached garages opening off alleyways, generally erected by homeowners some years after buying their house. At Ednor Gardens the 9-1/2-foot-wide garage bay left plenty of space for the laundry, a bathroom, and the furnace room at basement level. And under the sunporch jutting out at the front of the house lay a spare bedroom.

Edward Gallagher Jr., achieved a village-like atmosphere by giving the façades in each row varied rooflines and window arrangements, thus emphasizing the individuality of every house. Above each front sunporch was either a cross-gable or gambrel-roofed second story. Paired or triple sash windows set within the gable made the master bedroom light and airy. In some rows Gallagher paired the gabled or gambrel roofs, in others he seemingly placed them at random. The rough-faced dark grey, black, or tan stone of the first story vividly contrasted with the white stucco and dark grey roof above. The stone masonry, executed in a coursed ashlar, included a keystoned Roman arch over each front door. Corner columns framed the tall arts-and-crafts style casement windows in the sunporch. A slit attic vent mimicked English cottage attic windows; the chimneystacks running up the front between houses also contributed to the English aura. The Gallaghers built houses in this stone-and-stucco English style at Ednor Gardens from 1925 to 1928. In 1929 they switched to "Normandy Style cottages," again emulating more expensive suburban houses (FIGURES 108 AND 109). The new design proved cheaper to build because the first-floor façade was in brick rather than stone, and simple entry porches had replaced the large sun parlors. The houses still had cross-gables and gambrels, but the stuccowork was more colorful, enhanced by half-timbering and randomly scattered decorative brickwork.

The rowhouses in Ednor Gardens were distinct from others the Gallaghers had built: all streets were equally desirable and all the rowhouses were the same size—20 feet wide by 36 feet deep. Compared to their upscale counterparts at Guilford, the first Ednor Gardens houses were a bargain: $9,850 with a $120 ground rent. All buyers but one had white-collar occupations—business owners, chemists, a contractor, newspaperman, engineer, and florist—the exception being a marble worker who had lived in a Gallagher house on North Lakewood Avenue. They also relocated from good addresses: the Emersonian and Gilman Apartments, North Charles Street, and East 33rd Street.

The houses in Ednor Gardens sold quickly. The net profit/loss on the first twenty-seven houses on East 36th Street was similar to that Gallagher received from the sale of earlier houses: a 6 percent loss on house sales alone, and a 13 percent profit overall. The lower profit (he had been netting 30 to 40 percent) was a result of the high number of fee-simple purchases (for an extra $2,000 there would be no ground rent), a practice common among buyers of expensive houses. In his very best year, 1924, he also built 276 moderately priced houses at a cost of $1,221,562, and netted an overall profit of 33 percent. The economics of rowhouse building had changed somewhat. Although the lion's share of his profit still came from the sale of the ground rents, the unusual demand for housing in the 1920s allowed him to raise purchase prices. As a result, he averaged a 5 percent profit on the sale of the houses alone instead of the usual 5 percent loss. The financial health of his company improved as a result: in 1918 he had had assets of $174,815; by 1929 they had increased to $1.3 million.

Transit and the Automobile

One of the major changes to occur in the 1920s came about with the advent of the automobile. Since 1915 the automobile page had been a standard feature in the Sunday *Sun*. Usually next to the sports page, it ran stories on specific models of cars, mechanical advice, and a great many automobile and tire ads. A decade later it filled four pages and had a regular column, "News from Automobile Row," featuring the major car dealerships. A Chrysler Touring Car sold for $895; the much more affordable Ford Model T was priced at less than $300.[24] As car prices dropped, more middle-class householders came to consider the car a necessity and bought one. The Gallaghers understood this when they built Ednor Gardens; for the first time, a Gallagher site lacked public transit access—heretofore a major prerequisite for development—and it was twelve blocks to the main shopping area at Greenmount and 33rd Street. The Gallaghers included basement garages in the design of every house (FIGURE 110). They also paid for a bus to transport residents of Ednor Gardens back and forth to the shopping area at Greenmount and 33rd and the streetcar stop. The same bus met prospective buyers and drove them to the model unit.[23]

Baltimore's only electric streetcar company had no plans to offer service to Gallagher's neighborhood. Hurt by its own over-extension and the city's refusal to increase the nickel fare, the struggling United Railways could not afford to expand service. Some years earlier property owners along Liberty Heights Avenue, after pleading unsuccessfully to have a new line built to that region had deposited $32,500 as a guarantee against loss; and United built a line for $100,000. Their ploy worked and the sixteen acres that had failed to find a buyer at $8,500 soon sold for $18,000. But few neighborhoods could afford to make such an offer, and indeed the ailing company was not in a position to build. In 1925 it even refused to extend service to the affluent Homeland. United Railways executives had believed early on that automobiles would be used only for business purposes, not by households. But they were proven wrong by the facts. As early as 1921 the number of building permits for garages outstripped those for houses. Between 1920 and 1940 car registrations tripled, from 50,000 to 150,000.[25]

The success of Ednor Gardens was testimony to the Gallaghers' prescient view of the automobile's use. The English style houses there also spurred other large-scale builders to create "new and most pretentious developments of English group homes." To the west, James Keelty built English-style rows (priced at $7,000 each) in Wildwood, his large-scale development adjacent to "the beautiful Gwynns Falls Park," and slightly smaller versions (priced at $4,500 to $5,450) in Lyndhurst (FIGURE 111). Ephraim Macht's Welsh Construction Company built stuccoed, detached "English Type Homes" in Nottingham and Group Homes in Burleith, off Liberty Heights Road in West Baltimore. Smaller companies erected groups of English rows near Windsor Hills and Irvington on the west side, out the York Road beyond Guilford to the north, and, to a much lesser degree, in northeast Baltimore. But unlike Ednor Gardens, these projects targeted more moderate-income families, with houses priced in the $4,000 to $5,000 range; none equaled Ednor Gardens in size or brand-name identification. Ednor Gardens would remain the most clearly identified village of English style homes in Baltimore.

Zoning

Gallagher and his competitors had more than land and building costs and selling prices to worry about in the 1920s. After many attempts a city zoning ordinance had passed and, although immediately challenged, it threatened for the first time to limit where rowhouse developers could build. When Gallagher bought the first of the Jacobs tracts in 1923, it was designated with the letter "E" on the city's zoning map, meaning the developer could only build detached homes on the property. Up in arms, developers circulated among themselves a pamphlet entitled "How Zoning Will Reduce Present and Future Real Estate Values" (published in Philadelphia in 1922), warning of the dangers of zoning: "zoning is an imported idea. It came from Europe with the label on it—Made in Germany.... [In] attempting to shoot a few offenders such as owners of offensive garages, undesirable motion picture theatres or objectionable factories, [supporters of zoning] are using a gun loaded with buckshot that will hit many innocent bystanders."

Land-use regulations had been tried before in Baltimore, but without success. In 1890 a builder applied for a permit to construct six three-story houses and was refused on the grounds that the permit could be denied if the building would depreciate the surrounding property. A court ruled in the builder's favor, saying the city council had no power to pass such an ordinance. For the most part exclusionary ordinances failed as well, but efforts to pass them foreshadowed the zoning restrictions on rows that were enacted three decades later.[26]

The impetus for zoning came from an unexpected source: suburban residents. Suburban development encouraged a class segregation that had previously been almost imperceptible. It allowed an informal regulation; families could build near others of "their kind." This in turn spawned an architectural and economic homogeneity that suburbanites sought to maintain. The 1910 construction of six pairs of semi-detached houses in affluent Forest Park prompted the suburb's civic improvement association to petition the Maryland legislature for relief. The residents explained to the legislature that rowhouses presented a fire and health hazard. An assistant health commissioner of Baltimore City even testified that two-story brick rowhouses would drive up the mortality rate. All this rhetoric was simply the pretext to ensure a uniquely upper- and middle-class prerogative—the protection of property values. The legislature in 1912 responded with a law prohibiting row construction in the suburbs. Three years later the Maryland Court of Appeals declared the law unconstitutional and expressed its disapproval of the intent of the law to segregate on the basis of class. The residents of Forest Park responded by banding together to buy a parcel from a builder who had intended to build rows; the new owners subdivided the property for cottages, "to sell them to persons known to the community to be of the right sort."[27]

The rowhouse became the whipping boy of real estate advertising. The marketing tactics of some suburban developers boldly attacked the traditional concept or rowhouse living. "Do you live in a tunnel?" asked the headline in 1909 for Alissa Terraces off Harford Road. Walbrook's Beulah Villas announced that its domain was "one place where brick rows cannot invade." The developers also pronounced that temperatures were 10 percent cooler in Walbrook than in the city. Other advertisements stressed the healthful, rural nature of various suburbs, noting that "people lived in these parts because higher ideals may often be attained here." Ads for West Arlington noted the elevation, 250 feet above sea level.[28]

An annexation in 1918 increased the area of Baltimore City by fifty square miles and drew the battle lines anew; most of the new land was vacant, which meant that the development potential was enormous. City managers, led by Mayor James Preston, were determined that the development should be detached houses, not rows: "The row of houses is always unwelcome in the community based on the cottage plan. Such an invasion is invariably followed by a conspicuous display of "for sale" signs and consequent drop in real estate value."[29] Preston even attacked one of Gallagher's finest rows—in the 700 block of East 33rd Street, built in 1917—, which he condescendingly called, "residences entirely inadequate for the dignity and beauty and cost of the street."[30] But in 1917, Gallagher could build what he wanted and what he knew his customers wanted, regardless of Preston's assessment. He went on to build sunparlor houses with green tiled roofs in the 800 block of East 33rd a few years later.

Meanwhile Baltimore's zoning commission was formed, and it hired Edward Murray Bassett, the leading force behind New York City's 1916 zoning ordinance, to help write its ordinance. His opinion of rowhousing was uncompromising: "The first advantage to Baltimore from zoning . . . is protection for suburban detached houses. You have beautiful suburbs here. These houses which have ground all around them need protection against block houses and multi-family houses." Bassett created separate rowhouse and cottage districts based on density. Zones *A*, *B*, *C*, and *D* permitted rowhouses, but *E* and *F*, which included most of the newly annexed land, permitted only detached and semi-detached houses. Apartment were restricted but allowed in affluent areas like Druid Hill, Lake Drive, and Charles Street.[31]

The heated debate left a great deal of uncertainty about the constitutionality of Baltimore's first zoning ordinance in 1923, and many builders decided that the zoning maps were not necessarily enforceable. Frank Novak's parcel to the east of Ednor Gardens (what would become Lakeside) had an *E* designation, meaning a density of no more than sixteen houses per acre and all houses had to have two sideyards, each not less than 10 feet wide. This fit in with his plans because he wanted to build cottages. It was his first major effort at detached housing. Gallagher's Jacob tract was also labeled *E*, but he was determined to stick with building rowhouses. On January 14, 1924, the Board of Zoning Appeals passed twelve ordinances proposing changes in classification in small sections of the city, of which the city council approved five. The Jacobs Tract went from *E* to *D*, which meant that Gallagher could build 40 houses per acre, with no sideyard requirement. No written record of Gallagher's efforts to secure the zoning change exists in the company's archives, but he was a major builder with political influence.

The zoning laws also affected other aspects of city life. All Baltimore neighborhoods had long enjoyed some mix of uses—with a retail section, movie houses, schools, and apartments—even including the suburban villa developments like Roland Park; but under the new zoning regulations, with a *D* classification, Ednor Gardens could not have corner stores within the development. In new developments mixed use of land was outlawed; in older districts, existing businesses were grandfathered in and allowed to remain. For the residents of Ednor Gardens the nearest shopping district was at Greenmount and 33rd Street, a long walk. The *Sun* touted this as progress: "a man can buy a house secure in the knowledge that his property value will not be destroyed by the encroachment of business."[32] But for entire regions of the city it meant an end to the village quality of going around the corner for groceries or a haircut. City officials wanted separate and distinct commercial nodes with newsstands, drugstores, movies, and groceries concentrated together. Their decision hastened the age of the automobile.

Over the next few years the Zoning Board of Appeals unanimously rejected any and all plans for "solid" rows of houses in cottage districts, no matter how many rowhouses already existed in the particular suburb. Stores in residential areas became a matter of discretion; one woman was allowed a confectionary in her basement while another man was denied a grocery on the first floor of his house even though twenty-seven residents consented to the use; a movie house with a bowling alley was rejected for the 2400 block of St. Paul Street. Uses guaranteed to draw in protesters were applications for gas stations and household garages; even these facilities for homeowners' cars, ironically, were banished from the neighborhood (FIGURE 111).[33]

Restrictive covenants, a close cousin of zoning, which affected homebuyers more than builders, also came into play around this time. Families had always been allowed to alter their houses to suit their tastes, but generally most houses in any one row looked identical for several years after construction. Then owners began to individualize them, some slowly, others rapidly. By the mid-1920s and the 1930s, builders were attaching restrictive covenants to the sale of rowhouses, which contained provisions to ensure that a development retain the uniformity of the original row, at least for a period of time. The Gallaghers stipulated in their 1936 covenants that the houses in the 900 block of East 37th Street remain in their original condition including the paint color for ten years. Porches could not be built above the second-floor windowsills nor could an addition be built in front of the house extending further than the original porch. The front setback had to be kept as a lawn in perpetuity. Builders almost unanimously accepted the premise that this sort of covenant sustained and raised property values. As a 1926 Roland Park Company advertisement explained to prospective purchasers, the value of land in Guilford was protected by Guilford restrictions and would not be affected by the court decision that had lately nullified the city's zoning ordinance.[34] A five percent increase in lot prices in that garden suburb was evidence of the power of the covenant.

Restrictive covenants also were used to enforce segregation. Whereas individualized exteriors might weaken the sales price of nearby houses, and the introduction of a gas station might be a curse on property values, a black resident moving into the neighborhood was seen as the death knell. In 1921 C. Arthur Eby advised members of his Maryland Avenue Association, "We have some hope that in the new zoning ordinance a measure protecting purely white neighborhoods from a negro invasion will be incorporated." When Robert Banborg moved into 1009 McDonough Street, an all white block in 1922, the neighbors attacked his home. About the same time sixty residents on Harlem Avenue petitioned Mayor Broening to enforce some kind of legal order that would keep blacks out of their neighborhood. When the Harlem Avenue Christian Church was sold to blacks, white owners in the neighborhood sold their houses to blacks and left the area. Tensions worsened when in 1925 a crowd of 500 persons (half of them female) assaulted a white man who had leased property to a black on Lamont Avenue.[35]

Escalating racial tensions between black and white residents in the 1920s stemmed from the arrival of a great number of blacks, who had migrated to Baltimore from Southern rural farms, lured by the promise of higher factory wages and year-round work. The city's African-American sections, already heavily populated, were quickly overfilled as the 1910 black population of 85,000 rose to 108,000 by 1920. Many white residents, especially those in the middle class, were already nervous because the U.S. Supreme Court had thrown out Baltimore's segregation law in 1917, and blacks were crossing the city's defacto racial boundaries. Much to the regret of Eby and many others, the city's new zoning ordinance was silent on the issue of race.

Some neighborhood associations responded by adopting even more restrictive covenants. Residents of Lanvale Street from Mount Royal Avenue to Eutaw Place, for example, signed an agreement in which neither they nor any other persons to whom their property might pass would sell to blacks. To their relief, in 1924, the Maryland Court of Appeals ruled that a covenant barring blacks was binding on all residents and constitutional. Sellers and agents alike commonly gave a homebuyer a page of restrictions at the time of sale. The restrictive covenant remained the mainstay of segregation efforts until after World War II. A typical restriction read: "at no time shall the land included in this lease, or any part thereof, or any building erected thereon, be occupied by any negro or person of negro extraction."

Large numbers of white residents left the central city nonetheless. And as whites moved to newer rowhouses or the suburbs, blacks began renting or purchasing the older houses. Seldom did blacks move into newly constructed homes; it was rare to see the 1924 announcement that a parcel on North Gilmor Street was acquired to become the site of 30 "porch front dwellings for negroes." But then Gilmor Street was in the path of black expansion, so the only value it had was for black housing. The purchasers still had to rely on their own network of building and loans, few other institutions would lend money to blacks who wished to buy homes or commercial properties.[36]

A Depressed Rowhouse Market in the 1930s

The 1929 stock market crash had little immediate impact on Baltimore's economy—building went on for nearly a year. By late 1930, however, the production of machinery, petroleum products, and clothing had plunged 20 to 40 percent, throwing many factory employees out of work. And by 1932, the unemployment rate had risen to 19 percent; textile, steel, clothing, and the construction sectors were hit especially hard.[37] The Gallaghers continued building in Ednor Gardens, but they reduced the number of houses they constructed in one year—from 68 in 1929 to 33 in 1930, and 30 in 1931. Sales declined too: 54 houses in 1930, 31 in 1931, and, astonishingly, none between 1932 and 1935. It seems a sad close to a highly successful, forty-eight year development career. Edward J. Gallagher died on January 19, 1933, and the Edward J. Gallagher Realty Company suspended operations to wait out the Depression. The Jacobs tracts sat idle. (Fueled by the initial success of Ednor Gardens, Gallagher had purchased a third tract of twenty-eight acres from Mrs. Jacobs for $139,455 in May 1929. Three payments of $37,151 came due in the early 1930s.)

In Baltimore as nationwide, banks refused to make new real estate loans or refinance old ones, and called in loans for immediate repayment. The tactic led to collapsing markets and caused many banks to fail, which in turn meant that the depositors lost their savings and were bankrupt. Without available financing, real estate values plummeted. By 1933, half of all mortgages in America were in default; housing starts dropped to 93,000 in 1933, 90 percent below the high of 937,000 in 1925.[38] The federal government stepped in to reorganize and stabilize the nation's savings and loans, which had lent $15 billion in home mortgages during the 1920s. The Home Owners' Loan Corporation, created in 1933, refinanced more than $3 billion of mortgages and introduced the self-amortizing fifteen-year loan. It was a concept unfamiliar to most Americans, but one well known to owners of Baltimore's rowhouses. The self-amortizing term loan was quite similar to arrangements many local building and loans had used for decades: a 90 percent loan-to-value ratio, constant loan payments, and a 20-year repayment schedule.

The Federal Housing Administration (FHA) became the main financing vehicle for buyers and saved the homebuilding industry in Baltimore and the rest of the nation. Without it, large-scale developers would have been unable to sell houses in volume as they had done before. Edward Gallagher Jr., explained the terms to a prospective customer:

PURCHASE PRICE	$5,000
CASH DOWN	$ 700
BALANCE BY A LOAN	$4,300
FHA LOAN—20 YEAR PLAN	
LOAN $4,300 @ 6.81% A.P.R.	$ 29.28 per month
ANNUAL EXPENSES	
TAXES (1938)	$ 145.95
GROUND RENT	$ 90.00
WATER—METERED	
INSURANCE—9 POINT POLICY	
ON $4,300 @ $0.20 PER YEAR	$ 8.60
TOTAL ANNUAL EXPENSES	$ 244.55
	or $ 20.38 per month
TOTAL MONTHLY PAYMENT	$ 49.66

The fifteen-year direct reduction method required $1,000 cash down with a $33.76 payment per month with the same expenses. A prepayment penalty of 1 percent of the original loan amount was paid if the homeowner paid off the loan principal during the first eighteen years. Only a very few buyers were able to pay the purchase price in cash, and so the FHA 15-year and 20-year mortgages were widespread. The terms were basically no different from the ones Wesolowski had secured from Kosciuszko Building and Loan twenty-five years earlier. The $49.66 monthly payment was a realistic amount for a working man. In addition, the payments were constant and the loan could not be called. With federally insured mortgages, the FHA became a standardized financing mechanism for housing in Baltimore as well as the rest of the United States.

After the Gallaghers resumed business in 1936, homebuyers purchased the rest of the Ednor Gardens houses with government-backed loans. Only the names of the company's two favorite building and loans had changed: Sterling Building and Loan Association became the Sterling Federal Savings and Loan and Patterson Park became Liberty Federal Savings and Loan, the word "federal" reflecting their administration of FHA loans. Yet FHA underwriting guidelines strongly favored single-family houses in the suburbs over central city housing, a preference that only become stricter in the late 1930s. The rowhouse was deemed an outdated and undesirable dwelling type. In 1939, when the FHA set a minimum standard for lot size, setback, and house width, the 16-foot rowhouse was eliminated from eligibility for loan guarantees. According to the *Baltimore Real Estate News* of November 1938, Congress wanted to just stimulate new construction and not put the government in the position of insuring mortgages as a means of refinancing all mortgages on existing homes.

During the depression years the Gallagher firm had undergone changes. Sons Edward and Norman Gallagher took over the business upon the death of their father, who had left an estate appraised at just over one million dollars, mostly stocks and land holdings. They waited for the economy to improve before recommencing building in Ednor Gardens. In the meantime, property values plummeted. All the Ednor Gardens homes lost more than 50 percent of their original value. Houses in the 3600 block of Rexmere Road, which originally sold for $8,250 in 1928, resold in 1939 for $4,000.

Builders recognized that the homebuyer market had virtually evaporated: only 171 properties sold in all of Baltimore during 1933. Similar to other builders, James Keelty rented rather than sold as many as 300 of his houses, with a policy of applying the rent toward an eventual down payment. Many of the Gallaghers' customers were also hard hit. Thomas Parker who lived at 3315 Elmora Avenue fell behind on his mortgage payments and from 1937 to 1943 was continually in arrears. Since he often acted as a guarantor for his customer's loans, Edward Gallagher Jr., went to see Parker at his home to try to work out an arrangement. Parker's reply to a late payment notice summed up the troubles every homeowner faced: "I would glady [sic] increase my payments if I had imployment [sic] but I have bin [sic] out of work since Dec. 1." Parker eventually lost the house.

Thomas Parker, though, was more the exception locally than the rule locally: mortgagees in Baltimore fared better than those elsewhere in the country, largely because so many of the buyers rented the ground on which their houses were built. Land value was excluded from the total mortgage amount, and thus Baltimore homeowners did not have the large monthly mortgage payment obligation that their counterparts in other cities faced. Most were able to come up with the ground rent money, and builders did not have to take back many houses.[39]

The New Style: American Neocolonial

Builder James Keelty, who during the depression resorted to renting his newly built rowhouses with an option to buy, was one of the few developers to continue to build during these years. In 1924 he had purchased a 200-acre tract in Dumbarton Farms, a Baltimore County estate just a few blocks north of the city line (and thus beyond the reach of the zoning commission). He renamed it Rodgers Forge, after a long-time smithy located on a corner of the property, and in 1932 began building rowhouses there. Some rows he constructed in the English and Norman styles, similar to those he had built at Wildwood in the last few years, but for others he emulated the newly fashionable red brick American neocolonial style, a popular suburban house type being built at the Roland Park Company's Homeland, a half-mile south of Rodgers Forge.[40]

Homeland's architecture was influenced by happenings in Williamsburg, Virginia, an almost forgotten town in the southeastern reaches of that state. There, in 1926, Standard Oil heir John D. Rockefeller Jr., began acquiring properties in the pre-Revolutionary capital of the Virginia colony, with an eye to preserving a part of the nation's colonial heritage. In the 1920s the town was relatively small, its isolation having discouraged much in the way of economic advance or industrialization. By 1935 his staff had restored sixty-six buildings to their eighteenth-century form, and re-created forty-four others on their original foundations. National magazines, such as *Architectural Record*, published many laudatory articles about the restoration and Americans watched closely. Rockefeller's work at Williamsburg generated a revived interest in America's colonial architecture, which offered a comfortable alternative to contemporary European-inspired modernism. Nationwide, architects and builders alike leaped to create Early American designs for houses, banks, churches, and college buildings, offering traditional red brick structures, symmetrical Georgian style plans, pedimented doorways, white trim and shutters, and pitched gable roofs. These were often explicitly described as being "the Williams-burg type of architecture."

In Baltimore, James Keelty built a large house for himself in Homeland; directing his architect to create a massive brick colonial house modeled on Carter's Grove near Williamsburg.[41] Keelty's "Early American" rows at Rodgers Forge, sold for much less than their freestanding counterparts at Homeland, but had many similar features: red brick (at Rodgers Forge a mix of regular and glazed bricks laid in running bond); elaborate, white-painted neocolonial doorways (with broken pediments, broken scroll pediments, or segmental pediments supported by paneled pilasters); bay windows framed in fluted pilasters; multi-pane sash with white shutters; dormer windows on some units; brickwork angle quoins; and half-round lunettes set in the attic story in units with their gable ends to the street (FIGURE 113). Like the rows the Gallaghers had been building at Ednor Gardens, Keelty gave the Rodgers Forge rows deep front lawns and wide rear alleyways, for access to backyards or for parking. Unlike the Gallaghers' houses, Keelty's rows did not include built-in garages. By the 1930s cars had so increased in size that a basement garage would have used up considerably more space, leaving an insufficient area for the increasingly popular recreation or clubroom. Instead Keelty built an "individual garage" at the rear of the lot, opening onto the alley.

Keelty began offering Rodgers Forge homes for sale in the summer of 1934. He never mentioned a price in his ads (the end units sold for $4,500 and inside units for $3,400), but instead stressed that in this community, "just across the city line [with] low county taxes [and] 1 car fare...these beautiful Colonial homes have each been individually designed with a view to suiting the tastes of the most discriminating of buyers. Built with a view to the future." Keelty chose the right style that had the most appeal among buyers. Rodgers Forge became one of the most successful rowhouse communities in Baltimore, attracting white-collar, young professional buyers.[42]

Keelty's successful adoption of the neocolonial style quickly influenced other rowhouse builders. In 1938 the Gallaghers abandoned the English style in Ednor Gardens and switched to neocolonial for the remainder of the lots (FIGURE 114). Those that went up in the 3700 blocks of Kimble and Yolando Roads were more modest colonials than Keelty's, but they had such identifiable neocolonial characteristics as red brick, white trim, pedimented entranceways, and six-over-six sash. Besides being a new style preferred by homebuyers, the neocolonial vocabulary was also a cost-saving design for builders because it did not require the English style's elaborate materials, rooflines, and trim.

The Gallaghers also tried their hands at building single-family houses in Ednor Gardens in 1936; it was an experiment undertaken by force. Frank Novak, long considered a major rowhouse builder, had built detached cottages in accordance with zoning as early as the 1920s in Lakeside, a large tract of land southeast of Ednor Gardens; Novak objected to the zoning variance the senior Gallagher secured for Ednor Gardens in 1924. Convinced that the Ednor Gardens rows devalued Lakeside, Novak took the Gallaghers to court. He won the suit in the early 1930s, and forced the firm to build cottages on the remaining acreage that adjoined Lakeside. It was ironic that Novak, who was the recognized king of Baltimore rowhouse builders, suddenly became a spokesperson in favor of detached homes.[43]

The Gallaghers labeled their detached house "The Bride's Cottage," and boasted that each was "large enough for spacious, luxurious living— small enough and scientifically arranged to make the 'art of keeping house' a joyous adventure." Most had a daylight floor plan, with the stairhall and living room in the front of the house, the kitchen and dining room at the rear; a few had a center hall plan. The brochures for both highlighted the "Colonial stairway," the "real open fireplace and mantel" in the living room, and "wide, many-paned windows." The Gallaghers furnished the model house with Federal style furniture, lighting fixtures, and wallpaper, as well as Oriental-style rugs, and in true Gallagher fashion promoted the homes as "designed to be owned and enjoyed by the family to whom a moderate first cost is essential." In 1936 these brick and brick-and-frame neocolonials could be purchased "for as little as $6,450," his advertisements boasted. Similar houses in the Roland Park Company's original Northwood, their next development after Homeland, *started* at $7,750 and brick neocolonials in the exclusive suburb of Ruxton were priced in the neighborhood of $15,000.

Henry Singewald moved into a cottage like this when, after nearly a decade, his family outgrew their Gallagher-built daylight house on Howard Street. His was a Dutch neocolonial residence on Atwick Road, in a small development bordering the oldest section of Roland Park. The 1920s had been a prosperous time for him; he had a secure position with the Fidelity Trust Company and in 1926 helped organize the Real Estate Trust Company, which he served as Vice-President-Secretary. He had higher aspirations for his family than another rowhouse. If he was too frugal to buy in Roland Park or Homeland, he could still live next door. His house had a gambrel roof, a brick and stucco façade, a detached garage, and stood on an eighth-acre of land. The house's additional space allowed

Singewald room for his hobbies of photography and model trains; he set up a darkroom in the basement and shared the full-height attic space with his daughters. One half was devoted to model train gardens, the other to dolls and dollhouses. Singewald could have moved to Ednor Gardens, as well, but he had reached a new social level. A rowhouse was not befitting a banker of his income and professional stature. Still, rowhouses made up the vast majority of new housing built in both the city and expanding suburbs in the late 1930s and 1940s.

By 1940 manufacturing was again booming, a result of the war in Europe, and workers had money to buy houses. Indicative of the strong economy, plant investment amounted to $92 million, with 40,000 new personnel employed chiefly at the Glenn L. Martin aircraft plant and the shipbuilding division of Bethlehem Steel. (By the end of 1942 an additional 30,000 would be hired.) To accommodate the new buying power of these consumers, most of whom needed a house to live in, rowhouse builders increased their production accordingly.[44] Homebuilding nationwide regained its pre-depression-era vitality. Builders could afford to outfit their rowhouses with more pretentious colonial design features, which gave the rows a more handsome and substantial appearance. They eschewed maintenance-free, iron-spot or tapestry brick, and instead chose "Homewood Colonial Brick." Doorways were framed with pedimented, broken-pedimented, or flat entablatures supported by fluted pilasters. Elegant bay windows graced many living rooms. The wider end units usually had a front porch. Other colonial touches included angle quoins, half-moon or ocular attic vents, columned porches, and slate roofs (FIGURE 115).

Inside, the neocolonial daylight rowhouse of 1940 offered a basement "Club Room beautifully decorated in real knotty pine with Johns-Manville asphalt tile floor, equivalent to another living room for entertaining and fun!" According to the advertisement, the clubroom came equipped "complete with lavatory, toilet, and shower" to make entertaining even easier, or to provide an extra bedroom. Behind a nearby door, at least in a Gallagher-built house, sat "the American Radiator oil-burning heating plant with its summer and winter hook-up, its beautiful modern finish, [and] the Thrush circulator—all designed for marvelous efficiency and economy." (The "more costly built-in radiation" gave all rooms extra space.) The houses boasted "an abundance of electric outlets," and a buyer was told, "you do not need to buy even an electric bulb when you move in—nor linoleum for the kitchen floor."[45] The Gallagher brothers built 276 neocolonial houses in Ednor Gardens between 1940 and 1943, at which point wartime restrictions kept them from continuing. Priced between $3,980 and $4,790, the houses represented the middle tier of rowhouse choices. Other such houses located further from the city, along the major arteries, could be bought for as little as $3,390, and those in the greater Northwood area, along Loch Raven Boulevard, which had a higher social profile, from $4,150 and up.

Because corner stores were no longer a part of the rowhouse developments built after 1920, savvy developers followed the concept pioneered by the Roland Park Company back in 1894 and began to build shopping centers nearby or within their new automobile suburbs. Baltimore's first supermarket—a Food Fair—opened in 1936 on the York Road at 36th Street, a few blocks west of Ednor Gardens. A few years later the Roland Park Company opened the Northwood Shopping Center, the city's first modern shopping block—with food store, department store, movie theater, and large parking lot—to serve the company's last major development, Northwood, which opened in 1931 about a mile east of Guilford and Homeland (FIGURE 116). Designed to offer "more medium priced lots," the company developed only 25 acres of the original 526-acre tract; it sold the rest to different developers that filled street after street with neocolonial rows while noting in their advertisements that their rowhouses were "near the Northwood shopping center."[46]

Following America's entry into the war, only officially designated Defense Housing could be built. The Gallagher brothers acted quickly. Within three weeks of the bombing of Pearl Harbor they successfully petitioned the U. S. Office of Production's Division of Priorities to qualify 192 proposed units in Ednor Gardens as wartime housing since so many war workers were moving to Baltimore to work in the shipyards and aircraft factories. But when these units were completed in 1943, the Gallaghers had to stop building and wait out the war. One of the last houses built by the Gallaghers in Ednor Gardens was purchased by an individual who had previously lived in an earlier Gallagher house. This was nothing out of the ordinary; repeat buyers were commonplace. But the former address of this buyer was 515 South Glover Street, in Park Side—a house built in 1909 along one of Baltimore's last narrow alley streets. (In the story of the social mobility of Baltimore's working-class and immigrant population, the buyer could have been Bronislaw Wesolowski, who prospered and moved up to Ednor Gardens, but Wesolowski came upon hard times in the 1920s and had to move back to his old Fells Point neighborhood.) Instead, it was a second-generation Pole who was successful and decided to move up to a new house in a much better neighborhood. Dr. Michael Kozubski paid $4,775 for his new neocolonial home on Andover Road in 1942 with the help of an FHA loan. Kozubski had made the great leap from an old, predominately Polish block to one of the city's better neighborhoods in one bound. He moved to a 20-foot-wide, three-bedroom house with a one-car garage.[47]

By war's end in 1945 there was a tremendous pent-up demand for housing. All the major builders stood poised to fill their lots with new rows of neocolonial houses. In only twenty-five days in the spring of 1946, 259 rowhouses went up. Another federally sponsored housing program had been created to help homebuyers. The Servicemen's Readjustment Act of 1944, more popularly known as the GI Bill, created the Veterans Administration (VA) home loan guarantee program. It helped finance the housing boom that swept across Baltimore and the rest of America. Congress originally scheduled the home loan guarantees to expire in two years but in 1946 extended them to ten. The production of housing skyrocketed in America with five times the number of houses built in the 1950s as had gone up in the 1930s. The FHA and the VA funding put home financing within reach of families of all social classes, the money being made available through savings and loans, life insurance companies, and mutual savings banks. The amounts increased year by year with savings and loans lending $1.5 billion more in 1950 for home financing than they had in 1949.[48]

The last phase of construction in Ednor Gardens in the late 1940s included 116 neocolonial rowhouses and a handful of semi-detached cottages in the 3800 and 3900 blocks of Loch Raven Boulevard on the eastern edge of the development. The Gallaghers had no trouble selling the houses. When word circulated that Ednor Gardens was building again, inquiries flooded in. Veterans had preference and almost every sale was financed by a 4 percent GI loan. For example, GI loans financed thirty-two of the thirty-six houses in the 3900 block of Rexmere Road. Because of the demand, house prices soared. In 1949 the lowest-priced new house in Ednor Gardens sold for $10,500, and the monthly payments for a twenty-five year mortgage (based on a $2,000 down payment) stood at just over $75, which included an annual ground rent of $96.

The postwar era signaled a change in the leaders among Baltimore rowhouse builders. Ephraim Macht and James Keelty both died in 1944; the former was succeeded by his son and nephew; the latter by his sons. Frank Novak died in 1945, and his land was sold to the Machts' Welsh Construction Company. Edward and Norman Gallagher were growing tired of the building business; in 1950 they sold the rest of the Jacobs tract to other builders and retired. Although Norman's sons continued to build cottages near Ednor Gardens, by 1955 they too left the building business.

Government sponsorship of homebuilding created a change in the scale of the industry nationwide and made it possible for some firms to rapidly expand the size of their operations at their competitors' expense. By 1949 four percent of the builders in America constructed 45 percent of the homes. Such concentration occurred early in Baltimore: in June of 1946 and again in 1947, just five firms initiated three-quarters of all housing starts.[49] Rowhouse building continued in Baltimore in any area zoned for rowhouses, particularly in the northeast and northwestern sections of the city and the county beyond. Housing starts never dropped below 3,000 a year and they rose to 8,000 in 1954–1955. Builders continued offering the popular neocolonial style, which sold so well in the early 1940s. James Keelty's sons built out the original acreage of Rodgers Forge; Welsh Construction Company built some 1,000 homes a year in the late 1940s and 1950s on land they acquired in northeast Baltimore from the Frank Novak Realty Company; and the Roland Park Company completed original Northwood. But a whole new generation of younger builders created entirely new rowhouse developments along the major arteries running out of the city and into the county. In the northeast, on land that had been part of the Roland Park Company's Northwood, the Joseph Meyerhoff Company constructed homes in Walker Heights, a large development along Loch Raven Boulevard near the county line. Each house was built with a floor-to-ceiling picture window in the living room; a first-floor powder room with a mirrored wall; a chair rail lining the dining room wall; choice of inlaid kitchen linoleum; a twin basin bathroom with twin medicine cabinets; a basement ready for a clubroom conversion; an electrical circuit breaker with eight circuits (rather than former fuse box); and proximity to the Loch Raven Boulevard bus route.[50]

Loch Raven Village—the quintessential suburban rowhouse community of the 1950s—totaled 500 houses (**FIGURE 117**). In a multipage brochure of photographs, site plans, floor plans, and a bird's eye view, the developers called attention to what they believed was important to buyers.

> The village was planned as a complete community, including a new modern public grade school built on the property. A complete shopping center is planned. The homes are distinctive, in colonial style, and are built to attract people who are interested in better living standards…people who will make good neighbors…people who appreciate big lawns…winding streets… homes that have real charm. Located in pleasant country surroundings, yet providing every city convenience and modern facilities, LOCH RAVEN VILLAGE is only a 20 minute drive from City Hall! Just 4 minutes from city line.

The Wedgewood Building Company built another community, Wedgewood, "in the handsomely built Edmondson Avenue section" in West Baltimore. In 1951 a half-page ad for the development ran in the *Sun*, led by breathless, headline news:

> See Right Through the X-Ray House at Wedgewood. Just Opened!
> You have looked at homes before—but now you'll *see right through one!*
> Yes, Wedgewood brings you Baltimore's first X-Ray House—a dramatic demonstration of the quality construction that makes these homes a permanent investment of lifetime pride. Construction features, step by step, are all laid bare. You can see through walls—see through floors—see through ceilings—see through corners—see through plumbing—see through the roof! And you don't need X-ray vision to appreciate the wonderful location of Wedgewood...situated on high ground with a sweeping view...convenient to schools, churches, shopping centers... with Baltimore Transit busline just half-a-block away.

The developer, never one to miss a marketing opportunity, also added in large type, "Free Pony Rides for Children." The "6-Room All-Brick Colonial Group Homes" were priced reasonably at $8,700 ($67.70 monthly for war veterans).[51]

Several of the old business practices remained unchanged after the war. Builders used their own capital to purchase land, as banks remained reluctant to lend on raw land. Some savings and loans offered construction mortgages for 70 to 90 percent of the value of the finished project. The loan committee would look at a developer's track record, the product, and location to determine whether the project seemed sound. As in the past, money was lent essentially on the basis of a builder's reputation. The savings and loan disbursed the funds in staged payments, and the builder used his own money for the up-front costs of site engineering and legal fees. The sale of the ground rents created still remained the developers' major profit source, as well as a supply of capital for future projects. (And some developers still preferred not to sell their ground rents, thus receiving extra annual income from them).

Levittown and the Suburban Tract House

Tract houses built in the suburbs after World War II meant the end of the rowhouse. The relative low-cost of VA loans made owning one's house within reach of thousands of returning GI's. The loans could be used for the purchase of an existing or a new house, but it was a single-family detached house on a grassy lot to which most veterans and their families aspired. This dream grew out of the success of Levittown, a huge development of one-story homes on small lots, built by Levitt and Sons on Long Island between 1947 and 1950. Within a decade, the Baltimore *Sun*'s real estate pages were filled with photographs of ranchers, ramblers, and split-level houses that might come in "9 breathtaking styles" and "7 Different Floor Plans."[52]

From 1940 to 1950, Baltimore City's growth fell behind that of the surrounding county. A study in 1951 looked at 100 city residents who had moved to the county. Sixty-nine purchased a single-family residence. Twice as many had moved up from a rowhouse to a detached house, than vice versa; fewer than one-half had never owned a house before. Their reasons for leaving the city varied. Some first-time homeowners chose the county because they feared the quality of life in the city would deteriorate. Lower county taxes did not loom large as a reason because this savings was offset by the higher transportation costs of getting to work in the city. Instead, 68 percent of the respondents cited the appeal of more room, more privacy, and quieter neighborhoods in the still rural county. Only 4 percent said a change in the racial composition of their neighborhood prompted the move.[53]

The most vivid indicator of the changing nature of housing appeared in the Sunday *Sun*'s expanded real estate section: advertisements for ranchers and Cape Cods outnumbered ads for rowhouses, especially in listings for newly built structures. But there was still a market for moderate-priced rows. Ranchers in suburban Ruxton sold for $22,000 to $30,000, and those in less posh neighborhoods for $13,000 to $15,000; but three-bedroom rowhouses in many sections of the city still sold for less than $10,000, and smaller, stripped-down models for $7,000. Some builders continued to build reasonably priced rows for the working-class buyer. Yet the number of new rowhouses in the city dwindled. Developers built out all the land zoned for rowhouses and moved on to construct garden apartments and detached houses, which were in higher demand and proved more profitable. Planners decided that the rowhouse had seen its day as a successful urban dwelling and sought new ideas for ways to house the city's population, particularly growing numbers of low-income residents.

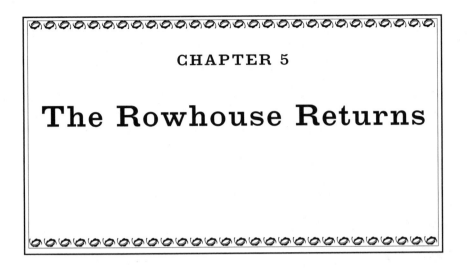

CHAPTER 5

The Rowhouse Returns

It doesn't look like public housing, and that's the whole idea. It looks like
Baltimore and that's the whole idea, too.
Phillip Mayfield, OKM Associates, architect and planner

The high-rise towers of Lafayette Courts before and during demolition in 1995 (Baltimore Sun)

TRAUGOTH SINGEWALD'S GREAT-GREAT-GRANDSON, Robert Tarring, Jr. returned to Baltimore in the early 1970s. At twenty-eight years old and having worked in New York City for a few years as a stockbroker, he sought an affordable home for his young family. Many of his childhood friends encouraged him to consider Rodgers Forge, just north of the city in Baltimore County: it was reasonably priced, conveniently located, near good schools for his five-year-old son, and was even near his parents' house in Homeland. Robert Tarring was a graduate of the University of Virginia, Thomas Jefferson's neoclassical academical village, and he knew and liked the neocolonial design of the rowhouses at Rodgers Forge. His son could play in the alley behind the house or in the nearby "tot lot" and could walk to school. There was a safe and attractive fenced-in yard and good neighbors. And he could afford the $230 monthly mortgage payment on the $33,000 house. He moved into the house in 1973 and soon after repainted the exterior trim Wedgewood green.

Rowhouse living remained an attractive and affordable option in Baltimore after 1955, yet only in the later rowhouse developments located well beyond the central city. Indeed, it was a major turn of events that occurred in Baltimore housing's history, which would enable Richard Gibson in 1997 to move into a red brick neocolonial rowhouse in Pleasant View Gardens, a new neighborhood in sight of City Hall. Gibson's daughter rides her bike on relatively traffic-free streets and walks a block to the fenced-in play yard. His wife gardens in their fenced back yard. The street-scape is serene, with all the comfort that neocolonial architecture, Williamsburg colors, wide sidewalks, and period street lighting can offer (FIGURE 118). For his three-bedroom house, Richard pays $152 a month and has available all the amenities city rowhouse life can offer—a safe neighborhood that has a community life in keeping with the scale of the street.

It was not always this way. Only a few years before, Lafayette Courts, a public housing project of tall and monolithic towers, rose on the site of Pleasant View Gardens. Such buildings stood in several sections of the city. The transition from rowhouse-centered neighborhood life for the city's low-income residents to life in high-rise apartments occurred over several decades. In Baltimore it began during the New Deal years of the 1930s and 1940s, when the U.S. Housing Authority introduced public housing there. Fifty years later, it would be declared a failure. Beginning in the mid-1990s, these anonymous towers were replaced by lower-scaled rowhouse communities that offered units for rent and for sale to low-income families. Planners and architects reestablished the importance of the street—its scale and multiple activities—to encourage the kind of social interaction that makes up successful neighborhoods. In Pleasant View Gardens, the houses are two stories and face the street, thus reinstating the use of sidewalks for pedestrian circulation and the front stoop for neighborly communication. In fact, architects did nothing more than revert to the spatial organization of the nineteenth-century American city, a successful concept long before the advent of zoning. If the middle class could enjoy living in a safe rowhouse community, with schools, sidewalks, and playgrounds nearby, then so too could Baltimore's low-income residents, such as those who had lived in the high-rise towers of Lafayette Courts, the largest public housing complex in the nation outside of Chicago and a stark symbol of the country's failed attempt to "warehouse the poor."[1]

In the 1940s, architects and planners of high-rise public housing—which was then a new form of low-income housing—considered the original "tower in the park" concept Utopian. It was a European invention, first espoused by August Perret, the French architect and engineer famous for his pioneering work in reinforced concrete. His pupil, Swiss-born architect Le Corbusier, elaborated on the concept with his *Villa Contemporaine* in 1927. Obliterating the existing street grid of the city, towers of housing were arranged in superblocks amid parklike settings that allowed every resident access to sunlight and greenery. Around 1924, Hungarian architect Marcel Breuer developed the first slab block, the form Baltimore's high rises eventually took, into a form for low-cost housing. Walter Gropius, the influential German modernist transplanted to America when he became head of Harvard's Graduate School of Design proclaimed the high rise to be "a direct embodiment of the needs of our age." The design concept took hold of the imaginations of American planners and architects starting in New York City in 1941 with the building of the East River Houses.

The high cost of land and new construction favored high-rise development—less land and less building area for higher density. Phillip Darling, director of development for the Housing Authority of Baltimore City, summed up the situation in 1952: "Slum sites have become so expensive that more dwellings per acre are needed to absorb site costs." This meant building upward to achieve density. As urban sociologist William H. Whyte noted, most urban redevelopment projects were, "in scale and spirit...the diametric opposite of the old blocks. With little variation from city to city the process was the same; not only were blocks razed but streets as well, and huge superblock projects grouped colonies of high-rise towers in abstract green space."[2]

The high-rise projects of the 1940s and 1950s were part of a modernist design experiment, which visionary architects and planners believed would have a positive impact on the urban social order. Low-income residents, most in need of assisted housing, were the reluctant subjects of the experiment. After years of total failure of the towers in the park, architects and planners came to learn that the poor did not want to be in the vanguard of modern urban design, nor did they necessarily want to live in high-rise towers. In Baltimore, currently as much as historically, they wanted to live like everyone else—in a rowhouse.

Central City Rowhouses Razed for High-Rise Public Housing Towers

National attention to conditions of urban blight had begun in the late nineteenth century with progressive reformers like Jacob Riis who focused on overcrowding, lack of sanitary facilities, and the prevalence of disease. In 1907 Janet Kemp published *Housing Conditions in Baltimore*, which pinpointed four problem areas—in Fells Point, Federal Hill, Old Town, and in northwest Baltimore—all noted for their high housing densities and high rates of tuberculosis. During World War I, the federal government first became directly involved in homebuilding, producing homes for war workers through the United States Housing Corporation. In 1919 housing reformer Edith Elmer Wood advocated low-cost, subsidized government housing for the poor. Yet through the prosperous 1920s homebuilding remained the domain of the private sector. Not until the Depression of the 1930s, when the private housing industry collapsed nationwide, did the federal government take a significant role in building housing for American citizens.

Beginning in 1933 with the Public Works Administration's (PWA) Housing Division, a product of President Franklin D. Roosevelt's New Deal, the federal government started building houses, either providing the funds for private contractors to do the work, or acting as the developer itself. Two years later the PWA published Wood's *Slums and Blighted Areas in the United States* and it had a lasting effect on New Deal policy. Wood averred that more than one-third of Americans were living in substandard housing that was overcrowded, without proper sanitary facilities or basic amenities like electricity and central heating. In his 1937 inaugural address Roosevelt repeated this statistic, calling for immediate action.[3]

Baltimore's "ring of blight," which an influential 1934 city canvass of housing documented, was concentrated in the city's oldest areas, within about a mile radius of the central business district. Here, in many of the same areas found to be overcrowded in Kemp's earlier 1907 study, lived the city's most disadvantaged citizens, forced to rent in crowded quarters owned by absentee landlords who had allowed their hundred-year-old properties to deteriorate. Many of these residents belonged to Baltimore's most recently arrived immigrant groups, including large numbers of blacks moving up from the rural south. The situation that faced new black residents was exacerbated by the fact that de facto segregation was still alive in Baltimore.

Although Jim Crow laws, which restricted where blacks could live, had been struck down by the courts Baltimore remained a Southern city, in culture as well as geography. As the *Sun* wrote in 1943, blacks had nowhere to live but the "Negro Archipelagoes."[4] These included historic black communities in South Baltimore (Sharp-Leadenhall), East Baltimore (just beyond Old Town), and West Baltimore, along Pennsylvania and Druid Hill Avenues—long the hub of Baltimore's black life. As the new Daylight suburbs offered better housing to the children and grandchildren of immigrants who had arrived in the 1880s and 1890s, the old housing stock they left behind in the city became residences for new arrivals. In 1940 African-Americans made up one in five residents in the city; because of segregation, though, they crowded together in only one-fiftieth of the city's total land area. Despite such dense and deteriorated housing conditions, the black residents forged bonds and made communities work (FIGURE 119).

Even with this, established, white Baltimoreans felt threatened by the growing black population and the crowded conditions under which they lived. Federal initiatives that recommended clearing "slums" and building new housing for the poor became an attractive option. The "geography of blight" covered different urban areas; one, on the west side, included 232 dwellings (most two-and-a-half stories) in which 138 lacked bathing facilities, 140 lacked an indoor toilet, and seven had no water supply. Canvassers identified "a ring of blighted residential tracts of the most serious importance and size." The housing stock had deteriorated so badly that slum clearance was recommended (FIGURE 120).[5]

Baltimore's rowhouse builders strongly opposed the federal housing program, claiming it constituted "unfair competition" that would "lessen individual incentive." The Baltimore *Real Estate News* summed up the homebuilding sector's position: "It is hardly expected that the many thousands of owners of small homes and those who are paying their own way, all taxes included, are going to be willing to pay more taxes to provide better homes than they now enjoy for use by those now residing in slum areas." Some realtors even spread rumors that public housing would force integration. Mayor Howard Jackson, who hated New Deal policies, vowed the federal government would not be allowed to compete unfairly against private enterprise and opposed a state or local housing authority. Nonetheless, the Housing Authority of Baltimore City was finally founded with an $18 million housing program targeted for five blighted sites in the central city, all identified in the 1934 survey.[6]

On a national scale, Baltimore's stock of substandard housing was third worst behind St. Louis and Chicago (and second when rental units alone were compared). The older residential sections, which immediately surrounded the center city, were full of houses that rented for less than $15 a month and had a high rate of tax delinquencies and foreclosures. Nevertheless, residents usually protested the idea of demolition. The first public housing project planned—298 three-story garden apartments in the same block as Edgar Allan Poe's house during his years in Baltimore (and thus named Poe Homes)—met with some community resistance. A coalition of homeowners denied that their neighborhood was a slum and demanded that their houses be "reconditioned not destroyed." But the city's planners saw old, crowded rowhouses as breeding grounds for crime, disease, and poverty, and wanted them gone: 226 rowhouses built in the 1820s and 1830s were razed. The historic Poe house was the only one saved in a two-block area and 1,000 residents had to be relocated before those who wished to could move into their new apartments.[7]

If some white Baltimoreans resented spending tax money for new black housing, they also insisted that such housing should be built within the boundaries of existing black neighborhoods. The only other politically acceptable solution was to build public housing in a physically isolated area like Cherry Hill, a peninsula across the Middle Branch of the Patapsco River. Since one of the hidden agendas of slum clearance was the prevention of black encroachment into white neighborhoods, the sites chosen for black public housing simply reinforced existing segregation patterns. One Housing Authority manager recognized that the McCulloh Homes project planned for West Baltimore would create "a splendid barrier against the encroachment of coloreds" into the adjoining white neighborhood of Bolton Hill.[8]

Poe Homes was just the start. In 1941 and 1942 six additional low-rise apartment projects opened, four for black tenants in traditionally black neighborhoods and two for white tenants in areas of the city still predominantly white. Once the sites for new housing were chosen, the housing authority tore down all existing buildings within their boundaries. The need for slum clearance and re-building was questioned by more than the residents displaced and moved. In 1940, under the headline, "They're Doomed," the *Sun* printed photographs of rows in the 1500 block of North Mount Street and 1600 block of Baker Street, both slated to be torn down for the low-rise Gilmor Homes in West Baltimore. Although "there are some bad spots confined to the alleys," the reporter noted, "for the area as a whole our Architectural Correspondent reports a level of habitability not noticeably lower than is to be found in block after block of the surrounding territory and in other sections of the city as well.... Large numbers of the dwellings on the Gilmor Homes site could be made more livable by renovation... [and] we see no point in tearing down good houses merely to replace them with other good houses, when the same money could be used to eliminate *worse* houses and build *better*.... No houser except perhaps a complete visionary would dream of tearing down" houses that could be brought up to decent standards.[9]

This criticism fell on deaf ears. Visionaries spurred on the nation's housing policy in the postwar era. Between 1940 and 1945 thousands of houses were razed in Baltimore's central district and a new type of high-rise housing planned (FIGURE 126). By breaking with the "old Baltimore tradition that every entrance must open on a public sidewalk," planners would be able to "give tenants grass, large interior courts, playgrounds, and facilities for community gatherings." The high-rise project would be the key to solving urban housing ills and its density would help solve the

"Negro housing problem." In 1945 the Housing Authority announced a program of creating housing for 4,500 blacks. Executive director Yewell W. Dillehunt explained, "since Negro housing in Baltimore is in a very critical condition, the postwar plan will cover 30.4% of the need for Negro housing and only 17.85% of the expected white housing needs." The plan called for the erection of four different high-rise projects, all to be built on cleared land where slums had previously stood and near the various low-rise projects built in the 1940s. Three of the projects were for blacks, one for whites.[10]

On December 15,1952 with Mayor Thomas D'Alesandro pulling down the first bricks, the slum clearance for Lafayette Courts was set in motion. A demolition crew then knocked down a wall on the northeast corner of Aisquith and Lexington Streets. Over 550 homes were coming down, to be replaced with six eleven-story buildings, the first use of high-rise towers by the Housing Authority. The slum that was coming down covered 60 percent of the site, but the new buildings would cover only 16 percent. In addition to the 105-foot-tall high rises, ten three-story garden apartments and seven two-story rowhouses would be built for big families. "On each floor of the skyscraper apartment buildings are tot lots where children can be watched by their mothers from their kitchens." In all, there were 110 one-bedroom, 406 two-bedroom, 252 three-bedroom, and 42 four-bedroom units planned to house 807 families. It would be the largest public housing complex in the nation, outside of Chicago.[11]

The Housing Authority initially selected tenants that "use the benefits of public housing to tide them over a time of crisis or low earning power." In 1955, to be eligible to get into Lafayette Courts, a three- or four-person family could earn no more than $2,800 annually and would get preference if a veteran or serviceman headed it. The average rent in the low rent program was $34.99 a month. As the city's first high-rise tower, Lafayette Courts attracted the press's attention, which focused on what was wrong with the design rather than the towers' harbor views. The *Sun* reporter noted the concrete floors and chain-link fencing that enclosed the outdoor corridors to prevent children from falling gave "something of the effect of a well kept prison."[12]

Five years later, in 1957, the head of the city's new Urban Renewal and Housing Agency, Oliver C. Winston, said he did not want to see Baltimore ringed with tall buildings that are clearly public housing projects; it "would be undesirable from the architectural and aesthetic viewpoint." High-rise projects remained in the pipeline for future construction. Just a week earlier the city had let the contract for the Lexington Terrace project, which included one fourteen-story and four eleven-story buildings, also for blacks. For the upcoming George B. Murphy Homes project, Winston scaled down the towers to only eight stories. Flag House Courts, the high-rise project designed for whites that opened in the same year as Lafayette Courts, had only three towers.[13]

Residents soon discovered that high-rise living, contained within such fencing, was an invitation to vandalism, littering, and petty crime. Project management files in the Baltimore City Archives reveal increasing discontent among stable families who lived in the projects. A widow with four children applied for a transfer from Lafayette Courts in 1963: "I would like to transfer from 1364 East Fayette to anywhere else in the city.... this neighborhood is affecting me and my children physically and mentally." The seriousness of the crimes committed within Lafayette Courts escalated until a private security firm was hired to patrol the project in 1965. By the late 1980s, 87 percent of the children in Lafayette Courts were living in poverty.[14]

Demolition was not the only avenue tried to improve housing in Baltimore. On the same day in 1952 that the *Sun* announced the razing ceremony for Lafayette Courts, Mayor Thomas D'Alesandro unveiled the "Baltimore Plan," a pilot program to rehabilitate a twenty-seven-block area. After all, as G. Cheston Carey of the Housing Authority noted, "The physical tearing down of the slums is not difficult. The tough problem is relocating the people." (Of the 480 families who had lived on the site of Lafayette Courts, 174 remained to be housed.) The idea was "to apply the plan not to rock bottom slums but to some 27 blocks in East Baltimore that might be saved permanently from sinking to the condition where razing is the final answer." In the 27-block area, about 720 out of nearly 800 houses were deemed "substandard" by the U. S. Public Health Service and of these over 300 were "seriously deteriorated." On a house by house basis, property owners were told to upgrade their buildings to an acceptable living standard. On average, bringing each house up to code cost $1,000. Homeowners took pride in the improvements; landlords tended to feel victimized, and as no city laws required central heating, bathtubs, or even one toilet per unit, kept repairs to an absolute minimum.

Housing reformers hailed the Baltimore Plan and the *Encyclopedia Brittanica* even made a documentary film of the whole process in 1953. The city continued its program in other targeted areas, but in the end the numbers were overwhelming. Twenty percent of the city's 277,880 units were substandard, according to the Housing Authority and by 1960 enthusiasm for the Baltimore Plan had died.[15]

Renovating Rows, Homesteading in the City

Of all the types of rowhouses in Baltimore's history, the oldest—the two-and-a-half story Federal style rows—played a pivotal role in the revitalization of the inner city. These 120- to 170-year-old buildings in Federal Hill and Fells Point had deteriorated to slums by the 1960s. During the 1930s and 1940s immigrant Polish, Czech, German, Ukranian, and Italian families living in these areas had developed strong, close-knit working-class neighborhoods. But as industrial jobs vanished, so too did the economic base of these communities and grown children of original residents moved out to suburban areas. The physical condition of the rows deteriorated as mostly elderly homeowners had trouble maintaining their old properties. In 1967 the city condemned the houses nearest the waterfront in each community so that a major highway could come through Baltimore's inner harbor area (FIGURE 122).

Proposals to build highways through the heart of the city had been floated since 1942, but the highway in question in 1967 was Interstate 95, which was laid out to connect Baltimore with Wilmington to the north and Washington, D.C., to the south. The condemned houses comprised the city's earliest historic fabric. The battle lines between the housing authority and community preservationists were drawn: community activists committed to saving their local heritage promptly founded the Society for the Preservation of Federal Hill, Montgomery Street, and Fells Point, raised money, and drew public attention to their cause; Society volunteers researched properties and successfully prepared applications for listing the two neighborhoods in the newly created (1966) National Register of Historic Places. They filed suit against the federal government for agreeing to provide funds (in the form of highway dollars) to demolish nationally significant historical properties. The longer such tactics delayed the start of construction, the more expensive the proposed expressway became. In 1977 city authorities gave up the fight, moved the path of the roadway further south, and lifted the condemnation ordinance. By litigation, protests, and sheer determination, a group of community activists had stopped the road. A small group of citizens had opposed one of the country's most powerful interest groups—the highway lobby—and won. The historic fabric of Baltimore's earliest rowhouse neighborhoods had been saved. Perhaps more importantly, the fight had drawn attention to the value of the city's historic waterfront and sparked its incipient renaissance.[16]

176

During the ten years the condemnation ordinance was in effect, the city acquired many historic properties from owners eager to sell to the city for the highest price. Enclosed in chain-link fencing, these early-nineteenth-century rowhouses sat vacant for years, continuing to deteriorate. In 1977, through efforts of the city, community groups, and the mayor, the condemned houses in Federal Hill and Fells Point received a second life (FIGURE 123). In Fells Point alone, the city found itself with 78 vacant houses (28 dating from 1776 or earlier and 50 from 1800–1830). Mayor William Donald Schaefer turned the matter of what to do with the houses over to a committee of eight residents. Their recommendation was to first offer to sell houses back to the original owners for what the city had paid them—around $2,500 to $5,000; only two of the original owners bought back their houses. The Preservation Society then persuaded the city housing department to maintain the properties and seek tenants. The tenants would have the first chance to buy the houses at the price the city had paid, as long as they paid the taxes that had accrued. The general public in a sealed bid auction could purchase any remaining properties. The preservationists created design guidelines for the rows to insure sensitive historic rehabilitations.

The neighborhood involved was exactly the one Traugoth Singewald had called home one hundred years earlier. In those days Fells Point was a community of many enterprising German immigrants who established neighborhood churches, businesses, and social clubs. They shared the streetscape with a flourishing African-American community, which followed the traditional maritime occupations of the Point. Shipbuilding remained a thriving industry and shipbuilders, ship captains, and droves of sailors also called Fells Point home. In fact, not much had changed since the houses had been built in the 1790s and early 1800s. Baltimore had grown, but life on the Point still centered around the waterfront, one's family, and earning a living. Then, in the 1880s and 1890s, immigrant Poles began settling in the area, soon after their arrival in Baltimore via a North German Lloyd steamer. Men worked on the docks, in can-making plants and other related industries; their wives and children worked long hours in the canneries, processing fruits and vegetables. These families rented cheap rooms from fellow countrymen in the old houses within a short walk of the waterfront and the canneries. If they could save enough and were able to achieve homeownership, many stayed in the neighborhood they had known so long.

A century later, resident renters who wanted to remain in the area bought almost half the Fells Point properties the city sold. Hundreds more houses were restored as new stores, inns, and restaurants opened along the main commercial streets of Broadway and Thames. A similar process occurred in Federal Hill. Houses the city had acquired for demolition for the highway were auctioned to interested citizens committed to restoring them to National Register rehabilitation standards.

On the other side of the harbor, equally significant events in the late 1970s were re-creating rowhouse living in the city. Three entrepreneurial business partners, C. William Struever, Fred Struever, and Cobber Eccles (Struever Brothers and Eccles), two of whom had recently graduated from Brown University, combined their knowledge of historic preservation and urban development to create market-rate housing at reasonable cost. They set up a small office in an old house near the harbor and, with money lent by two of the partners' mother, bought a row of six small, deteriorated two-story Italianate houses on a narrow street south of Federal Hill Park. They worked together to gut the houses, repair exterior woodwork, and regrade lawns, and in six months they offered the newly refurbished four-room units for sale at an affordable $45,000 (FIGURE 124). It was just the beginning. The fledgling firm acquired a few more houses, renovated and sold them, and then acquired more. Because the houses were located in a National Register historic district, the cost of renovations made on investment properties (either rental units or storefronts) could be written off as tax credits and the units were readily sold to investors seeking offsets against taxes owed. Many others went to owner-occupants attracted by the idea of a return to convenient city living in a charming historic house. The firm acquired the old houses, sold them at a profit, and then received the construction contract for the renovations. In 1978 Struever Bros. and Eccles launched a major initiative for commercial revitalization in the area, acquiring many old storefronts along Charles and Light Streets, near the Cross Street Market. By setting an example (turning a three-story shopfront facing the market into a trendy ice-cream parlor, and converting two 1850s alley houses into a children's bookstore), they attracted a variety of investors to the area. The firm celebrated the neighborhood's heritage by sponsoring a local oral history project focusing on traditional market families, supporting a state-funded architectural survey of the properties in the National Register district, and producing a booklet telling of the area's interesting history. Property values rose quickly. A two-and-a-half story Federal style house built by John S. Gittings in 1838 on East Hamburg Street sold for $8,000 in 1977, resold for $18,000 in 1978, and then again for $35,000 in 1979. Today the same house, only a few blocks walk to the Inner Harbor, might list for $150,000.

By 1980 Struever Bros. and Eccles had taken on a new partner, Winstead Rouse, son of the esteemed developer and humanitarian, James W. Rouse, who had opened Baltimore's Harborplace the year before. Jim Rouse's vision of creating a festival marketplace on two plots of land north of Federal Hill, where rotting docks had stood until the 1960s, catapulted Baltimore's newly designated Inner Harbor into a national tourist destination. In recent years the city has recognized that tourism is its major growth industry and has made concentrated efforts to continue to attract national-level investment in the Inner Harbor area.[17]

A major factor in the success of Federal Hill and the reclamation of the Inner Harbor also placed Baltimore on the national stage. In 1973, Housing commissioner Robert C. Embry, Jr. announced the launching of Baltimore's homesteading program. Modeled after that of Wilmington, Delaware, (announced a month earlier), the goal of the program was to reclaim city-owned vacant houses that might sell to committed renovators if they only cost $1. With five thousand abandoned rowhouses in the reclamation inventory, Embry decided to improve upon Wilmington's plan, which, he claimed "didn't provide any financing for the owners and it was on too small a scale." He created a special homeownership development office in the city's Department of Housing and Community Development, which would give homesteaders technical and financial assistance. Because no private banks would risk lending money for the rehabilitation costs of these rows in marginal locations, Embry devised a city-backed loan program that would finance renovation and construction costs, with average loans of $20,000 at 7 percent interest, offered to qualified buyers/renovators of the $1 houses. The owners were given six months to bring their house up to code requirements and then had to live there a minimum of 18 months to have the house deeded to them. Wilmington had a three-year residency requirement; Baltimore's shorter term proved more attractive to prospective buyers.[18]

The initial 200 houses offered included 42 two-and-a-half story rowhouses in the 600 block of Stirling Street. The city had slated them for demolition, to be replaced by low-income housing. By focusing renovation efforts on an entire block, instead of on scattered sites, Embry believed the project would have a greater chance of success. Sixty-three homebuyers, most of whom already lived in the city, signed up. As renovations proceeded, the new owners formed a tight club, naming themselves the Stirling Street Neighbors. Many combined two adjoining twelve-foot-wide houses, built in the early 1830s, to create a larger, more livable unit (FIGURE 125). Some retained the traditional floor plan, others gutted the interiors into open loft spaces. The average cost of rehabilitation in 1975 came in at $27,000. Although the city housing authority's acting director for planning had claimed that "while they may look quaint, the information I have is that structurally the buildings are not worth saving," he was proven wrong. Stirling Street, with its quaint brick houses set on a gently curving street in Old Town (repaved with Belgian blocks and given period street lighting) and with a spectacular view at the end of the row of the downtown skyline, quickly gained attention in the national press as the first concentrated homesteading effort in the United States.[19]

Embry's next project focused on a group of more substantial early-nineteenth-century houses in an area called Otterbein (named after a 1780s German church), only a few blocks west of the harbor basin (FIGURE 126). The city had acquired over one hundred "slum" properties in this area with the hope of attracting Kenzo Tange to design a project here. When plans failed, Embry offered the houses on the same terms that had worked at Stirling Street—$1 for the houses and the opportunity to obtain low-interest city rehabilitation financing. In 1975 over 3,000 people showed up for the tour and 700 signed up to purchase and renovate a $1 house. The area thrived and showed that the success of urban homesteading lay in the development it sparked around it. Ninety-four households risked their time and money on what had been decreed a slum, and thereby encouraged other investors to follow. When the city auctioned off the several blocks of long-vacant houses, originally acquired for the highway in nearby Federal Hill, bidding was spirited. The houses were old and charming, overlooked the harbor, and were only a short walk from downtown. No matter how they might look, one had only to walk a few blocks west to Otterbein to see what could be done. Every year the Historic Harbor House Tour added newly renovated houses to its roster. People discovered that they enjoyed living downtown in small rowhouses on quiet streets, with shops, markets, and restaurants only a few blocks away, or around the corner (FIGURE 127). The uniformity of the rowhouses gave a cohesive neighborhood ambiance to the street. The lesson was that these rows were not dispensable. Baltimore's homesteading program, under the leadership of Robert C. Embry, was nationally and internationally hailed as an imaginative solution to cure inner city housing problems, turning whole neighborhoods around, and bringing middle-income residents back into the city.

118. TOP   1118–1124 Comet Street, Pleasant View Gardens, built 1997 and
designed by CHK Architects and Planners (Steven Allan)

119. TOP   Houses on Pine Street, built in the 1820s and demolished in the 1940s to make way for urban renewal (Maryland Historical Society)

120. TOP RIGHT   A blighted block, as illustrated in the book that documents the Baltimore Plan, *The Human Side of Urban Renewal*, published by Fight-Blight, Inc., 1958. Original caption: "A typical blighted block from the rear; a junk collector's paradise, with outdoor hoppers, three-foot alley, masses of filth, rubbish and raw sewage accumulated in the yards."

120. BOTTOM RIGHT   "Baltimore Homes of 1830" were identified as slums in the 1948 exhibition and catalog, *Baltimore Housing, Past, Present and Future*, held at The Peale, the city's municipal museum.

122. TOP   Rendering of proposed Inner Harbor highway, 1960 Baltimore City Planning Commission report; the highway would have cut through Fells Point and Federal Hill, destroying some of the city's earliest rows (Eric Holcomb)

123. BOTTOM   2–12 East Montgomery Street, built 1848, a row of two-story-and-attic houses in Federal Hill overlooking the harbor; condemned for the planned highway and stood derelict for years before renovation in the 1980s (Steven Allan)

124.   This group of tiny houses on Grindall Street in Federal Hill, built by John
T. Grindall in 1850–1852, became the first renovation project of the newly created development firm, Struever Bros. & Eccles, who pioneered the concept of
"sweat equity" in Baltimore and revitalized large sections of Federal Hill through
the use of historic tax credits (Struever Bros., Eccles & Rouse)

125. TOP   Stirling Street, built circa 1830; a long row of two-and-a-half story houses was one of the first renovated under Baltimore's $1 house program of the 1970s, a program that gained national attention (Jane Webb Smith)

126. top   Detail, *E. Sachse & Co.'s Bird's Eye View of the City of Baltimore*, 1869, showing the Otterbein neighborhood that would become the site of Baltimore's largest $1 house program; the site of the Camden Yards stadium, built against one wall of the old B & O Railroad warehouse, is located in the upper left (Maryland Historical Society)

127. BOTTOM   111–123 Welcome Alley, renovated $1 mid-nineteenth-century rowhouses in the Otterbein neighborhood; in the late twentieth century these are highly desirable and easily marketable houses in a secluded neighborhood within a short walk of Inner Harbor and downtown (Steven Allen)

128. LEFT   Advertisement for FormStone, 1950, the artificial stone product that covered brick facades of many Baltimore rowhouses in the 1950s and 1960s, from the Baltimore *Sun* (Enoch Pratt Free Library)

129. TOP   A block of two-story Italianate rowhouses in Sandtown-Winchester, renovated by Habitat for Humanity, 1996

130. TOP   Modular rowhousing in the 1200 block of North Stricker Street, part of the Nehemiah Housing program in the Sandtown-Winchester neighborhood of West Baltimore, built by The Enterprise Foundation and Ryland Modular Homes, 1992 (David Harp for The Enterprise Foundation)

131. TOP   Montgomery Square, Federal Hill, designed by D. W. Taylor, Associates, Inc. Architect, and built by Ryland Homes, 1994 (Steven Allan)

132. BOTTOM   Elevations of rowhouses at Spicer's Run, an in-fill development of 86 three-story units that replaced a 1960s public housing project, which had replaced elegant Queen Anne houses built by Joseph Cone and others in the 1880s (Artelier Design for D. W. Taylor, Associates, Inc. Architect)

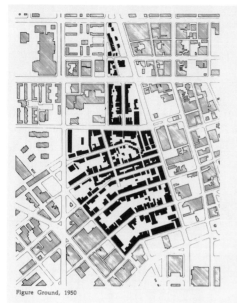

Figure Ground, 1950

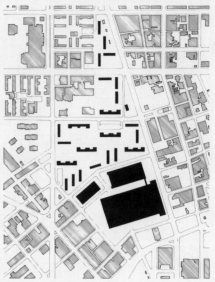

Figure Ground, 1960

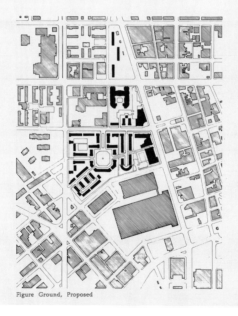

Figure Ground, Proposed

133. LEFT   Various site plans showing the evolution of the Lafayette Courts site: upper left, the rowhouse neighborhood in East Baltimore that would become the site of Lafayette Courts high-rises, 1950; upper right, the layout of Lafayette Courts towers, 1960; bottom, the site plan for Pleasant View Gardens, which replaced the towers, 1997 (CHK Architects and Planners)

134. TOP   Pleasant View Gardens in 1998, with the skyscrapers of downtown in the background and the community park at the end of the boulevard in the foreground (Alain Jaramillo)

THE WALKING CITY 1790-1855
The shaded area in the center city
shows the location of Federal and
Greek Revival style rowhouses. The
first rowhouses were built in the
Federal style near the booming
port–three-and-half-story houses for
wealthy merchants and two-and a-
half story types for artisan and labor
classes, many of whom worked in
port-related occupations. In the
1840s three-story Greek Revival
rowhouses appeared north of the old
business district, in Mt. Vernon
Place; not long afterwards two-
story-and-attic versions rose near
the Mt. Clare Yards of the new
Baltimore & Ohio Railroad in West
Baltimore and in neighborhoods
around the port occupied by newly
arrived German and Irish immigrants (Steven Allan)

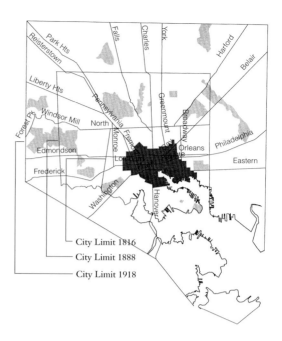

PARKS AND SQUARES 1850-1890
The shaded area around the center
city shows the location of Italianate
style houses built in the second half
of the nineteenth century. As
Baltimore industry prospered, mid-
dle- and upper-income residents
moved beyond the old central city
into new neighborhoods reached by
horsecar lines and filled with three-
story Italianate-style houses. Several
of the rowhouse neighborhoods on
the west and east sides of town bordered new public parks and squares.
Many lower-income residents filled
two-story Italianate rowhouses along
the narrow alley streets that bisected
principal blocks. Thousands of
unskilled factory workers, most
newly arrived from southern and
eastern Europe, made their homes in
two-story Italianate houses built
within walking distance of jobs on
either side of the harbor (Steven
Allan)

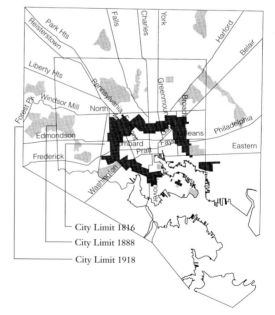

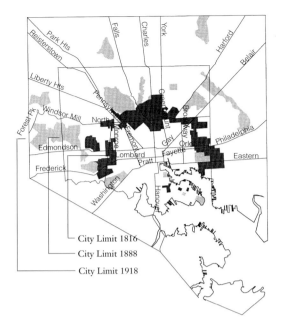

STREETCAR SUBURBS 1875-1915
The shaded area shows the location of Queen Anne, picturesque, and Renaissance revival style rowhouses that went up in Baltimore just as the streetcar was making commuting convenient and affordable. Nationally circulated periodicals, technological advances, and inexpensive mass-production made for a wide variety of styles available in three-story versions for affluent and two-story models for working-class residents. The extension of public services brought city water, gas, electricity, and plumbing to most households and led to improved living conditions for all Baltimoreans (Steven Allan)

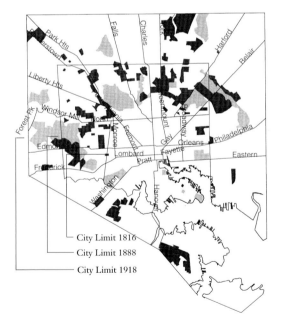

AUTOMOBILE SUBURBS AND DAYLIGHT ROWS 1915-1955
Streetcar lines and major automobile routes guided rowhouse development in the first half of the twentieth century. The shaded areas show the sections in which Daylight rowhouses went up during these years. With the advent of the automobile and further extension of streetcar lines, the city continued to expand in all directions. Many residents moved to Daylight rowhouses being built in large numbers on the city's edge and in the surrounding county. Daylight houses featured a wider frontage and shallower depth, every room had a window, and many had wide front porches, small front lawns, and a garage in back for the family auto. The shopping center replaced the neighborhood corner grocery in Daylight suburbs (Steven Allan)

135. TOP Richard Gibson, resident of Pleasant View Gardens, 1998 (Steven Allan)

Formstone: Friend or Faux?

As renovators went about improving their historic properties—all located within a few blocks' walk of the Inner Harbor and downtown business district—their first obstacle came in the form of a sparkly faux stone that covered many of the houses. Today, thanks in part to the movies of natives Barry Levinson and John Waters and to the nationally syndicated television series, *Homicide: Life on the Street*, Baltimore has become famous for Formstone, a simulated stone resurfacing material that covers thousands of the city's rowhouses. Invented in Columbus, Ohio, in 1929, "Perma-Stone," an ersatz, molded, stonelike wall facing, arrived in Baltimore in 1937 when L. Albert Knight patented a similar product he called Form-Stone. Advertisements claimed that the material was maintenance free, fireproof, and energy efficient (FIGURE 128). It appealed to Baltimoreans because the quality of early Baltimore brick was so poor that it required frequent and continuous painting. Builders like Edward J. Gallagher and Frank Novak switched to the hard-fired "iron-spot" brick when it became available in the early 1900s, advertising that their houses "never needed painting." Once formstoned, a brick rowhouse was basically maintenance free. Another appeal was Formstone's stonelike appearance. Many of the homeowners in East Baltimore, where the Formstone salesmen did especially well, had roots in various Eastern European countries where stone buildings lined block after block. Proud first-time homeowners in Baltimore, they worked hard to maintain and improve their houses. When they saw neighbors getting a Formstone job that made their homes look like "little castles," they eagerly followed suit. One East Baltimorean nicely captured Formstone's benefits: "It looked like shantytown when it was red brick. The man came and Formstoned it...made it look like Hollywood. That's...the God's truth."[20]

Stone had always signified wealth and status to Europeans and the least expensive way to have the look of stone was to apply stucco, which was two-thirds less expensive than stone. Formstone became a more creative form of stucco, which protected the house as well but was even more colorful and could be shaped into different textures. Formstone, which is still used today, is applied in three layers (each $3/8$ to $3/4$ inches thick) on metal lath attached to the brick. The finish layer contains the colored mortar cements to imitate the appearance of stone. Before the last two layers have set, waxed paper is applied to the wall and an aluminum roller with a crinkled surface creates the look of stone. Other methods, such as Perma-Stone, use pressure molds to imitate stone. Applying Formstone to a mid-row house cost about $325 in the 1950s. It came with a plate stating that the product was "genuine FormStone"; often a congratulatory letter arrived soon after from the local utility company.

Regardless of Formstone's historic precedents, preservationists in the 1970s hated it. As soon as rehabbers acquired a city house they hired a contractor to rip the Formstone off. The process was time-consuming and dirty; big chunks of cement fell to the street and the glittery surface pulverized into dust. When the metal lathe came off, it left the mortar joints full of holes and the brick looking pock-marked. A thorough cleaning and then repointing was necessary, which added significantly to the restoration cost. Formstone, the preservationists argued, masked the authentic style of the façade and often resulted in the loss of architectural details that might have to be removed during installation. Long-time neighbors, however, remained committed to the aesthetic choice *they* had made and resisted pleas for removal.

Formstone served as an indicator of the health of city neighborhoods in the 1950s and 1960s, showing where rates of homeownership were high and people were committed to staying in the city. In contrast, where blocks of older rows retained their original red brick, it was a sure sign that absentee landlords were in control. Even today, blocks covered with Formstone still have a high rate of homeownership and stability. In the late 1970s, it was, ironically, the removal of Formstone that became the new barometer of a neighborhood's health. Revealing the original "historic" red brick underneath meant gentrification was in process, which to the city government meant new vitality and higher property values.

To others, of course, the designation of revitalized neighborhoods as "historic districts" came at a price. Long-time homeowners were forced to sell because of rising property taxes or chose to because they could not afford to turn down high purchase offers. Historic urban neighborhoods that had formerly belonged to the working classes now gentrified to become attractive to often younger, better-educated middle-class men and women. Marie Pabst Zalk, a Fells Point resident for over 90 years, reflected, "Yeah, historical. It's historical the way it is now. It's laughable. It wasn't historical when I lived here...."[21] Longtime homeowners were amazed at the prices people would pay to live in houses they had always felt were second class. Ongoing redevelopment of the Inner Harbor shored up Federal Hill and Fells Point real estate values even during the national recession in the early 1990s. Generally, any row near the waterfront escalated tremendously in value.

New Rowhouses for
Low- and Middle-Income Families

Baltimore was a national leader in urban homesteading in the 1970s, and again in the 1980s with the development of better housing for low-income families. In 1982 James W. Rouse's Enterprise Foundation initiated plans to improve housing conditions for low-income households nationwide. The foundation creates affordable housing through public-private housing partnerships, and by arranging financing packages from a variety of sources. More than 1,100 local nonprofit housing groups across the country currently participate in the program. Enterprise commenced its first Baltimore project in 1990, in the city's most concentrated and historically significant black neighborhood. Located in West Baltimore, along the major commercial strip of Pennsylvania Avenue where jazz greats Billie Holliday, Cab Calloway, Louis Armstrong, and others regularly played, the neighborhood known as Sandtown-Winchester comprises that part of the city where blacks were "allowed" to live when legal segregation was still in effect, and where they virtually were forced to remain even after segregation was declared unconstitutional. The 72-block area is lined with deteriorating, mostly three-story Italianate houses built in the 1870s and 1880s for middle- and upper-middle-income Germans. Two-story "alley" rowhouses stood on the narrow, mid-block streets, but the city tore down many of these in the 1970s to clear land for what became derelict and abandoned playgrounds.

Rouse and Enterprise believed the area's residents needed decent, affordable housing so through a variety of local partnerships and a mix of private, federal, and city funding, an eight-year effort culminated in the reclamation of nearly a hundred previously vacant houses and the construction of over 300 new ones. All were ultimately purchased on liberal terms by people who previously had little hope of owning their own house. In the early 1980s Rouse gained the support of then President Jimmy Carter and the U. S. Department of Housing and Urban Development, which agreed that low-income city residents should be offered the chance of homeownership. Habitat for Humanity, founded in Americus, Georgia in 1976 by philanthropist Millard Fuller, uses donated labor, materials, and money to build and renovate decent houses for low-income people. In a quarter-century, more than 700 Habitat organizations have sprung up nationwide. Baltimore's Habitat, headquartered in Sandtown and begun in 1988, receives annual funding from Rouse's Enterprise Foundation.

In 1992 former President and First Lady Rosalynn Carter personally assisted in the renovation of ten Sandtown rowhouses, which Habitat for Humanity had reclaimed together with city-wide volunteer and neighborhood groups. Seeking to bring in more volunteers, Carter announced, "The next time I come back with Rosalynn we'll be carpenters working side by side with families that are going to have a decent house perhaps for the first time." Since then, ten houses have been restored each summer. One resident, Linda Greene, 35 and a mother of four who worked as a $5.50-an-hour truck driver for a paint supply company, said as she was working on her own house, "I've struggled from day one up to now. I've always been determined. If you want something, you have to work for it. Nothing's handed to you on a silver platter unless you're the Queen of England." Before Habitat began renovating rows for low-income households, Greene thought about owning a house but concluded, "I'd probably be fifty or older or maybe never—with the price of houses, credit checks, banks, settlement costs, and everything." Greene joined up with Habitat and volunteered with her fifteen-year-old son. "You're working on your own house. You actually see it. Its beyond words," she says. "I think about planting a flower garden and putting some tomatoes and collard greens out back. My daughter and son are already fighting over the bedrooms."[22]

Linda Greene and other low-income families became homeowners through Habitat's program combining no-profit home building, interest-free loans, donated materials, volunteer labor, and at least 250 hours of "sweat equity" work. Most residents have average annual incomes of $10,000 or less, which is below the level to qualify for government housing programs. In the Habitat program, the average house costs about $30,000 and Greene pays about $200 a month to own hers (FIGURE 129).[23] In the words of Rev. Mark R. Gornik, president of the Sandtown Habitat board in 1992, the process amounts to "biblical economics."

Enterprise also partnered with a local coalition of some forty-five churches seeking to help restore inner-city neighborhoods, which operates under the acronym BUILD (Baltimoreans United in Leadership Development), to build houses in the Sandtown-Winchester neighborhood as part of the federally funded Nehemiah Housing Opportunity Program. In 1991 the coalition hired Struever Bros., Eccles & Rouse, and Ryland Modular Homes to construct 300 new rowhouses. Funding for the $22 million project combined federal, state, and local funds. A combination of federal and city subsidies was used to write down monthly mortgage payments and taxes on the houses in the Sandtown-Winchester community to as low as $250, thus enabling a family with an annual income of $11,000 to qualify.[24]

The two-story, three-bedroom rowhouses were built 18 feet wide and 30 feet deep, with 1,100 square feet of living space and an unfinished basement. They also included two bathrooms, central heating and air conditioning, and carpeting. The developer set the houses back fifteen feet from the street, which gave each family a front yard—perceived as a special amenity of the suburbs (FIGURE 130). One distinct feature was the modular construction; each house arrived at the site 90 percent complete, packed in four boxes, two for the first floor, two for the second. A crane lifted the units into place and at the end of the same day, the house could be locked. With kitchen cabinets and bathrooms installed, modular units accelerated the construction period and also prevented theft of materials, a chronic problem for inner-city builders.

New Market-Rate Rowhouses

Among young, middle-income urban dwellers, the newly built rowhouses of the 1990s provided an attractive neotraditional option for city living. With redevelopment around the Inner Harbor, Federal Hill, and Fells Point gaining momentum, in 1994 Columbia-based Ryland Homes returned to downtown Baltimore (having built modular houses in the Sandtown-Winchester community) to develop Montgomery Square in Federal Hill, an infill project of forty-two "historic" townhouses. Montgomery Square was good evidence that houses designed to harmonize with the city's oldest rows (yet adapted for the car) could be successful for residents and profitable for the developer.

Ryland laid out the brick, two- and three-bedroom houses, located at Charles and West Montgomery Streets, in a traditional Baltimore block pattern—rows face both main streets and side streets, and also run along the narrow alley street bisecting the block. Each half block has an interior court, which provides access to the rear-entry garages. Similar to Edward J. Gallagher's Ednor Gardens in the late 1920s, the garages are built into the back of the first floor of the house. Although the driveway takes up the rear yard in Montgomery Square, a large deck off the main living area on the second level (as well as some on the third) offers space for outdoor living. The architects D. W. Taylor Associates designed the 20-foot-wide townhouses with about 1,500 square feet of living space and an initial sales price of $155,000. Carefully planned to fit into the historic community of mostly Federal style rowhouses, the designers positioned the houses flush with the front lot line, provided arched sally ports between units to access the rear, set the houses on high basements, and used traditional fenestration patterns (FIGURE 131). Attempting to blend with the mix of architectural styles in the area, they combined both Federal style gable-roofed units with plain cornices and shed-roofed Italianates with segmental-arched window lintels and a modillion cornice. Both styles, however, are dressed with neocolonial features—six-paneled doors, multi-pane sash, shutters, Williamsburg paint colors, and carriage lights. There are notable differences between the construction techniques of these 1990s townhouses and the authentic nineteenth-century rowhouses around the corner: the original houses have wooden cornices and trim; the window mullions do not pop out (as do the new flexi-mullions), and the exterior wooden shutters are truly operable.[25]

A few blocks from the Sandtown neighborhood, development of new rowhouses for moderate-income families got underway in 1997 on 6.7 acres at the corner of Eutaw Place and North Avenue and extending south to Robert Street. This area was filled in the late nineteenth century with several blocks of picturesque rowhouses, many of them built by Joseph Cone; indeed, a few surviving Queen Anne style houses originally built by Cone still stand (SEE FIGURE 65). As part of the city's urban renewal efforts, the historic rows were condemned and razed in the early 1960s, to be replaced with public housing garden apartments. Thirty years later, by the early 1990s, the public housing apartment complex known as Eutaw Gardens had deteriorated to such a state that it too was razed in the summer of 1997, one of the first low-rise public housing projects the city demolished.

The City awarded development rights to a team that proposed to build owner-occupied rowhouses on the site, to be called Spicer's Run in honor of a small stream that once ran from the area to Jones Falls. The plan is designed "to enhance the community and bring middle-income people to the area," said Wendy Blair, the project's co-developer with Derek McDaniels, which calls for houses priced in the $115,000 to $130,000 range. Similar to Pleasant View Gardens, the designers of Spicer's Run re-instituted the original street grid of the four-block parcel and drew up plans for eighty-six 20-foot-wide three-story houses, with depths ranging from 30 feet to 36 feet. The architects, D. W. Taylor and Associates, who also designed Montgomery Square, created rowhouses that combine modern, cost-saving materials and traditional Italianate-style elements—tall, narrow windows, bracketed cornices, and arched doorway surrounds—to match the nearby historic neighborhood of Bolton Hill (FIGURE 132). Cornices and door surrounds will be made of fiberglass and instead of a traditional Italianate-style shed roof, the roofs will be gabled, a more practical configuration. As at Montgomery Square in Federal Hill, most of the houses are designed with a built-in garage at basement level, accessed from the rear. The integral garage is economical to construct and an important security measure, which commercial lenders increasingly are requiring when they finance development projects.[26]

The Enduring Baltimore Rowhouse

More than any other type of urban dwelling, the rowhouse can foster one aspect of urban living that is absolutely critical to a neighborhood—the sense of community where residents on a block look out for one another. A neighborhood will not function as a block of strangers. Because the rowhouse is close to the street and sidewalk, and offers low-height and low-density housing, it preserves the important human scale. The odds for strong urban neighborhoods seem to increase as the number of stories in a dwelling decreases; homeownership cements this neighborhood bond. Such is the argument in favor of building and renovating rowhouses.

When the city slated Lafayette Courts for demolition in 1994, it involved the community in the decision of what would take its place. Father John Roche of St. Vincent de Paul, the Roman Catholic Church three blocks away, remembers the community's unanimous response: "Give us rowhouses." Another resident, Janice Bagwell said, "We just want to live in the same kind of housing that everybody else has." No apartment blocks or low-scale units like the Poe Homes, but the Baltimore tradition of the front door opening out to the public street. Daniel P. Henson III, the city housing commissioner, in 1995 said the project "removes the stigma of living differently from the rest of your neighbors. It gives people a good place to raise their families. Its designed to give people the will to move on with their lives, as opposed to feeling trapped." U. S. Senator and long-time Fells Point resident Barbara Mikulski added, "Lafayette Courts was a dangerous place to live, a dangerous place for kids to play and no place to raise a family. The new housing will help remedy a failed urban policy and give a hand up to those who want to help themselves."[27]

Designers CHK Architects and Planners, part of Lafayette Court's redevelopment team, called for restoring the qualities of community. "Care was taken to maintain the essential characteristics of the Baltimore rowhouse," planner Cheryl O'Neill recalled. "The stoop, the continuity of wall surface between units, the heavy cornice, the vertical proportions of

the windows, and the repetitive and constant rhythm of window spacing."
The architects also adopted neotraditional planning concepts—part of the
new urbanism—such as the use of narrow streets to slow down traffic, sidewalks to encourage walking about the community, on-street parking, and
public areas where neighbors can gather (FIGURE 133). For residents, their
own backyards were of prime importance, as opposed to the nebulous open
space that surrounded the old towers. Because of the failures of life in the
towers, site planning also incorporated residents' concerns for security and
defensible space, such as eliminating thru-traffic (which led to drug trafficking). In addition to the rowhouses, a day care center, recreation center,
community center, and senior center make up the public buildings on site.
In early 1998 the Boys and Girls Clubs of Central Maryland opened a $3
million educational center for up to 225 local children, which provides a
computer lab, an arts and culture program, and help with homework, in
addition to physical fitness and recreation programs.[28]

CHK's redesign for the Lafayette Courts site—the new rowhouse
community Pleasant View Gardens—was one of the first projects nationwide to apply the principles of the new urbanism to public housing design
and in 1997 won the American Institute of Architect's Honor Award for
Urban Design. The rowhouse was only one among several basic parts of
the solution to create a livable neighborhood. Baltimore housing commissioner Henson understood the importance of identity for a community. A
study of neighborhoods in Chicago found lower rates of violence in urban
neighborhoods with a strong community fabric. In addition to homeownership, the Chicago study concluded, community stemmed from a combination of shared parental supervision and ownership of public space. CHK
planner O'Neill suggests that this intangible but very real community
identity is a major aim of Pleasant View Gardens: "The larger goal of the
new project...is to make this public housing neighborhood just like the
other residential neighborhoods of the city, such as Little Italy or Fells
Point (FIGURE 133)."[29]

Baltimore planners' recent enthusiasm for the rowhouse derives from
the historical record: Edward Gallagher's neighborhoods survived for a
century or more while Lafayette Courts failed within three decades. Over
the years, Gallagher's and other rowhouse neighborhoods have provided
many city dwellers an affordable house, and also the sense of community
that is essential to the survival of a neighborhood. Among Gallagher's
developments throughout Baltimore, some have fared better than others,
but the residents of each one can define a distinct neighborhood character,
well beyond a collection of houses.

Gallagher's first large-scale development, Park Side, survives completely intact. Glover Street, the narrow mid-block street where Bronislaw Wesolowski bought his first house, looks essentially the same as it did in Gallagher's 1909 advertising brochure. The iron-spot brick façades, which builders claimed would never need painting, show no signs of wear. Families can still walk across Eastern Avenue to Patterson Park in a few minutes. True to Baltimore tradition, most of the houses on Glover and the surrounding streets are owner-occupied. Along with other Poles, Wesolowski was a first-time buyer in a brand new development. Almost ninety years later the housing pattern has come full circle. New residents in Park Side are also young and buying their first homes, but unlike Wesolowski, they are mostly single. The health of the neighborhood is due to the rejuvenation of Canton, an area a few blocks south on the edge of the harbor. The revitalization of Baltimore's Inner Harbor has moved eastward into this once industrial neighborhood and it is now becoming gentrified. Young professionals, some just graduated from college, live in rowhouses near the descendants of Wesolowski's Polish neighbors. The old factories where Gallagher's working-class buyers once toiled, like American Can or the Tin Decorating Company, are being rehabilitated into upscale housing and retail space. Restaurants, bookstores, health clubs, and nightspots catering to a young, urbane market, are opening at a rapid pace. Wesolowski's $700 four-room house is now about eighty times more expensive, with houses on Glover Street selling for around $55,000.

Saint Clair, on Belair Road across from Clifton Park, was Gallagher's development priced especially for the working class in the 1920s. For $3,900, a purchaser could own a porch-front house with a tiny front yard, a park across the street, and a daylight plan squeezed inside. Today, the same house can be acquired for $30,000 to $40,000, mostly by black families who are just as eager to move out of crowded East Baltimore into a neighborhood near a city park as Gallagher's German and Polish buyers were over seventy years ago. Because there is a high percentage of homeowners, the neighborhood is generally well maintained.

Ednor Gardens is still considered by many realtors and rowhouse experts to be the best rowhouse community in Baltimore. The design of the houses, the landscaping, and the siting of the rows combine to give Ednor Gardens a sense of place that every resident now and in the past has strived to preserve. It also enjoys a strong sense of neighborhood identity, which has made it a desirable place to live. Quality construction, spacious interiors, and quick commuting to downtown offer unmatched value to buyers, for an average house price of $80,000. By contrast, comparable houses in surrounding suburbs sell at more than twice the price.

Gallagher's marketing theme, the "cottage in the city," turned out to be quite accurate, and enduring. Ednor Gardens is in the midst of the city yet its ambiance is that of a small village remote from the congestion of the central city. While many among Baltimore's middle class have moved out of the city to seek small town environments, Ednor Gardens' residents have found it here—and this within a ten-minute commute of downtown. Ironically, the presence of the city's major league baseball and football stadium next door (until the 1992 opening of Camden Yards) did not detract from Ednor Gardens' value or livability. On summer nights the cheering of the crowds at a baseball game became a background sound as familiar as music on the radio.

The argument that contends that homeownership engenders pride of place continues to be proven in Baltimore's old and new rowhouse neighborhoods. Ednor Gardens was always a neighborhood of owners who recognized the distinction of their community. Beyond the activities of the community association, which helps to maintain city services, such informal acts as next-door neighbors trimming bushes on a vacant property waiting to be sold are telling signs of the neighborhood's health. The quality of the architectural and landscape design is also crucial. The English, Norman, and neocolonial rows at Ednor Gardens have retained their handsome appearance, and residents are proud to own them.

Baltimore's rowhouse neighborhoods have an enduring quality. In 1993, when Robert Tarring's son, Robert III, was first looking for a place to live he chose Rodgers Forge, the same community of neocolonial rowhouses his father had chosen twenty years earlier. In 1999 the first residents of Pleasant View Gardens are settling into their newly built neocolonial rows. Many will be offered the chance to become homeowners because of the goals of the city and the federal government. Richard Gibson is optimistic (FIGURE 135). He has a front door, a front stoop, and a back yard. His daughter walks across the street to the tot lot and down the street to the village circle, where ice-cream trucks stop regularly. He has air-conditioning and cable television, and a parking space in front of the house. Frances Foster, 77, who lived in the high-rise tower for forty years, settled into her new two-bedroom house with the help of her six children and at least six grandchildren, one of whom will be sharing the house with her. "I feel good," she said. "I feel real good." Many of her friends from the tower will be coming too, to live next door to one another, in a neighborhood. Hazel Carter, 54, who spent thirty-one years at Lafayette Courts says, "It's going to be quiet, and it's small, and it's my dream."[30]

Notes

CHAPTER ONE (PAGES 9-17)

1. That he was able to do this within such a short time gives credence to the family tradition that he and his brother arrived with substantial funds in hand. Information regarding house sales and Singewald's neighbors comes from Baltimore City Land Records, Clarence J. Mitchell Courthouse, Baltimore (hereafter referred to as BCLR) and Hall of Records, Annapolis and the Baltimore City Directories. The entire range of directories is available at Maryland Historical Society and Enoch Pratt Free Library, Baltimore. The titles and publishers vary from year to year; they will hereafter be cited as Directory. Traugoth Singewald's three different house purchases are documented in BCLR, Liber AWB 365, folio 374 (Liberty Alley, 1846); Liber ED 15, folio 473 (east side of Broadway, 1852); and Liber ED 134, folio 94 (west side of Broadway, 1857). Directory 1818, 1822–1823, 1847, 1851, 1855–56, 1858, 1860. For information on Baltimore's German community see, Dieter Cunz, *The Maryland Germans, A History* (Princeton, NJ: Princeton University Press, 1948).

2. The various occupants of Singewald's block in Fells Point, running from Broadway west to Bethel and then Bond Street, and from Lancaster north to Alicanna Street can be found in BCLR, Block Index, vol. 1, under block 1811. Directory, 1851, 1852, 1853–54, 1855–56, 1858, 1860.

3. For further information on English rowhouse prototypes, see Stefan Muthesius, *The English Terraced House* (New Haven and London: Yale University Press, 1982), and John Summerson, *Georgian London* (London: Pleiades Books, 1945; Rev. ed., Pelican Books, 1962 and Penguin Books, 1969). Citations will be to the Penguin edition.

4. Summerson, *Georgian London*, 126. According to drawings done by R. Elsam and Peter Nicholson in 1823–25, class I was 4-1/2 stories, 3 bays wide, had a rusticated basement, *piano nobile*, and two floors of bedrooms (marked by graduating window sizes.); class II was 4 stories high and 2 bays wide; class III was a slightly narrower version, and class IV was 3 stories high and 2 bays wide. Class I and II houses extended back the full width of the main house; class III houses had narrow, one-room deep extensions, and class IV houses had no rear extension. See Muthesius, 82–83 for drawings.

5. The efforts of building craftsmen (many of whom earned 21 shillings a week for six months of the year) to become small-scale developers did not always meet with success but this did not deter a great many of them from trying. The most notable exception to the two-unit construction approach was Nicholas Barbon, who in 1686 built Red Lion Square, one of the first large-scale rowhouse developments in which the units were identical in design down to the staircase detailing. The Duke of Westminster is one of the few men from outside the builders' ranks to try his hand at these projects. Summerson, *Georgian London*, 44–51.

6. For further information on ground rents, see Frank A. Kaufman, "The Maryland Ground Rent—Mysterious but Beneficial," *Maryland Law Review* 5, no. 1 (December 1940): 1–72. For a more recent study see Garrett Power, "Parceling Out Land in the Vicinity of Baltimore: 1632–1796," pts. 1 & 2, *Maryland Historical Magazine* vol. 87, no. 4 (Winter 1992): 453–462, & vol. 88, no. 2 (Summer 1993): 150–173; Garrett Power, "Entail in Two Cities: A Comparative Study of Long Term Leases in Birmingham, England and Baltimore, Maryland 1700–1900," *Journal of Architecture and Planning Research*, vol. 9, no. 4 (Winter 1992).

7. Walter Muir Whitehill, *A Topographical History of Boston* (Cambridge: Harvard University Press, Belknap Press 1968), 42, 85; Willliam John Murtagh, "The Philadelphia Rowhouse," *Journal of the Society of Architectural Historians* 16, no. 4 (December 1957): 8, 13.

8. Whitehill, *Topographical History*, 42–77.

9. The authors are indebted to Dr. Jeffrey A. Cohen for information regarding Philadelphia rowhouses. See also Kenneth L. Ames, "Robert Mills and the Philadelphia Rowhouse," *Journal of the Society of Architectural Historians* 27, no. 2 (May 1968): 140–146. A drawing of 1809 showing eleven houses designed for Capt. John Meany closely resembles Soane's Plate XI in *Sketches in Architecture* (London, 1798). Monumentally-scaled rowhouses came late to New York City. Along St. John's Park rows of three-and-a-half story, three-bay wide Federal-style houses went up in the 1820s, but the first planned imposing blockfront, or terrace, appeared in 1827–28 on Bleecker Street—the Le Roy Place houses. Also three-and-a-half stories and three bays wide, the houses sat on high basements and were faced with granite. Depau Row had three-story houses with hipped roofs. See Charles Lockwood, *Bricks & Brownstone: The New York Row House, 1783–1929, An Architectural and Social History* (New York: McGraw-Hill, 1972).

10. This information is gleaned from the records of the city's first fire insurance company, Baltimore

Equitable Society, which opened for business in 1794. Since only one row appears in 1795, another in 1796, and one other in 1798, it is assumed that the form was only just becoming a popular method of house construction in this decade. Until the early 1800s even paired houses were unusual, at least as reflected in the insurance records. Of course, as the practice of insuring houses against damage by fire was a new concept, one cannot assume that these records document all major building activity in the town. However, most major buildings and residences do appear in the records *and* the records reflect both substantial, large-scale dwellings and extremely modest examples, which suggests the sample offered by the Equitable Society's policies provides a relatively accurate view of what kind of building was going on in Baltimore in this period.

11. Baltimore Equitable Society, Policies, vol. A, 281–288; vol. B, 70–71. Directory, 1800–1801.

12. Baltimore Equitable Society, Policies, vol. A, 281–288. Directory, 1804.

13. *Baltimore American*, March 24, 1801.

14. Baltimore Equitable Society, Policies, vol. A, 195–212. Directory, 1804.

15. Baltimore Equitable Society, Policies, vol. A, 180–185. Directory, 1804.

16. Baltimore Equitable Society, Policies, vol. B, 126–127. Directory, 1804.

17. Those craftsmen of the period who identified themselves as master builders in city directories and newspaper notices include the following. Their original trade is noted in parentheses: John Ash (carpenter), Christian Baum (carpenter), James Campbell (artist), Joseph Clark (architect), Thomas Coulson (inlay worker), John Donaldson (carpenter), James Hannan (carpenter), Leonard Harbaugh (engineer), Robert Cary Long (carpenter), James Mosher (bricklayer), John Ready II (carpenter), John Sinclair (carpenter), Robert Sinclair (carpenter), Jacob Small (carpenter), Josias Thompson (carpenter). This information was gleaned from the research files at the Museum of Early Southern Decorative Arts, Old Salem Village, North Carolina.

18. Baltimore Equitable Society, Policies, vol. D, 319, 332, 403, 409. Directory, 1818.

19 Baltimore Equitable Society, Policies, vol. B, 126–127. Directory, 1804.

20. In 1783, Howard leased two lots on Montgomery Street in Federal Hill to a John Ermane with the stipulation that Ermane "within the term of four years from the date hereof, erect and build a good and substantial dwelling house on the premises of the yearly value of 24 pounds current money." Ermane defaulted and surrendered the lease back to Howard. BCLR, Liber WGSS, folio 240. For a more detailed discussion of rowhouses in

Federal Hill see Mary Ellen Hayward, "Urban Vernacular Architecture of Nineteenth Century Baltimore," *Winterthur Portfolio*, vol. 16, no. 1 (Spring 1981).

21. BCLR, Liber WG, no. DD, folio, 502; Liber WG 63, folio 477; Liber WG 71, folio 4. An example of which is the advertisement placed by house builder and carpenter Horatio Berry in 1811 for the house adjoining his own: "To Let, a convenient two story BRICK DWELLING house situated on the corner of Green and German-streets, western precincts. Enquire [sic] of the subscriber living next door." *Federal Gazette and Baltimore Daily Advertiser*, April 11, 1811.

22. BCLR, Liber WG 147, folio 442; Liber WG 156, folio 349, 652; Liber WG 158, folio 93. Directory, 1822, 1824. Speculatively built houses were commonly sold to investors, as an advertisement of 1810 makes clear: "Three small brick houses . . . they will be sold together or separately—those persons who are desirous of holding property on account of interest, will find very little, if any, in this city, equal to that now offered. The price for which it may be had at private sale will produce from 11 to 12 per cent per annum." *Federal Republican and Commercial Gazette*, May 9, 1810.

23. For the English background of this practice, see Summerson, *Georgian London*.

24. *Baltimore American and Commercial Daily Advertiser*, June 29, 1822.

25. *Baltimore American*, September 3, 1800.

26. John Moxon, *Mechanick Exercises, or the Doctrine of Handy-works, Applied to the Art of Smithing, Joinery, Carpentry, and Turning* 3rd Edition (London: J. Moxon, 1700), 1977 microfilm reproduction of original, Bodleian Library; William Chambers, *Treatise on Civil Architecture* (London, 1759); Batty Langley, *A Sure Guide for Builders* (London, 1729).

27. Moxon, *Mechanick Exercises*. For further information on eighteenth-century building practices, see Summerson, *Georgian London;* Charles E. Peterson, ed., *Building Early America: Contributions Toward the History of a Great Industry* (Radnor, PA: Chilton Book Co., 1976); George Balcomb, *History of Building: Styles, Methods and Materials* (London: Batsford Academic and Educational Press, 1985); and Martin Briggs, *A Short History of Building Crafts* (Oxford: Claridon Press, 1945).

28. Compare this to Batty Langley's *A Sure Guide for Builders* (London, 1729), in which houses were ranked from first to fourth rate with the thickness of front and rear walls specified for each ranking. For first-rate houses (equivalent to most two-and-a-half story Baltimore rows) a cellar wall needed to be 18 inches thick, walls of the next two floors 14 inches thick, and the garret wall 9 inches thick. The fourth-rate house, "being chiefly for Nobelmen and etc. Have

their Thickness left to the Discretion of the Architect," a notion that most structural engineers today would find amusing. Roofs of early rows had 3"-by-4" rafters spaced 24 inches on center, covered with 1"-by-8" planking, spaced 4 inches apart to allow for ventilation of the wood shingle roof. Although the roofs of Georgian London were slate, Baltimore's were mainly wood.

29. In 1798 the city had passed an ordinance requiring inhabitants of every dwelling to keep two leather fire buckets hung near their front door or pay a $5 fine. Ordinance No. 109 (approved December 12, 1798), *Ordinances of the Corporation of the City of Baltimore* (Baltimore: Thomas Dobbin, 1798); Ordinance No. 22 (approved June 11, 1799). *Ordinances of the Corporation of the City of Baltimore* (Baltimore: Thomas Dobbin, 1799); Ordinance No. 31 (approved February 9, 1826), *Ordinances of the Corporation of the City of Baltimore* (Baltimore: William Warner, 1826).

30. For further information on the brickmaking industry see Harley J. McKee, "Brick and Stone, Handicraft to Machine," in Peterson, ed., *Building Early America*, 74–91; Ralph J. Robison, "Brick in Baltimore," *Baltimore*, September 1952; Lee H. Nelson, "Brickmaking in Baltimore, 1798," *Journal of the Society of Architectural Historians* vol. 18, no. 1 (March 1959): 33–34.

31. The number of ordinances in Baltimore regarding penalties for unswept chimneys and the need for periodic inspections of fireplaces, stove pipes, and chimneys reflected this constant fear of fire. The superintendent of chimney sweeps had to approve all installation of stovepipes as well. See Ordinance No. 109 (approved December 12, 1798), *Ordinances of the Corporation of the City of Baltimore* (Baltimore: Thomas Dobbin, 1799).

32. As in other early residential architecture, early-nineteenth-century rowhouse life centered around the traditional fireplace, even though it was an extremely inefficient heat source. Beginning in the early eighteenth century, inventors tried to improve the traditional English fireplace by adding jamb stoves (boxes made of five iron plates set in the rear wall of the fireplace), parabolically curved fireboxes (to reflect more heat into the room), and dozens of other designs. In America, the most notable of these was Benjamin Franklin's Pennsylvania Fire-Place—an open-front cast iron firebox that could stand well forward in an existing fireplace and radiate much more heat. Between the plates of cast iron, smoke and heat rose against the front surface of the airbox, descended along its back surface, and then rose to the chimney. See Cecil D. Eliot, "Heating and Ventilation," *Technics and Architecture* (Cambridge: MIT

Press, 1994); Eugene S. Ferguson, "An Historical Sketch of Central Heating: 1800–1860," in Peterson, ed., *Building Early America*, 165–181.

33. *Baltimore Gazette and Daily Advertiser*, January 1, 1822. Eliot, "Heating and Ventilation," 274.

34. Eliot, "Heating and Ventilation," 275. Such stoves remained in use in rowhouses until the advent of gravity air or steam furnaces which first were used in expensive rowhouses by the mid-nineteenth century. They did not become available for working class rows until the late nineteenth or even early twentieth century.

35. Alfred Quick, "Baltimore Water Works," in *Baltimore, Its History and Its People*, ed. Clayton Coleman Hall (New York: Lewis Historical Publishing Co., 1912), vol. 1, 413–23.

36. Quick, "Baltimore Water Works," 414. Metal pipes for supplying water initially used the same manufacturing methods as those used for making gun barrels, and early installations often made use of inexpensive gun barrels or ones rejected because of inferior quality. Wells continued to be a source of domestic water until 1915 and the last of the spring-fed fountains remained until 1945.

37. Maureen Ogle, "Domestic Reform and American Household Plumbing, 1840–1870," *Winterthur Portfolio*, vol. 14, no. 3 (Autumn 1979); advertisements *Baltimore Gazette and Daily Advertiser*, June 1, 1820

38. Ordinance No. 11 (approved March 18, 1817), *Ordinances of the Corporation of the City of Baltimore* (Baltimore: William Warner, 1817). In 1819 John Hignat, a Baltimore brickmaker, publicly complained about "the excrements, dead horses and other nuisances which are deposited in the neighborhood of my brickyard," stating that the City Council would not respond to his petitions to "get the evil removed;" in *Morning Chronicle and Baltimore Advertiser*, July 28, 1819.

39. In the 1870s when the public health movement proved that sanitary engineering greatly reduced disease, the public finally gave strong support for building a sewer system. In Baltimore's case, however, it came far later than most cities of her size. See Eliot, "Heating and Ventilation," 219; Sam Bass Warner, *Streetcar Suburbs* (Cambridge: Harvard University Press, 1978), 31.

40. Penn's design, in turn, had been based on that of London after the Great Fire of 1666, and had a regular grid and public squares (but not Sir Christopher Wren's diagonal vistas). For further information on the Poppleton plan, see Richard J. Cox, "Trouble on the Chain Gang: City Surveying, Maps, and the Absence of Urban Planning in Baltimore 1730–1823; With a Checklist of Maps of the Period," *Maryland Historical Magazine*, vol. 81, no. 1 (Spring 1986).

Unlike New York City's 25-foot-by-100-foot lots, Baltimore's followed no set dimensions and all varied in size.

41. Baltimore Equitable Society, Policies, vol. E, 35–37, 152. Directory, 1822–23. See also William Voss Elder, *Robert Mills' Waterloo Row—Baltimore, 1816* (Baltimore: Baltimore Museum of Art, 1971).

42. Baltimore Equitable Society, Policies, vol. E, 228–230.

43. Baltimore Equitable Society, Policies, vol. D, 410. Directory, 1818.

44. Baltimore Equitable Society, Policies, vol. E, 249, 291–91. Directory, 1822–23.

45. Thomas W. Griffith, *Annals of Baltimore* (Baltimore: W. Wooddy, 1833), 250–51.

46. For further information on the Greek Revival in New York, see Charles Lockwood, *Bricks & Brownstone, The New York Row House, 1783-1929: An Architectural and Social History* (New York: McGraw Hill, 1972).

47. Maryland Historical Society Library, Washington Monument Papers, MS 876.

48. Griffith, *Annals*, 280. It remains unclear as to how closely Howard and Small collaborated. See Robert L. Alexander, "William F. Small, 'Architect of the City,'" *Journal of the Society of Architectural Historians*, vol. 20, no. 2 (May 1961): 66–68.

49. (Baltimore: John Murphy, 1840.) The Maryland Historical Society Library and the Library of the Peabody Institute both possess copies of the 1840 and 1848 editions.

50. Baltimore *Sun*, June 2, 1848.

51. BCLR, Liber TK 140, folio 164; Liber TK 270, folio 83.

52. BCLR, Liber AWB 351, folio 525; Liber AWB. 429, folio 354.

53. BCLR, Liber AWB 427, folio 318; Liber AWB 462, folio 175; Liber AWB 463, folio 260; Liber AWB 467, folio 82. Roche went on to build stylish Italianate houses in the 1870s in the upper Mt. Vernon area and was consistently noted in the *Sun* as being the city's most prolific builder of fine houses.

54. Baltimore *Sun*, December 13, 1850.

55. By the mid-1850s several omnibus lines served the city. The People's Line ran west to east between Franklin Square, Baltimore Street, Gay Street, and Madison Square; the Accommodation Line ran south from Pennsylvania Avenue to Baltimore Street and then east to Broadway and Fells Point; and Messrs. Zimmerman & Co.'s Citizens' Line ran south from Madison Street to Howard, Baltimore, and Gay, and Pratt Streets, and then east to Broadway. Each of these lines was in service during business hours on weekdays, with the coaches running every five minutes. On June 2, 1854, the *Sun* noted that "Johnson's Accomodating [sic] Line" now had "fourteen first class coaches," including four new ones, built in New York that were "amongst the handsomest coaches we have yet seen on our streets." The writer went on to add: "Baltimore is now pretty well supplied with these lines, there being six lines traveling the city from the extreme points—east, west, northeast, and south—besides the cemetery lines and some other independent coaches. It is comparatively but a short time since the first coach was introduced, and their rapid increase goes to show the popularity they have achieved. They are emphatically the 'people's carriages,' and everybody rides." If one didn't live near an omnibus line, a hackney coach could be hired, but they were expensive. The fare of 50 cents for one passenger (37-1/2 cents for two or more) from any steamboat landing or railway station to a hotel or residence or vice-versa was doubled when the coach was sent specifically from the stables. See William A. House, "Street Car System and Rapid Transit," in Hall, ed., *Baltimore, Its History and Its People*, vol. 1, 542–58. See also Baltimore *Sun*, July 18, 1853; June 2, 1854; May 28, 1856

56. BCLR, Liber AWB 464, folio 525. Directory, 1850. Slightly larger two-story-and-attic houses in Federal Hill (13 feet front by 30 feet deep, with a one-story back building) rented for $100 annually. Baltimore *Sun*, July 10, 1848.

57. BCLR, Liber TK 296, folio 322; Liber ED 36, folio 102; Liber TK 316, folio 49. Directories 1842, 1849–50.

58. Baltimore *Sun*, June 29, 1850.

59. Baltimore *Sun*, August 3, 1853.

60. Gittings obituary, vertical clipping file, Maryland Historical Society Library.

61. BCLR, Liber ED 32, folio 99.

62. John Ahern, the proprietor of the Cecelia Furnace in Canton built tightly packed rows of 11-foot and 12-foot wide gabled-roofed houses on Spruce Alley, which he laid out in the early 1850s, and on adjoining Castle and Washington Street, which he sold for $200 to $250 to both Germans and Irish laborers, tailors, shoemakers, and porters among others in the years 1851–1855. Today all the houses are Formstoned, but all are lived in and well cared for. BCLR, Liber AWB, folio 477; Liber ED 75, folio 471; Liber ED 124, folio 361; Liber ED 131, folio 16; Liber ED 140, folio 67, 69, 111. Directory, 1855–56, 1858, 1860.

63. Even a few two-and-a-half-story half houses were built in Baltimore, probably in the late 1830s. A distinctive group stands on West Montgomery Street in Federal Hill.

CHAPTER TWO

1. William Tufts Bingham, *Baltimore Hats, Past and Present: An historical sketch of the hat industry of Baltimore from its earliest days to the present.* (Baltimore, 1890). Only Edward, the youngest son, did not enter the business. Instead he went to medical school at Johns Hopkins in the 1880s and became a physician in Baltimore in the 1890s.
2. Baltimore *Sun*, August 7, 1860.
3. Baltimore *Sun*, January 5, 1853. For an overview of Baltimore's economic growth in this period, see Gary L Browne, *Baltimore in the Nation, 1789–1861* (Chapel Hill: University of North Carolina Press, 1980), and Dennis M. Zembala, ed., *Baltimore: Industrial Gateway in the Chesapeake* (Baltimore: Baltimore Museum of Industry, 1995); and Charles Hirschfield, *Baltimore, 1870–1900: Studies in Social History* (Baltimore: The Johns Hopkins University Press, 1941).
4. Baltimore *Sun*, December 11, 1858.
5. Baltimore *Sun*, July 31, 1872.
6. Baltimore *Sun*, January 2, 1873.
7. Dieter Cunz, *The Maryland Germans* (Princeton: Princeton University Press, 1948).
8. Baltimore *Sun*, July 20, 1872; August 25, 1877; November 9, 1880; July 2, 1881; January 17, 1941. See also Alfred Quick, "Baltimore Water Works," in Hall, ed., *Baltimore, Its History and Its People*, vol. 1, 413–23.
9. Baltimore *Sun*, October 10, 1894.
10. For further information on Baltimore's streetcar system, see Michael Farrell, *The History of Baltimore's Streetcars* (Sykesville: Greenberg Publishing Co., 1992); and William A. House, "Streetcar System and Rapid Transit," in Hall, ed., *Baltimore, Its History and Its People*.
11. The Rogers property was three-quarters-mile beyond the city limits and its acquisition provoked outcry, but city fathers were planning for future expansion of the city. They believed, rightly so, that the initial growth would come in the form of suburban houses for the well-to-do, and eventually long lines of rowhouses that would slowly encircle the park. Baltimore *Sun*, July 25, 1909.
12. Baltimore *Sun*, February 22, 1843.
13. Baltimore *Sun*, February 19, 1845.
14. For further information on Baltimore's cast-iron architecture, see James D. Dilts and Catherine F. Black, editors, *Baltimore's Cast-Iron Buildings and Architectural Ironwork* (Centreville, MD: Tidewater Publishers, 1991). New York architect Robert G. Hatfield worked with Bogardus on the design of the Sun Iron Building.
15. The romantic impulse soon spread to other realms. Cemeteries had Egyptian obelisk burial stones, Egyptian style mausoleums, castellated gates, and tall Gothic mortuary chapels. Jails looked like stone castles in which even the prisoners' dining room was decorated with a vaulted ceiling.
16. A. J. Downing, *The Architecture of Country Houses* (New York: Dover Publications, 1969), 317.
17. Baltimore's Athenaeum housed the newly founded Maryland Historical Society, the Library Company of Baltimore, and the Mercantile Library.
18. Baltimore *Sun*, May 5, 1844.
19. Baltimore *Sun*, February 23, 1839.
20. Baltimore *Sun*, June 11, 12, 1839.
21. Baltimore *Sun*, March 8, 1847.
22. Baltimore *Sun*, June 4, 1850; June 21, 1852.
23. Baltimore *Sun*, May 16, 1850; June 21, 1852.
24. Baltimore *Sun*, April 11, 1850.
25. Baltimore *Sun*, September 30, 1851.
26. BCLR, Liber AWB 445, folio 440; Liber AWB 456, folio 4' Liber ED 64, folio 328; Liber ED 42, folio 306; Liber ED 50, folio 312. Baltimore City Directory, 1853–54; 1855–56.
27. BCLR, Liber TK 285, folio 55; Liber AWB 342, folio 33.
28. BCLR, Liber ED 42, folio 64; Liber ED 73, folio 35; Liber ED 116, folio 466-71; ED 128, folio 548. Directory, 1855–56, 1858, 1860.
29. BCLR, Liber ED 55, folio 475; ED 72, folio 222–23; Liber 93, folio 434, 440, 446. In October and November 1855 William Thomas executed leases for the three houses at the western end of the row to Samuel Black, a stonecutter; John L. Reese Jr., a brickmaker; and Henry M. Fitzhugh, a clerk of the Circuit Court for Baltimore County. Thomas gave Black and Reese $4,000 mortgages. Since the two men never lived in the houses, and since they assigned them back to Philip Thomas in 1857, it seem likely that these transactions represented a pay-off for construction work: Black supplied the brownstone and Reese the brick. They received houses worth $8,000 for the price of $4,000, and had only to pay the mortgage interest on a $4,000 loan and the ground rent, while being able to rent the houses for probably $600–$700 annually. Fitzhugh lived at Waverly Terrace and undoubtedly bought his house as an investment; he sold it a year-and-a-half later to a merchant tailor, who lived there. Fitzhugh acquired another house in the row in 1860, a unit that William Thomas had leased originally to David Carson, a builder who may have constructed the row.
30. Baltimore *Sun*, December 13, 1850; July 5, 1852.
31. Account book kept by Decatur H. Miller for building his house on Cathedral Street, 1849, made available to the authors by Charles B. Duff. See also Charles Lockwood, *Bricks &*

Brownstone, The New York Row House, 1783–1929: An Architectural and Social History (New York: McGraw Hill, 1972).

32. Charles T. Davis, "Pressed Bricks and Ornamental Bricks," *American Architect & Building News*, vol. 17, no. 487 (April 25, 1885); Ralph J. Robinson, "Brick in Baltimore," *Baltimore*, vol. 45, no. 11 (Sept. 1952): 37–43; Walter S. Kunz Jr., "The Use of Gauged and Pressed Brick in the Baltimore Vicinity," unpublished paper, 1980; *American Architect & Building News*, vol. 23, no. 634 (February 17, 1888).

33. Baltimore *Sun*, January 12, 1858; BCLR, Liber ED 136, folio 370–372; Liber ED 137, folio 157–160. Directory, 1860. The Donnells leased the lots with $155 ground rents and offered an advance mortgage of $1,750 to the builders for each house. Each advance mortgage contract specified that the houses erected were to be "similar to houses on the south side of Hollins Street west of Fremont, or the south side of Fayette between Calhoun and Stricker previously built by Mallonee."

34. Baltimore *Sun*, January 24, 1871. The number of building permits soared from 1,384 in 1866 to 3,430 in 1870. The financial recession of 1873 slowed the pace to about 1,500 annually, but in the next decade the number rose again.

35. Baltimore *Sun*, July 12, 1856; *Republican and Argus*, April 24, 1857.

36. Baltimore *Sun*, August 1867; January 15, 1859.

37. Henry L. Mencken, *Happy Days* (New York: Alfred A. Knopf, 1936, 1969 edition), 8–10, 63–64, 69. Basement hot-air furnaces were a decided improvement over free-standing cast-iron stoves in every room. Flues installed in the walls allowed the hot air to rise, or a central grate in the first floor allowed gravity heating. Furnace gases were expelled through the chimney. That the house also had a bathroom, demonstrates how much had changed for the middle and upper classes. In 1855 there were only 720 "water closets" and 2,055 baths in the entire city; fifteen years later the number was over 8,000.

38. Mencken, *Happy Days*, 27–28.

39. BCLR, Liber GR 507, folio 269, 274; Liber GR 510, folio 79–80; Liber GR 511, folio 523 [Gilmor, Pratt, and Lemmon Streets]; Liber GR 653, folio 207; Liber GR 779, folio 482 [Lombard Street]. Directory, 1872, 1875, 1876, 1877. For an overview of activity in this block, see Block Index, vol. 1, block 246.

40. BCLR, Liber GR 560, folio 87; Directory, 1873.

41. BCLR, Liber RTA 976, folio 331; Liber RTA 983, folio 92 [Hollins Street]. Directory, 1873, 1875, 1878, 1884–85.

42. In an ironic twist, in 1878 Thomas Winans hired builder George Blake to build twenty-three *three-story* dwellings in South Baltimore,

each with "pressed brick fronts, with halls and verandas, nine rooms with all modern conveniences." The houses were to be "pioneers of a complete square of dwellings," which Winans intended to erect on Marshall Street, "for the accommodation of business men in that section of the city who have heretofore been compelled to seek dwellings in the western and northwestern sections of the city." The houses were within a few blocks of Riverside Park and commanded "a fine view of Fort McHenry, the Patapsco River and the Chesapeake bay." Baltimore *Sun*, March 30, 1878.

43. This material was published originally in Mary Ellen Hayward, "Urban Vernacular Architecture of Nineteenth- Century Baltimore," *Winterthur Portfolio* vol. 16 no. 1 (Spring 1981).

44. Baltimore *Sun*, October 9, 1885; September 16, 1897.

45. See Cecil D. Eliot, "Heating and Ventilation," *Technics and Architecture* (Cambridge: MIT Press, 1994); Harley J. McKee, "Brick and Stone: Handicraft to Machine," in Peterson, ed., *Building Early America*, 74–91.

46. William L. Sims, *Two Hundred years of the History and Evolution of Woodworking Machinery* (Leicestershire, England: Waldren Press, 1985); J. Richard, *A Treatise on Construction and Operation of Woodworking Machinery* (New York and London: E. and F. N. Spon, 1872); Jeff Tunney, interview by Charles Belfoure, Baltimore, March 1998.

47. For further information on Joseph Cone and his building operations see Martha J. Vill, "Residential Development on a Landed Estate: The Case of Baltimore's 'Harlem,'" *Maryland Historical Magazine* vol. 77 no. 3 (Fall 1982): 266–178; and Martha J. Vill, "Building Enterprise in Late Nineteenth-Century Baltimore," *Journal of Historical Geography*, vol. 12, no. 2 (1986), 162–181.

48. Baltimore *Sun*, April 20, 1878.

49. Baltimore *Gazette*, October 1, 1878.

CHAPTER THREE

1. For further information on Baltimore's streetcar system, see Michael K. Farrell, *History of Baltimore's Streetcars* (Sykesville, MD: Greenberg Publishing Company, 1992). Horsecars could travel twice the speed (6–8 miles per hour) as omnibuses. See also "The Street Railway System of Philadelphia: Its History and Present Condition," *The Johns Hopkins University Studies in History and Political Science*, vol. 15, nos. 3, 4, 5 (1897).

2. Richard Plunz, *A History of Housing in New York City* (New York: Columbia University Press, 1990); Robert G. Barrows, "Beyond the

Tenement Patterns of American Urban Housing 1870–1930," *Journal of Urban History*, vol. 9, no. 4 (August 1983).

3. For further information on Baltimore's industrial growth, see Allan D. Anderson, *The Origin and Resolution of an Urban Crisis, Baltimore, 1890–1930*. (Baltimore: Johns Hopkins University Press, 1981); Eleanor F. Bruchey, "The Development of Baltimore Business, 1880–1914," parts 1 & 2, *Maryland Historical Magazine* (Spring and Summer, 1969): 18–42; 144–160; and Charles Hirschfield, *Baltimore, 1870–1904: Studies in Social History* (Baltimore, Johns Hopkins University Press, 1941). See also the 10th, 11th, and 12th reports of the United States Census Bureau (Washington, DC: U. S. Government Printing Office, 1880, 1890, 1900).

4. *Daily Record*, September 19, 1891.

5. The Baltimore *Sun*, May 11, 1878.

6. Henry Hudson Holly, "Modern Dwellings: Their Construction, Decoration, and Furniture," *Harper's New Monthly Magazine* 52 (1875–76): 855–67. Holly goes on to describe the Queen Anne revival as showing, "the influence of the group of styles known as the Elizabethan, Jacobite, and the style of Francis I, which are now, indeed, to be arranged under the general head of 'free classic,' but the Queen Anne movement has also been influenced by what is known as the 'cottage architecture' of that period. These cottages are partly timbered, partly covered with tile hangings, and have tall and spacious chimnies of considerable merit. Their details partook strongly of the classic character, while the boldness of their outline bore striking resemblance to the picturesque and ever-varying Gothic. Nevertheless they were very genuine and striking buildings, and have been taken freely as suggestions upon which to work by Mr. Richard Norman Shaw...."

7. For further information on the Aesthetic movement and the Queen Anne style, see Robin Spencer, *The Aesthetic Movement: Theory and Practice* (London: Studio Vista, 1972), and Robert A. M. Stern, ed., *The Anglo-American Suburb* (London: Architectural Design, 1981).

8. Baltimore *Sun*, November 21, 1877.

9. *American Architect and Building News* vol. 12, no. 355 (October 14, 1882): 183.

10. *American Architect and Building News* 27, no. 743 (March 22, 1892): 188.

11. Baltimore *Sun*, July 22, 1886.

12. Although Augustus Welby Pugin's archaeologically correct Gothic Revival, mainly an ecclesiological phenomenon, had challenged ideals of the picturesque in the 1830s and 1840s, creative freedom had reasserted itself in the mid-1860s, largely because of the writings and ideas of John Ruskin, whose *Stones of Venice* (1851) and *Seven Lamps of Architecture* (1859) called attention to the beauties of Italian (specifically Venetian) Gothic buildings.

13. Baltimore *Sun*, December 24, 1873.

14. Baltimore *Sun*, June 22, 1886; October 31, 1877.

15. Baltimore *Sun*, May 2, 1881; For information on George Blake, see *Baltimore: The Book of its Board of Trade* (Baltimore: 1895), 56.

16. Baltimore *Sun*, August 24, 1883.

17. Baltimore *Sun*, April 4, 1885.

18. To create an academic look for the Villard houses, McKim, Mead, and White recommended the façade be of light-colored limestone, but Villard insisted on brownstone. Nonresidential examples of the firm's use of the Renaissance Revival style include two mens' clubs in New York City, the University Club and the Century Club.

19. *American Architect and Building News* 27, no. 743 (March 22, 1890): 188.

20. Baltimore *Sun*, October 12, 1895. Baltimore's swell fronts also closely resembled the Federal era bow fronts built by Charles Bulfinch in Boston, a similarity that suggests their popularity in the 1890s was part of the neocolonial revival.

21. A decade earlier, a city dweller had written to the *Sun*: "Now that the fall is drawing near and builders are looking for eligible sites on which to build, I would like to offer a few suggestions. Instead of building rows upon rows of marble-trimmed houses, why not vary the intense monotony by building several squares of houses with porches across their fronts, like those on Mt. Royal avenue? A home of this style is certainly comfortable in summer, and besides, nothing would add so much to the appearance of a street as a row of houses in cottage style, with a small garden in front of each. Where so many uptown lots are 140 or 130 feet long the builder could lop off a little of those long yards, of which there is no necessity, and have a small garden in front;" in Baltimore *Sun*, April 21, 1895.

22. There were three tiers of architects in Baltimore: the first included those who designed such commissions as churches, museums, houses for the wealthy, and large mercantile buildings; the second designed commercial work; and the third designed housing, usually for builders. Rowhouses were designed by third-tier architects that were effectively rowhouse specialists, most often draftsmen with no formal architectural training or college education. Beginning in 1900 the *Sun* often listed the name of the architect along with that of the builder of the rows in its daily real estate column. Gerwig's name appears as architect for 142 rowhouse projects between 1900 and 1920.

23. All of the financial data cited in this section of the chapter has been extracted from the Gallagher Archives, Langsdale Library, University of Baltimore; and the Land Records of Baltimore City. Gallagher founded the company in 1886; under the direction of his two sons, the company built rowhouses for Baltimoreans until the mid-1950s. Gallagher, a wealthy man, had an annual salary from 1917 to the late 1920s of $25,000, a large sum compared to a bricklayer's $1,200 annual wages.

24. Census of Manufactures, 11th U.S. Census (Washington, D.C.: U.S. Government Printing Office, 1890).

25. Agreement of February 1891, Gallagher Archives, EJG 1, Box 54: deeds, leases 1886–1914.

26. *American Architect and Building News* weighed in with its opinion in 1888: "It is obvious what an excellent investment these rents are when only safety and moderate income is desired. The very large amount of Baltimore capital that is buried in them, which might be more advantageously employed in commercial or manufacturing enterprise, is somewhat typical of the traditional spirit of the community." *American Architect and Building News*, vol. 23, no. 639 (March 24, 1888); abstract of 12th U.S. Census (Washington, DC: United States Government Printing Office, 1900).

27. Baltimore *Sun*, August 27, 1895.

28. Building permits began to be published regularly in the *Daily Record* in 1888. They list the builder's name, the location and number of houses built, and the estimated total construction costs. Beginning in about 1900 the *Sun* also began to note building permits, but these entries also listed the architect, if any, involved with the project. Some of the largest rowhouse builders in Baltimore used one architect consistently for their projects. Frank Novak, the biggest developer, employed Joseph Hirt to design his houses and Walter Westphal used Samuel Bersterman. Frederick Beall designed many rows in the early 1900s and was James Keelty's architect for Rodgers Forge in the 1930s. If a first-tier architect ever designed low-priced rows, he did so early in his career when he would take on any work.

29. Gallagher's records reveal that installation of vestibules and kitchens with stamped sheet metal ceilings averaged $4 per house. To control costs Gallagher formed his own building supply company and purchased materials in volume at wholesale prices. For construction costs, see Gallagher's Ledger book, 1904–1915, Gallagher Archives.

30. Baltimore *Sun*, January 28, 1891.

31. Janet Kemp, *Housing Conditions in Baltimore* (Baltimore: Federated Charities, 1907).

Baltimore *Sun*, September 12, 1907; June 20, 1908.

32. Baltimore *Sun*, August 21, 1910.

33. Baltimore *Sun*, September 5, 1893. Poles were not a large percentage of the city's population, but they were a considerable presence in the Fells Point section. Most had grown-up in the agricultural sections of Poland and by the lights of industrializing Baltimore were unskilled workers. They came to form the backbone of the laboring classes, finding work as longshoremen and stevedores, fruit pickers, cannery workers, garment workers, and general laborers. As the Baltimore *Sun* reported, "The learned Polish men of Baltimore say there are 23,000 of their countrymen in the Polish colony here.... About 1,500 arrive annually in this city, but they all stay here. The cause of this is that the Poles have found that Baltimore furnishes an exceptional market for unskilled labor." Baltimore's textile industry expanded dramatically in the mid-1890s. By the early 1900s it employed more than 10,000 workers and produced $17 million worth of men's clothing. Wesolowski was one of these 10,000, and like most of them he was doing repetitive piece-work under the supervision of skilled tailors, and may well have been one of the 2,500 employees who worked in Henry Sonneborn and Company's 8-story building at Paca and Pratt Streets. There were also many other such clothing factories nearby in the northwest portion of the city's central business district.

34. For further information on building and loans, see Martha J. Vill, "Land Tenure, Property Ownership and Home Mortgages in the Late Nineteenth Century, a Case Study of Baltimore's Germans," Ph.D. dissertation, University of Maryland, 1976. The authors are grateful to Josephine D. Fisher who shared her work on "Baltimore's Ethnic Building and Loan Associations, 1865–1914," a graduate paper presented to Johns Hopkins University; W.A. Linn, "Building and Loan Associations, " *Scribners*, vol. 2 no. 65 (1888); Edmund Wrigley, *The Working Man's Way to Wealth, A Practical Treatise on Building Associations: What They Are and How to Use Them* (Philadelphia: James K. Simon, 1869); Baltimore *Sun*, August 21, 1910; May 6, 1923; *Baltimore of Today* (Baltimore: Baltimore Board of Trade, 1915).

35. The records of the Kosciusko Savings and Loan Association are housed at the University of Baltimore Archives. Their original Polish was translated by Charles Belfoure's mother, Kris Belfoure.

36. Baltimore *Sun*, March 31, 1903; Twentieth Annual Report of the Bureau of Statistics and Information of Maryland, 1911.

37. *Industrial Survey of Baltimore, Report of Industries Located Within the Baltimore Metropolitan District* (Baltimore, 1915).

38. Although the Supreme Court struck down segregation ordinances in 1917 and the Maryland Court of Appeals did likewise in 1918, *de facto* segregation persisted in Baltimore until the 1960s. Gallagher and other large-scale building developers would not have considered selling houses to African-Americans under any circumstances and continued to try to shape the character of the neighborhoods they built by selling only to those deemed acceptable. See Garrett Power, "Apartheid Baltimore Style: The Residential Segregation Ordinances of 1910–1913" *Maryland Law Review*, vol. 42 no. 2, 1983; Cynthia Neverdon Morton, "Black Housing Patterns in Baltimore City 1885–1953," in Sari J. Bennett and Charles M. Christian, Ed., Baltimore: A Perspective on Historical Urban Development (Baltimore: American Association of Geographers , 1989); Baltimore *Sun*, October 10, 1910; May 6, 1911.

39. Baltimore *Sun*, April 16 and May 20, 1907.

40. *The First Colored Professional, Clerical, Skilled and Business Directory of Baltimore City* (Baltimore: Robert W. Coleman, published annually 1913 to 1946).

41. Developers were often large investors in urban transit systems. Gallagher's financial records, however, show no investments in Baltimore transit: he instead invested in August Belmont's Interborough Rapid Transit (the first subway in New York City), and Detroit's transit system.

42. Information on the sewerage system in Baltimore comes from Calvin W. Hendrich, "Sewerage Systems" in Hall, ed., *Baltimore: It's History and its People*, 424–28; Baltimore *Sun*, November 9, 1880; December 28, 1901; December 19, 1903; June 28, 1906; August 16, 1908; September 24, 1911; M. J. Ruark, *The Disposal of Night Soil in Baltimore* (Baltimore: American Society for Municipal Improvement, 1923).

CHAPTER FOUR

1. Since the new houses were wider, fewer could be fit into the same parcel of land. But since developers set ground rent prices on a front footage basis, they did not lose money by providing a wider house—they simply charged a higher ground rent (commonly about $90 in the 1920s).

2. This was a national phenomenon. By 1901, $420 million had been spent on land acquisition for suburban developments in America and $60 million had been spent by street railways to extend service to the new regions. See Vincent J. Scully, *The Shingle Style: Architectural Theory and Design from Richardson to the Origins of Wright* (New Haven: Yale University Press, 1955).

3. For a comprehensive study of the Roland Park Company's various developments, see James F. Waesche, *Crowning the Gravelly Hill* (Baltimore: Maclay and Associates, 1987).

4. Guilford embodies the Georgian colonial revival that swept America starting in Newport in 1885 with McKim, Mead, and White's H. A. C. Taylor House. The style became the final imprimatur for upper- and middle-class respectability and elegance.

5. *Architects and Builders Journal*, vol. 3 (September 1901); *Daily Record*, September 19, 1891. The 1908 police census of buildings showed 114,000 homes and 49 apartment buildings. Baltimore *Sun*, January 1, 1908; November 12, 1911.

6. For further information on English cottage architecture, see Gavin Stamp and Andre Goulancourt, *The English House, 1860–1914: The Flowering of English Domestic Architecture* (Chicago: The University of Chicago Press, 1997), and Robert A.M. Stern, "La Villa Bourgeosie," *The Anglo-American Suburb* (London: Architectural Design, 1981).

7. Waesche, *Crowning the Gravelly Hill*.

8. *Roland Park Review*, vol. 6, no. 4 (January 1914).

9. *Roland Park Review*, vol. 1, no. 4 (January 1909) and vol. 3, no. 12 (September 1911). Palmer was on the architectural cutting edge when he experimented with concrete for residential use. Introduced at the turn of the century, poured-in-place concrete was thought to be a material that would replace bricks and wood in residential construction. In 1901 Thomas Edison opined that all houses in the future would be poured not built. His prediction proved wrong; although concrete construction was often adopted for commercial and industrial applications, it was rarely used for residences. Palmer did not use it again. *Architect and Builders Journal*, vol. 3 (September 1901).

10. Baltimore *Sun*, November 30, 1911.

11. Baltimore *Sun*, July 19, 1914.

12. Baltimore *Sun*, November 18, 1917.

13. Baltimore *Sun*, February 6, 1914; Baltimore *News*, April 1, 1916. Port Sunlight was a social housing venture to improve living conditions for workingmen in Liverpool. Most houses combined two materials—a brick or stone base with roughcast, a stucco-like material, above. Despite Mueller's boast that his rows were finer than those abroad, the design of Port Sunlight houses is far superior to any of the English style rows built in Baltimore.

14. Baltimore *Sun*, September 10, 1925.

15. *Baltimore Gas & Electric News*, June 1917.

16. Baltimore *Sun*, April 19, 1914.

17. Baltimore *Sun*, October 15, 1915.

18. Baltimore *Sun*, July 9, 1914; August 11, 1920; August 16, 1920; Gallagher Archives, UB, House cards.

19. In 1916 he built a record 280 houses, but in 1917 and 1918 together he built only 106 houses. Many of the design features he added to the upscale houses eventually found their way (sometimes in a much watered down fashion) to his lower-end rowhouses. His working-class developments during this period included McElderry Park (in East Baltimore) and Saint Clair (near Clifton Park).

20. All figures regarding purchase prices of houses, land acquisitions, and occupations of residents, from the Gallagher Archives, UB.

21. This form of transaction resembles a contemporary land purchase agreement.

22. Baltimore *Sun*, July 1, 1923.

23. Allan D. Anderson, *The Origin and Resolution of an Urban Crisis, Baltimore, 1890–1930* (Baltimore and London: Johns Hopkins University Press, 1981); Baltimore *Sun*, April 15, 1923. Jitneys had made an appearance in Baltimore in 1915 and faded away, but with streetcar expansion over, the bus was the only viable means of new transit service.

24. Baltimore Sun, September 6, 1925.

25. Baltimore Sun, August 31, 1921.

26. *American Architect and Building News* (February 15, 1890).

27. For an overview on zoning laws and their effects on Baltimore development, see Garrett Power, "The Advent of Zoning," *Planning Perspectives* 4 (1989); Power, "The Unwisdom of Allowing City Growth to Work Out its Own Destiny," *Maryland Law Review*, vol. 49 no. 3 (1988); Power, "Anti-Rowhouse," unpublished paper; and Power, "Development of Residential Baltimore, 1900–1930," unpublished paper. For a contemporary view, see Joseph W. Shirley, "The Development of City Planning in Baltimore," *The Baltimore Engineer*, vol. I no. 9 (December 1926) and the Baltimore *Sun*, June 20, 1909; October 12, 1915; September 21, 1919; November 7, 1919; November 26, 1921; July 20, 1922; January 23, 1923; April 18, 1923; May 20, 1923; March 24, 1924; June 14, 1924; June 25, 1924; June 16, 1925; July 3, 1926; and November 23, 1926.

28. Baltimore *Sun*, May 25, 1909; *Architect and Builders Journal*, vol. 3 (December 1901).

29. *Baltimore Municipal Journal*, October 24, 1918.

30. *Baltimore Municipal Journal*, October 27, 1916.

31. Baltimore *Sun*, March 24, 1922.

32. Baltimore *Sun*, May 20, 1923.

33. Baltimore *Sun*, January 6, 1925. In 1922 Bassett had also promised "protection against the menace of garages. Zoning will assure a property holder that a garage will not be erected next door to his store or home." Baltimore *Sun*, March 24, 1922.

34. Although the city's zoning ordinance was passed in the early 1920s, the Maryland courts initially held that use restrictions on private property were unconstitutional and struck down the ordinance. Then the U. S. Supreme Court in 1927 upheld the constitutionality of zoning in *Euclid vs. Amber Realty Co.* The Maryland courts reconsidered and a comprehensive zoning ordinance was enacted in 1931. See Garrett Power, "The Advent of Zoning," *Planning Perspectives* 4 (1989): 1–13; "The Unwisdom of Allowing City Growth to Work out Its Own Destiny," *Maryland Law Review*, vol. 47, no. 3 (1988).

35. For contemporary discussions of the segregation issue, see Baltimore *Sun*, November 18, 1917; November 28, 1920; January 21 and 29, 1921; December 18, 1921; January 15, 1922; February 10 and 23, 1923; August 12, 1923; September 23, 1923; October 28, 1923; March 11, 1924; May 4, 1924; June 19, 1924; and August 18, 1925. See also Garrett Power, "Apartheid Baltimore Style: The Residential Segregation Ordinances of 1910-1913," *Maryland Law Review*, vol. 42, no. 2 (1983).

36. The houses were in the 1500 block of North Gilmor Street (Baltimore *Sun*, June 19, 1924). In the early 1920s the Homemakers Building Association took out half-page advertisements in *The First Colored Directory* promoting membership in their building and loan: "A high degree of safety, a rate of interest above that which banks can afford to pay, and the consciousness that every dollar entrusted to the Homemakers Building Association will be put to work at once in helping people of limited means to secure suitable homes, are factors which should appeal to many." The Association met every Monday evening at the Sharp Street Memorial Community House, Dophin and Etting Street, part of Sharp Street Memorial A. M. E. Church, one of the oldest black congregations in the city. *The First Colored Directory* (Baltimore: Robert W. Coleman, 1923–24).

37. H. Findley French and Ralph J. Johnson, "Baltimore's Industrial Development, 1919–1950 (Baltimore: Baltimore Association of Commerce, 1964); *The Baltimore Engineer*, vol. 4, no. 10 (January 1930); *The Baltimore Book: A Resume of the Commercial, Industrial, and Financial Resources and General Development of the City* (Baltimore, 1914).

38. For further information on federal financing, see Miles E. White, et al, *Real Estate Development Principles and Process* (Washington, D.C.: Urban Land Institute, 1991).

39. Frank Kaufman, "The Maryland Ground Rent, "Mysterious but Beneficial," *Maryland Law Review*, 4 (December 1940).

40. For further information on Rodgers Forge, see Jeanne B. Sargent, "The Enduring Rows of

Rodgers Forge," *Baltimore Magazine*, vol. 88, no. 7 (July 1995).

41. Frederick Beall was Keelty's architect. He had previously designed many rows for rowhouse builder Walter Westphal, including the city's longest on Wilkens Avenue.

42. In 1975 Keelty's grandson recollected the houses' selling prices; Baltimore *Sun*, December 12, 1937.

43. When he realized that he could not make as great a profit on cottages as he did on rows, since a cottage development created a far fewer number of ground rents on a given acreage than did rows, Novak never did another detached house development again.); Baltimore *Sun*, August 8, 1933.

44. Baltimore *Sun*, January 2 and 5, 1941; January 2, 1942.

45. Baltimore *Sun*, October 6, 1940.

46. For further information regarding Original Northwood, see James F. Waesche, *Beyond the Gravelly Hill*.

47. Gallagher Archives, UB, House cards.

48. Miles E. White, et al, *Real Estate Development Principles and Process*.

49. White, *Real Estate Development Principles and Process*; *Baltimore Real Estate News*, June 1946 and June 1947.

50. Baltimore *Sun*, May 30, 1954.

51. Baltimore *Sun*, June 24, 1951. Although the modern style of Frank Lloyd Wright and the European Bauhaus architects influenced design in postwar America, rowhouse builders never experimented with the style. Only one exception exists in Baltimore: a group of paired, flat-roofed international style houses built in northwest Baltimore in the mid-1950s.

52. Baltimore *Sun*, May 16, 1954.

53. Roland Eppley, *Residential Development in Baltimore City and Baltimore County* (Baltimore: Johns Hopkins University Press, 1953).

CHAPTER FIVE

1. Edward Gunts, "Lafayette Courts Building on Hopes," Baltimore *Sun*, August 18, 1995.

2. Richard H. Plunz, *A History of Housing in New York City* (New York: Columbia University Press, 1990); Baltimore *Evening Sun*, December 15, 1952; William H. Whyte, *City, Rediscovering the Center* (New York: Doubleday, 1988).

3. For further information on Baltimore during the 1930s Depression era, see Jo Ann E. Argersinger, *Toward a New Deal in Baltimore* (Chapel Hill: University of North Carolina Press, 1988).

4. Baltimore *Sun*, July 30, 1943.

5. Baltimore *Evening Sun*, May 10, 1937; April 12, 1939; The Housing Authority of Baltimore City, "Effects of the Post-War Program on

Negro Housing," a statement prepared by the Division of Public Relations Research and Special Studies, September 25, 1945.

6. *Baltimore Real Estate News*, November 1938: 9.

7. Baltimore *Sun*, February 5 and 28, 1939; June 16, 20, 25 and September 22, 1940; Baltimore *Evening Sun*, September 30, October 9 and 11, 1940.

8. Darling's statement came from his article, "HABC Considering Use of Elevator Buildings," *HABC Quaerterly Review*, January 1952, as quoted in Deborah R. Weiner, "From New Deal Promise to Postmodern Defeat: Two Baltimore Housing Projects," unpublished paper, July 1995. See also American Civil Liberties Union, "Background Regarding the ACLU's Lawsuit to Remedy Decades of Racial Segregation and Discrimination Against Baltimore City's Public Housing Residents," January 31, 1995.

9. Baltimore *Evening Sun*, September 4, 1940.

10. Baltimore *Evening Sun*, September 27, 1945; Housing Authority of Baltimore City, "Effects of the Post-War Program on Negro Housing"; Baltimore *Evening Sun*, April 28, April 30, October 10, 1945.

11. Baltimore *Evening Sun*, December 11 and 15, 1952.

12. Housing Authority of Baltimore City, "Baltimore's Housing Situation at a Glance," May, 1955; Baltimore *Sun*, February 2, 1955.

13. Baltimore *Sun*, January 18, 1957.

14. Deborah R. Weiner, "From New Deal Promise to Postmodern Defeat: Two Baltimore Housing Projects"; Baltimore City Archives, Housing Authority of Baltimore City Project Files, Record Group 48, Series 14, Box 41.

15. Martin Millspaugh and Gurney Breckenfeld, *The Human Side of Urban Renewal, A Study of the Attitude Changes Produced by Neighborhood Rehabilitation* (Baltimore: Fight-Blight, Inc., 1958); Baltimore *Sun*, December 11, 1952; January 27, 1953; February 6, 1953; January 4, 1954; March 20, 1955.

16. Lucretia Fisher, "They Stopped the Road" (editorial), Baltimore *Sun*, February 26, 1992; interviews with Lucretia Fisher (1996) and Robert Eney (1997), leaders in the fight to stop the road; Linda Shopes, "Fells Point: Community and Conflict in a Working-Class Neighborhood," in Elizabeth Fee, Linda Shopes, and Linda Zeidman, editors, *The Baltimore Book, New Views of Social History* (Philadelphia: Temple University Press, 1991).

17. Opened in August 1981, the National Aquarium at Baltimore now draws over one million visitors annually. In 1998 Planet Hollywood opened at Harborplace and both a Hard Rock Cafe *and* an ESPN Zone opened their doors two piers over. A Bubba Gump Shrimp Factory is in the offing. Current statistics show that

more people visit Baltimore's Inner Harbor annually than attend Disneyworld.

18. For an overview of Baltimore's homesteading program, see Lenora H. Nast, Laurence N. Krause, and R. C. Monk, *Baltimore, A Living Renaissance* (Baltimore: Historic Baltimore Society, 1952).

19. Interview with Robert Embry, January 1997; Leonore Nast, *Baltimore, A Living Renaissance*; Baltimore *Sun*, May 20, 1969.

20. Baltimore *Sun*, February 24, 1992; June 23, 1994; September 17, 1997.

21. Baltimore *Sun*, August 19, 1979.

22. Baltimore *Sun*, March 28, 1992; June 15, 1992.

23. Baltimore *Sun*, June 15, 1992.

24. Interview with Lee Rosenberg from Ryland Homes, July 1998; Baltimore *Sun*, April 28, 1991. What made the $62,500 houses affordable to people with incomes of between $11,000 and $35,000 was the package of low-interest mortgage financing that was available. With a down payment of $750, buyers could obtain a $37,500 four to five percent loan from the state as a first mortgage, a second, interest-free mortgage from HUD, and a third mortgage from a Baltimore community development block grant. They only had to pay monthly interest on the first mortgage, or about $250 to $350. The second and third mortgages only had to be repaid when the house was sold.

25. Interview with Jim Joyce, Ryland Homes, July 1997; Baltimore *Sun*, April 25 and November 21, 1993.

26. Interview with Gloria Mikolajcyzk, architect with D. W. Taylor and Associates, July 1998; Baltimore *Sun*, August 28, 1996; June 21, 1997.

27. Baltimore *Sun*, August 18 and 20, 1995.

28. Interview with Cheryl O'Neill, planner with CHK Architects and Planners, August 1997; Baltimore *Sun*, March 1 and 18, 1998.

29. During the summer of 1996 another high-rise complex came down, replaced by rowhouses that include a mix of subsidized rentals and lease-purchase agreements with market-rate rentals and sales, in order to bring an economic mix to the community. Here, at the Terraces, replacing Lexington Terrace, 100 of the rowhouses built in 1998–1999 will be offered at prices starting at $47,000. Recently the city received an additional $21.5 million from HUD to complete its five-year $293 million program to demolish all the high-rise public housing projects and rebuild rowhouses in their place. The same mix of subsidized rentals and sales with market-rate offerings are planned. The George B. Murphy Homes, with 800 public housing units, will become the site of 362 new rowhouses. Award-winning CHK has already been chosen as the architect for the 260-unit rowhouse community that will replace Flag House Courts, where half of the houses will be subsidized and half unsubsidized market-rate units. Baltimore *Sun*, October 8, 1997; March 1 and June 3, 1998.

30. Baltimore *Sun*, September 28, 1997

Appendix A

1. Bricks

Pressed — 304,543	$6905.43
Common — 5,278,300	$34,840.37
#2 pavers — 6,000	39.00
	$41,784.80

2. Bricklaying (average @ $3.25 & extra work)
19,253.20

3. Bellhanging — **330.65**

4. Bath-room fixtures — **51.90**

5. Casks (for toilets for 5 hos. W.s. Luzerne St.)
30.00

6. Cellar digging & grading — **5,728.87**

7. Carpenter work — **17,653.29**

8. Cement Work (labor only) — **7,181.32**

9. Cement (material) — **5,609.70**

10. Decorating Ceilings & vestibules — **753.75**

11. Electric light wiring — **72.04**

12. Flues (5246 ft.-8.5x13) — **680.64**

13. Gas fixtures — **2,747.33**

14. Gas ranges — **320.00**

15. Grilles — **445.40**

16. Gravel (693 dbl. Loads) — **1,131.35**

17. Hardware (inc. sash weights, joist hangers)
3,829.08

18. Hot water heating — **8,557.64**

19. Hair (1662 bushels) — **324.46**

20. Iron work — **126.37**

21. Joist irons — **98.29**

22. Lumber & Mill-work & stair-work
44,350.27

23. Leaded glass — **60.00**

24. Lathing & plastering work — **8,860.08**

25. Labor & watchman — **3,373.67**

26. Lime — **3,852.56**

27. Mantels, medicine cabts., & tiled work
4,989.90

28. Marble work — **9,428.00**

29. Mirrors — **281.93**

30. Numbering houses — **65.05**

31. Paperhanging work — **5,330.25**

32. Pipe (fittings & bends) — **351.12**

33. Plumbing & gas fittings — **27,321.58**

34. Painting & glazing — **9,078.59**

35. Plaster — **377.62**

36. Roofing & cornice work — **8,715.64**

37. Scrubber — **184.20**

38. Sewer work — **2,134.48**

39. Sand — **3,650.23**

40. Stone work — **34.50**

41. Sundries — **7,586.71**

42. Trees — **150.40**

43. Whitewasher — **234.50**

44. Windowphanie — **15.60**

45. Water supplies — **2,316.00**

46. Wire guards — **241.66**

Cost of 202 Houses — **$246,568.25**

$1,220 per house

Appendix B

Edward J. Gallagher Realty Company
Total Sales: 1915–1931

Year	Total Houses Built	Total Houses Sold	Net Value of House Sales, (Less Returns)	Ground Rents Sold	Net Value, Ground Rent Sales, (Less Brokerage)	Total Sales Value
1915	167	100	$ 165,465.00	152	$ 127,868.95	$ 293,333.95
1916	280	186	309,325.00	192	170,906.67	480,231.67
1917	68	178	299,362.46	157	139,731.22	439,093.68
1918	38	75	191,305.50	35	38,869.58	230,175.08
1919	144	83	321,795.00	86	108,227.64	430,022.64
1920	112	99	450,997.00	107	127,159.22	578,156.22
1921	34	49	215,521.75	99	111,423.34	326,945.09
1922	197	119	583,128.42	50	67,540.95	650,669.37
1923	128	211	923,873.32	242	254,663.04	1,178,536.36
1924	276	215	1,017,880.17	228	288,755.67	1,306,635.84
1925	208	210	949,060.66	184	210,973.22	1,160,033.88
1926	125	155	798,072.51	134	167,529.69	965,602.20
1927	98	94	559,920.79	159	218,365.82	778,286.61
1928	69	79	470,411.90	35	56,703.07	527,114.97
1929	68	88	598,439.10	80	117,637.67	716,076.77
1930	33	54	366,727.85	65	94,783.83	461,511.68
1931	30	32	213,702.75	48	75,041.63	288,744.38
	2,075	2,027	$8,434,989.18	2053	$2,376,181.21	$10,811,170.39

Index